The Idea of Private Law

The Idea of Private Law

Ernest J. Weinrib

OXFORD
UNIVERSITY PRESS

OXFORD
UNIVERSITY PRESS

Great Clarendon Street, Oxford, OX2 6DP,
United Kingdom

Oxford University Press is a department of the University of Oxford.
It furthers the University's objective of excellence in research, scholarship,
and education by publishing worldwide. Oxford is a registered trade mark of
Oxford University Press in the UK and in certain other countries

© E. Weinrib, 1995, revised edition with new preface first published 2012

The moral rights of the author have been asserted

First Edition published in 2012

Impression: 1

British Library Cataloguing in Publication Data

Data available

Library of Congress Cataloging in Publication Data

Library of Congress Control Number: 2012942996

ISBN 978–0–19–966581–5 (hbk)
ISBN 978–0–19–966479–5 (pbk)

Printed in Great Britain by
CPI Group (UK) Ltd, Croydon, CR0 4YY

To the memory
of my father
Percy (Pinchas) Weinrib

שְׁאַל אָבִיךָ וְיַגֵּדְךָ

Contents

Preface to the 2012 Edition   ix
Acknowledgments   xxi

1. Understanding Private Law   1
2. Legal Formalism   22
3. Corrective Justice   56
4. Kantian Right   84
5. Correlativity   114
6. Negligence Liability   145
7. Strict Liability   171
8. The Autonomy of Private Law   204

Index   233

Preface to the 2012 Edition

The Idea of Private Law emerged out of, but went beyond, the great controversies about tort theory that agitated legal scholarship in the last decades of the twentieth century. The origins and aspirations of the book are the subject of this retrospective preface.

That tort law became the site of fierce theoretical contention is not surprising. By its very nature tort law immediately raises an array of pressing theoretical issues. What justifies the law's coercive authority to impose obligations on persons who have not assumed them? On what basis does tort law protect certain interests and not others? Where is the line to be drawn between freedom of action and liability for the consequences of action? What is the normative significance of culpability? Can tort law succeed in bringing the arbitrary misfortune of unintended injuries under a rational juridical discipline? In tort law these questions, interesting enough on their own, play themselves out within a subject that has always been fundamental to legal education, so that tort theory resonates broadly within the intellectual culture of academic lawyers.

Contemporary tort theory initially burst forth in the 1970s, with the publication in the United States of a cluster of works that tugged in two opposite directions. On the one hand, the great pioneers of the economic analysis of tort law brilliantly articulated theories that focused on the promotion of efficiency. On the other hand, counter-vailing accounts suggestively thematized such values as justice, morality, fairness, or liberty. The conjunction of these developments with John Rawls's reinvigoration of political theory set the framework for theoretical writing about tort law. Rawls's work, with its explicitly

Kantian inspiration, rekindled the debate among political theorists about instrumentalism and its alternatives. The parallel debate among tort theorists aligned the instrumentalist proponents of economic analysis against those who were inspired by non-instrumental ideas drawn from moral theory. These competing perspectives led to vigorous disagreement across a range of issues: the nature of liability rules, the identification of tort law's underlying normative impulses, and the mode of discourse most appropriate to the theoretical enterprise. Also implicated were differences regarding the direction of the budding interdisciplinarity of legal studies. While tort scholarship had always rested on presuppositions about the relation of law to economics, morality, or politics, the theoretical disputes forced those presuppositions into the open.

The Idea of Private Law (as well as the articles preparatory to it published in the 1980s and early 1990s) was conspicuously on the "moralist" side of the economist-moralist divide. Its central message was that a particular conception of justice ("corrective justice") underlies the bases of liability in private law. The book and its predecessor writings were extended explorations of what that form of justice meant and how private law manifested it. Concomitantly, they repudiated economic analysis as incapable of providing an intelligible or coherent account of liability.

Although this body of work was not unique in rejecting the economic analysis of tort law, its grounds for doing so were distinctive. These grounds began with structure rather than substance. Instead of alleging that economic analysis was burdened with unattractive ideological baggage, riven with internal tensions, or ambiguous about whether its claims were normative or descriptive, the corrective justice argument highlighted the incompatibility of economic analysis with the bilateral structure of the plaintiff-defendant relationship. This structure requires that reasons for liability should be such as to link a particular defendant to a particular plaintiff. For in every case of liability what must be ascertained is not merely why the law should impose a burden on the defendant or provide a benefit to the plaintiff, but why it should simultaneously do both in a single operation. The reasons, in other words, have to embrace both parties in their interrelationship rather than deal with either of the parties independently. Economic analysis failed to do this, because the incentives that it postulated were necessarily directed to the parties separately. The consequence was that economic analysis could neither provide a theory for the nexus between the parties nor explain the legal concepts through which the law expressed that nexus. This critique obviated the need to determine whether economic analysis was sound in its own terms. All that was claimed was that, given the structure of the parties' relationship, economic analysis was incapable of illuminating the juridical nature of liability.

This repudiation of the economic analysis of tort law flows from the specific conception of corrective justice developed in *The Idea of Private Law* and its preparatory articles. Reflecting the truism that the liability of a particular defendant is always a liability to a particular plaintiff, corrective justice takes the relationship between the parties to be the central and pervasive feature of liability, and therefore the feature whose explication is the fundamental task of theory. Within this relationship the position of one party is always conditioned by the position of the other. Liability being a bipolar phenomenon, the theoretical analysis of it can therefore not come to rest at either pole. Accordingly, it is a mistake to explain liability by reference to considerations separately relevant to either of the parties (or even to both of them). Rather, the relational character of the reasons supporting liability has to match the relational structure of liability itself. A tort claim, for instance, is based on the plaintiff's suffering of a wrong done by the defendant. The book contends that the nature of that wrong, and of the liability that corrects it, is intelligible only if the doing and the suffering are regarded as comprising a single normative unit in which each party's position is the mirror image of the other's. Then the normative force of the reasons for assigning liability for the commission of the wrong is as applicable to the plaintiff as to the defendant.

The significance that corrective justice attaches to the parties' relationship is the precondition for the structural criticism of economic analysis. The criticism draws on the relational nature of liability to point to the inappositeness of accounting for liability on the basis of incentives directed separately to plaintiffs and to defendants. The argument against economic analysis thus highlights the mismatch between the operation of the incentives and the structure of the parties' relationship. Without engaging in economic disputes, it confronts economic analysis precisely at the point at which its claims move from efficiency to liability.

The relational nature of corrective justice has broad implications that allow *The Idea of Private Law* to go beyond the confines of the tort theory debate between the "economists" and the "moralists". Three points are worth observing.

First, the argument from structural incompatibility is not restricted to economic analysis; it extends to all instrumental approaches to private law. An instrumental approach postulates a goal (or a plurality of goals) that is desirable independently of private law and then understands liability either as promoting that goal or as being defective to the extent that it doesn't. Because the goal does not arise out of or reflect the bilateral unity of the plaintiff-defendant relationship, it can be promoted only by breaking that relationship apart through reasons for liability that refer separately to one or the other of the parties. Economic analysis, for example, assumes that efficiency is the goal that tort law should or does promote. Because this goal is unconnected with and indifferent to the bilateral structure of the parties' relationship, the reason for liability that economic analysis offers—that liability can act as an incentive to efficient conduct—refers to one party or the other but not to the relationship between them. A similar dynamic is in play whatever the goal. This is paradigmatically evident in the most frequently invoked goals of tort law, deterrence and compensation. Considered as reasons for imposing liability, the former of these refers only to wrongful actions without accounting for why tort liability requires injury; conversely, the latter refers only to injuries without accounting for why tort liability requires wrongdoing. Thus, the inadequacy that corrective justice identifies in economic analysis is general to all instrumental conceptions of liability. To the extent that these have dominated legal scholarship for generations, this book is an extended argument for a dramatic shift in theoretical orientation.

Second, the emphasis on the parties' relationship also affects the "moralist" side of the debate. One might be tempted to flesh out the "moralist" approach to tort law by elaborating general notions of personal responsibility and personal morality. Tort law, however, is replete with doctrines, such as the objective standard in negligence law and the absence of a duty to perform even an easy rescue, that are difficult to reconcile with these general notions. Corrective justice points in a different direction, to the existence of a special kind of morality that reflects the bipolar character of relationships of private law. From the standpoint of corrective justice, considerations geared to only one of the parties are as misplaced in the moral approach to tort law as they are in the economic approach. Excluded are considerations that treat the entire relationship from the standpoint of the subjectivity or the needs of one of the parties. Accordingly, this special morality matches tort law in having no room for a duty of rescue, because such a duty would obligate the defendant to respond to the needs of the plaintiff. Nor can it admit a subjective standard, because that would draw the border of the plaintiff's security at the limits of the defendant's particular abilities. As is the case with economic analysis, these considerations are dismissed on structural grounds without reference to their independent soundness or desirability. Corrective justice entails no denial that the needs or subjectivity of a particular person are relevant to moral deliberation in certain contexts or for certain purposes. Rather, the point is that these contexts or purposes are not germane to the understanding of the normative character of liability.

Third, by exhibiting the structure of the plaintiff–defendant relationship, corrective justice illuminates not merely tort law but all the grounds of liability in private law. A tort theory based on corrective justice is part of a wider theory of private law, because its point of departure is the conception of the relationship between the parties that is common to liability generally. To be sure, every ground of liability has a different set of requirements, but those requirements fit into a uniform conceptual structure that directly relates each of the parties to the other. By attending to the nature and implications of corrective justice, the book presents a general theory of private law rather than a theory of tort law alone. Indeed, when the book was originally submitted for publication, an astute reader noted the provocation in its title which, implicitly rejecting the legal realist notion that private law is merely public law in disguise, treats private law as a distinctive normative enterprise animated by its own organizing idea.

The book elaborates this idea through a series of complementary steps that deal in turn with the methodology of inquiry into the law's relational structures, the specific structure of private law relationships, and the content appropriate to that structure.

The methodology involves rehabilitating the long discredited notion of legal formalism. In contemporary legal discourse formalism is often identified with an interpretive stance growing out of a certain conception of positivism: this version of formalism requires strict or mechanical adherence to the authoritatively formulated rules of positive law without reference to the rules' normative underpinning. The formalism presented in this book has nothing to do with this justifiably maligned notion. The book's formalism is neither positivist, nor an interpretative stance toward verbal formulations, nor rule centered, nor divorced from normative underpinnings. Rather, it aims to elucidate the different ways in which legal relationships can coherently be ordered. Presented at their most abstract, these different ways are the most general structures or "forms" immanent within the operations of law. The earliest philosophical treatment of these forms is found in Aristotle's account of the distinction between corrective and distributive justice, an account that inspires much of this book. In the book's version of the legal formalist position, the positive law is relevant not because its rules are valid for a particular jurisdiction (as with positivism), but because it indicates the subject matter of inquiry and because the juristic experience of that subject matter provides insight into the specific character of the different kinds of ordering in different legal contexts. Moreover, the book's formalism is concerned not with the rules themselves but with the intelligibility and coherence of the reasoning that might support them. Far from being divorced from normative underpinnings, this formalism exhibits the various structures of reasoning operative in those underpinnings.

Within the formalist approach to legal ordering, corrective justice connotes the normative structure specific to the relationship of plaintiff and defendant. Correlativity is the defining feature of that structure, in that it specifies how, given the nature of liability, the parties to the bilateral relationship stand to each other. Liability consists in a finding that the parties are situated correlatively to each other as doer and sufferer of the same injustice. The reasons for such a finding can be coherent only if they too are correlatively structured. Otherwise, holding the defendant liable to the plaintiff would not reflect what the defendant is being held liable for; a correlatively structured correction cannot correct a non-correlatively structured injustice. Thus, correlativity constitutes the structuring idea not only for the correction of the injustice through liability, but also for the very conception of the injustice that liability corrects. Corrective justice operates to correct a corrective injustice.

This view of corrective justice has not been uncontroversial. The objection has been made that corrective justice refers only to the remedial operation that allocates back to the plaintiff. The norm whose breach is being corrected, so the objection goes, cannot itself be a matter of corrective justice because then the norm would be correcting something else, and so on in infinite regress.[1] This objec-

---

[1] John Gardner, "The Purity and Priority of Private Law," 46 U. Toronto L.J. 459, at 469 (1996); John Gardner, "What is Tort Law for? Part 1: The Place of Corrective Justice," 30 Law and Philosophy, 1, 23 (2011).

tion is either wrong or illusory. It is wrong if it holds that the correlativity of the correction does not presuppose correlativity in the reasons supporting the norm whose breach occasions the correction. For if those reasons are non-correlative, in that their normative force does not link the particular defendant who commits the injustice to the particular plaintiff who suffers it, then the law cannot coherently tie the defendant's liability to the plaintiff's entitlement. The objection is illusory if it merely disputes the meaning of the words "corrective justice." The objection assumes that these words refer narrowly to the justice that consists in the operation that corrects, whereas the book uses these words to refer more broadly to the system of norms and their supporting reasons within which such an operation makes sense. The illusion lies in thinking that stipulating a meaning determines anything of significance. Here, as elsewhere, one should think thoughts, not words.

What, then, is the content appropriate to this correlative structure of normative reasoning? Some have thought, because corrective justice is only a form of justice and not itself a substantive principle, that it is compatible with any content. Once one realizes, however, that corrective justice is a structure of reasoning, it is evident that it is not indifferent to its content, for at the very least it excludes content that is inconsistent with its own structure. For instance, the distinction that Aristotle postulated between corrective justice and distributive justice goes to the internal composition of their respective structures of reasoning: corrective justice signals a bipolar correlativity and distributive justice a numerically unlimited comparison along a criterion of distribution. The categorical difference between correlativity and comparison demonstrates that no distributive consideration can be the basis for liability. The structural arguments against economic analysis and instrumentalism that were mentioned earlier are further instances of the power of corrective justice to exclude certain kinds of content.

These examples illuminate the content of corrective justice negatively, by indicating what corrective justice disqualifies. The greater theoretical challenge is to characterize that content positively, in terms of what it includes. In this connection two requirements must be kept in mind. The first is, of course, that the normative force of the content should be correlative. The second is that this correlativity should be intrinsic to the reasoning that endows it with its normative character.

This second requirement, obscure though it might seem at first blush, is vital and needs further elaboration. As the normative structure of the private law relationship, corrective justice is implicit in the positive law but is not its creature. The positive law is composed of norms that are legally valid for a particular jurisdiction. Corrective justice, however, goes not to what makes the norms of private law valid but to what makes them coherent in the light of the reasons that support them. The non-positivist role of corrective justice carries over to its content, which contains the correlatively structured normative reasoning relevant to liability. Accordingly, a theory does not assign adequate content to correlativity by first postulating considerations that are not themselves intrinsically correlative (for example, distributional advantages or the interests of one or the other of the parties) and then setting them up as correlative through the fiat of the positive law (say, by encasing those interests within the bipolar litigational framework of private law).[2] This kind of theoretical move would produce the very incoherence that corrective justice is designed to avoid. This is because the litigational framework is not only the creation of the positive law in particular jurisdictions, but also the institutional manifestation of an anterior set of normative considerations that can coherently link the parties to each other. The correlativity of those considerations derives from the normative basis of the considerations themselves, and not from the operation of positive law upon them.

Reflecting these two requirements, *The Idea of Private Law* elucidates the content of corrective justice in terms of the robust conception of rights spelled out by Kant. This fulfills the first requirement, because a right immediately implies the existence of a corresponding duty, thereby fitting readily into corrective justice's structure of correlativity. Kant's account also makes correlativity intrinsic to the rights' normative significance in accordance with the second requirement. For Kant, rights and their correlative obligations are juridical markers of the conditions under which the action of one person can coexist with the freedom of another. Kant analyzes the relationship of doing and suffering, which is the concern of corrective justice, in terms of the equal status of the interacting parties as purposive and self-determining beings. Rights and their correlative obligations thereby become the vehicles through which private law expresses the relation of one free being to another. The Kantian account brings out the

---

[2] Examples of this move are Peter Cane, *The Anatomy of Tort Law* (1997), 10–15; Hanoch Dagan, *The Law and Ethics of Restitution* (2004), 224–28.

normativity inherent in the relationship of the doer and sufferer as such—that is, as interacting persons endowed with, and affecting each other through the exercise of, the capacity for self-determining freedom. This normativity constitutes a special morality that regards the interacting parties solely as purposive beings free to pursue their own purposes consistently with the purposiveness of others, without being obligated to act for any particular purposes, however laudable ethically or desirable socially. Accordingly, the normative significance of the Kantian system of private law rights is internal to the correlativity of the parties' normative positions within corrective justice. Rights so conceived provide the appropriate content for the correlative structure of corrective justice.

It is worth noting the role that Kantian right plays in this account of private law. One should not think that for purposes of this account Kant's legal philosophy is foundational, in the sense that it represents a truth from which one builds up the correct conception of private law. If that had been the intention, the book would have started with Kant on the assumption that nothing theoretically significant could be said about private law until the foundation on which everything rested was in place. Instead, the book starts with private law itself, raises the question of what it means for private law to be internally intelligible, and then proceeds through a discussion of formalism and corrective justice, reaching Kantian right only in the fourth of its eight chapters. Kantian right is introduced in order to address this question: corrective justice treats the parties as equal, but what is the nature of this equality? What ensues is a transition from the corrective justice's formal notion of equality to its presupposition of a Kantian conception of self-determining agency and then to the significance of rights as the juridical manifestations of agency so conceived. In this context what is important about the Kantian ideas of agency, freedom, and rights is not that they are true but that they are presupposed in a coherent conception of liability. Kant is not the foundation on which one erects a theory of private law, but a stage reached as one works back from the private law we already have to its structure and presuppositions.

The Idea of Private Law melds legal formalism, corrective justice and Kantian right into an integrated framework for understanding the relationship between the plaintiff and the defendant. In what sense does this yield a theory of private law? Given all the ways in which the phenomenon of private law could be theorized, what does the particular theory presented here aspire to accomplish?

The central aim of the book is to set out what it means for a system of liability to be normatively coherent. The normative coherence to which this aim refers is the coherence of the reasoning on which liability is based. The formalist attention to structure, the specification of corrective justice as the structure appropriate to private law, and the elaboration of the Kantian notion of rights are all directed to the structure and content of the coherent justifications for finding the defendant liable to the plaintiff. The idea of coherence is a stringent one; it requires that the justification occupy the entire conceptual space to which its normative content entitles it. If it fails to do so, then a determination that the defendant is liable to the plaintiff would involve either arbitrarily extending the justification, so that it occupies space to which its own normative force does not entitle it, or arbitrarily truncating the justification, so that it recedes from the space to which it is entitled. Within this conception of coherence the demarcation of the space that a justification occupies by virtue of its own normative force is crucial. Hence the preoccupation with the structure of the plaintiff–defendant relationship and with the kind of content that is adequate to that structure. The structure indicates the shape of the conceptual space that a justification for liability has to fully occupy if it is to be coherent. And the abstract formalism with which corrective justice presents that space affords an uncluttered view of the kind of normative consideration that would fill it without excess or shortfall.

Like every sophisticated system of private law, the common law values its own normative coherence and strives to achieve it. Inasmuch as it exhibits the theoretical structure of this coherence, corrective justice provides the basis both for understanding the law's own efforts and for identifying and criticizing its failures. It reflects and gives normative meaning to the master feature of liability, that liability of a particular defendant is always liability to a particular plaintiff. Corrective justice is implicit in the litigational and remedial framework that links the plaintiff to the defendant. It is also implicit in basic doctrines that on their face attest to the significance of the immediate nexus between the parties in various grounds of liability (causation in tort law, offer and acceptance in contract law, enrichment at the expense of another in the law of restitution, and so on). Corrective justice thus constitutes the structure of normative coherence immanent in the most general and pervasive features of private law. It thereby provides a basis for criticism, internal to the law itself, of whatever incoherencies the law has on the grounds that these fail to live up to the normative implications of those more general features.

Consequently, corrective justice is always attuned dynamically to the reasons for a particular legal doctrine rather than statically to the doctrine as a self-standing rule. The question with which corrective justice is concerned is whether a justification adduced in support of a given rule is consistent with the normative coherence upon which corrective justice insists. From the standpoint of this approach the common law is not viewed as a set of "data" that corrective justice has to "fit." Rather, the common law forms a culture of justification that aspires to its own internal coherence—that is, to live up to its own justificatory character. Corrective justice displays the kind of structure and content relevant to this aspiration.

The corrective justice approach honors the law's reasoning and concepts as good-faith attempts to achieve normative coherence. However, it also acknowledges what every student of the law knows, that this effort is not always successful. Corrective justice then supplies the critical perspective from which this lack of success can be evaluated in accordance with the law's own normative character. This critical perspective is not, as is sometimes incorrectly asserted and as the book expressly disavows, the search for an "essence" that determines whether a rule is part of private law.[3] The point of the enquiry into coherence is always normative and never ontological. What matters is not whether some set of legal arrangements is "really" private law, but whether it can coherently be justified within a coherent ordering of the relationship of plaintiff and defendant.

The book was written with the full awareness that both its content and its tone may well appear idiosyncratic. In a scholarly environment dominated by instrumentalism and an aversion to conceptualism, this book offers an approach to private law that is both non-instrumental and conceptual. And when the prevailing academic dogma proclaims law to be inherently political, the autonomy of law to be dead, and formalism to be arid, this book presents a formalist account of private law that attempts to give meaning to the autonomy of law by distinguishing the legal from the political. Readers who persevere to the final chapter will find there the argument that private law can be

---

[3] Cane, *The Anatomy of Tort Law*, 208–9; cf. *The Idea of Private Law*, 30–31.

autonomous without being detached from social reality and public without being political. Beyond the specific merits or demerits of that argument, the apparent idiosyncrasy of this book lies in reconnecting private law to the grand tradition of legal philosophy that treated it as an autonomous and inherently normative enterprise. In the contemporary academic world, this conception of private law has been thoroughly effaced, its conceptual repertoire ignored, and its vocabulary largely forgotten.

Styles of scholarship pass, but private law abides. As long as it does, the possibility of its normative coherence will never be an unimportant or obsolete topic of reflection.

Acknowledgments

Some sections of this book rework material that appeared in the following articles: "Law as Idea of Reason," in Howard Williams, ed., *Essays on Kant's Political Philosophy*, 15–49 (Cardiff, University of Wales Press, 1992); "Corrective Justice," 77 *Iowa Law Review* 403–421 (1992); "Liberty, Community, and Corrective Justice," in Raymond Frey and Christopher Morris, eds., *Liability and Responsibility: Essays in Law and Morals*, 290–316 (Cambridge, Cambridge University Press, 1991); "Legal Formalism: On the Immanent Rationality of Law," 97 *Yale Law Journal* 949–1016 (1988), reprinted by permission of The Yale Law Journal Company and Fred B. Rothman & Company; "Law as a Kantian Idea of Reason," 87 *Columbia Law Review* 472–508 (1987). I am grateful to the publishers of these articles for permitting me to make use of them.

During the long period of preparing this book, I happily accumulated many debts. Alan Brudner, Bruce Chapman, Jules Coleman, Izhak Englard, Owen Fiss, Steven Heyman, Ken Kress, Peter Lin, Jean Love, Tim Lytton, Dennis Patterson, Stephen Perry, Rob Prichard, Joseph Raz, Arthur Ripstein, Marshall Shapo, John Stick, Wayne Sumner, and Richard Wright helpfully commented—often by thoughtfully articulating their incredulity—on the ideas presented here or in the preliminary articles. I am additionally grateful to Ken Kress and Dennis Patterson for organizing the symposia on legal formalism that appeared in the *Iowa Law Review* and in the *Harvard Journal of Law and Public Policy*, and to Jules Coleman for organizing a very useful research conference on corrective justice. Mordechai Wasserman read through the entire manuscript, and his comments compelled many revisions.

Alice Woolley provided indispensable assistance in preparing the index. I have also benefited from long and continuing conversations over many years with Peter Benson and Martin Stone.

The research and writing of this book were greatly facilitated by tenure of the Killam Research Fellowship, the Connaught Research Fellowship in the Humanities and Social Sciences, and a Social Sciences and Humanities Research Council of Canada research fellowship. I thank the Canada Council, the University of Toronto, and the Social Sciences and Humanities Research Council of Canada for providing this assistance. I also thank Rochelle Vigurs for the cheerfulness and efficiency with which she coped with the endlessly successive drafts of the manuscript.

A version of this book formed the Julius Rosenthal Lectures for 1993 at the Northwestern University School of Law. I am grateful to the Northwestern University School of Law for inviting me to participate in this distinguished lecture series, and to the faculty and students of Northwestern for making my stay there enjoyable, stimulating, and productive.

1

Understanding Private Law

1.1. Introduction

In this book I address a single question: How are we to understand private law?

Private law is a pervasive phenomenon of our social life, a silent but ubiquitous participant in our most common transactions. It regulates the property we own and use, the injuries we inflict or avoid inflicting, the contracts we make or break. It is the public repository of our most deeply embedded intuitions about justice and personal responsibility. Private law is also among the first subjects that prospective lawyers study. Its position in law school curricula indicates the consensus of law teachers that private law is the most elementary manifestation of law, its reasoning paradigmatic of legal thinking, and its concepts presupposed in more complex forms of legal organization.

Consequently, an inquiry into how we are to understand private law opens onto the broadest vistas of legal theory and practice. At issue are the nature of legal justification, the limits of the judicial role and judicial competence, the difference between private law and other kinds of legal ordering, the relationship of juridical to ethical considerations, and the viability of our most basic legal arrangements. Indeed, if private law is as fundamental as law teachers suppose, misconceptions about it will affect our understanding of the entire field of law.

The most striking feature of private law is that it directly connects two particular parties through the phenomenon of liability. Both procedure and doctrine express this connection. Procedurally, litigation in private law takes the form of a claim that a particular plaintiff presses against a particular defendant. Doctrinally, requirements such as the causation of harm attest to the dependence of the plaintiff's claim on a wrong suffered at the defendant's hand. In singling out these two parties and bringing them together in this way, private law looks neither to the litigants individually nor to the interests of the community as a whole, but to a bipolar relationship of liability.

My concern here is with liability as the locus of a special morality that has its own structure and its own repertoire of arguments. Among the questions I shall consider are the following: What is the framework for understanding this morality? What kind of justifications constitute this morality? What is its structure and its normative grounding? And how does the operation of private law conform to its requirements? In these inquiries, my focus is on liability rather than on property. Of course private property is basic to private law, and this book includes a certain conception of property. But my principal aim is to consider the private law relationship not statically through what the parties own, but dynamically through the norms that govern their interaction.

The idea that private law constitutes a normatively distinct mode of interaction is not currently in favor. According to the standard view in contemporary scholarship, private law does not differ from other law: like all law, private law is normative only to the extent that it serves socially desirable purposes; and one understands private law by first identifying these purposes and then evaluating its success in serving them.

In this chapter I wish to introduce the themes of this book by contrasting the standard view with the approach I will be developing. My claim is that by focusing on the purposes that law might serve, the standard view regards private law from an external perspective that fails to take seriously the features expressive of private law's inner character. I suggest instead that one must understand private law from a perspective internal to it.

I orient us toward this internal perspective through the following steps. First I outline the role of purposes as independent grounds of justification in the standard approach. Recourse to such purposes reflects a set of widely held assumptions about law: that law is not an autonomous body of learning, that law cannot be separated from politics, that the law's concepts are not to be taken seriously in their own right, and that private law is not distinct from other modes of legal ordering. Then I delineate an alternative approach that challenges these assumptions. The alternative approach treats private law as an internally intelligible phenomenon by drawing on what is salient in juristic experience and by trying to make sense of legal thinking and discourse in their own terms. Crucial to this approach is the role of coherence both as an internal characteristic of private law and, more generally, as an idea that has no external referent. Attention to private law's internal features leads to a reconsideration of the standard view that law cannot be an autonomous discipline. Finally, I sketch the components of the theory that elucidates the internal perspective for understanding private law. This is the theory developed in the rest of the book.

1.2. Purpose in Private Law

The usual view of legal scholars is that one understands law through its purposes. To understand tort law, for instance, we must determine the goal or goals that tort law serves or ought to serve. Tort scholars accordingly examine tort law with the following questions in mind. Is the goal of tort law to compensate accident victims? Or is the goal to deter behavior that might produce injuries? If compensation is the goal, should the costs of compensation be spread as broadly as possible, or should they be allocated to the people wealthy enough to bear them easily? If deterrence is the goal, does this require the collective specification of the activities whose potential for injury makes them socially undesirable, or does it require the funneling of incentives through the market and its price structure? Or, alternately, is tort law a system of mixed goals that includes all these goals as well as others, in an elaborate network of mutual adjustments and trade-offs?

That one comprehends law through its goals—a notion we may call functionalism—is particularly well entrenched in American legal scholarship. A concern with the goals of law appears in an unbroken succession from the jurisprudence of Oliver Wendell Holmes to the realist revolt against Christopher Columbus Langdell's legacy to the current preoccupation with policy and with the weighing of social interests. Its most prominent contemporary manifestation is the economic approach, which has produced complex and sophisticated analyses of the incentive effects of different liability rules. The economic approach, however, provides only the most notable example of the current understanding of private law in terms of goals. Even those who disagree with the economic elaboration of those goals rarely regard goals as irrelevant in principle. Instead of emphasizing goals such as wealth maximization[1] or market deterrence,[2] they champion liberty[3] or community.[4] Their quarrel with the economists concerns the choice of goals, not the search for goals.

The functional approach to private law has an understandable appeal. The proposed goals specify aspects of human welfare—the compensation of injury, for instance, or the minimizing of the frequency and seriousness of accidents—that it is desirable to promote. The goal-oriented understanding of private law follows from the seemingly axiomatic proposition that "the object of law is to serve human needs."[5] The task for scholars is then to specify the goals relevant to the incidents regulated by a particular branch of private law, to indicate how different goals are to be balanced, to assess the success of current legal doctrine in achieving the specified goals, and to recommend changes that might improve that success.

Under this functionalism, the justificatory worth of the goals is independent of and external to the law that they justify. To continue with the tort example, deterring accidents and compensating accident victims are socially desirable quite apart from tort law. Indeed, tort law may be modified or even abolished should it be an unsuitable means of accomplishing these goals. If tort law forwards them, so much the better. The goals, however, are independently justifiable and do not derive their validity from tort law.

A consequence of the current focus on independently justifiable goals is that private law is only indirectly implicated in the functionalist inquiry. The functionalist starts by looking past private law to a catalogue of favored social goals. Private law matters only to the extent that it forwards or frustrates these goals. What the functionalist proposes is not so much a theory of private law as a theory of social goals into which private law may or may not fit.

Because they are preoccupied with independently justifiable goals rather than with private law directly, functionalist approaches to private law are radically incomplete. The functionalist is concerned with whether the results of cases promote the postulated goals. Private law,

---

[1] Richard A. Posner, *Economic Analysis of Law* (3rd ed., 1986).

[2] Guido Calabresi, *The Costs of Accidents* (1970).

[3] Richard A. Epstein, "A Theory of Strict Liability," 2 *Journal of Legal Studies* 151 (1973).

[4] Robert A. Bush, "Between Two Worlds: The Shift from Individual to Group Responsibility in the Law of Causation of Injury," 33 *University of California at Los Angeles Law Review* 1473 (1986).

[5] Guido Calabresi, "Concerning Cause and the Law of Torts," 69 *University of Chicago Law Review* 105 (1975).

however, is more than the sum of its results. It also includes a set of concepts, a distinctive institutional setting, and a characteristic mode of reasoning. These aspects are components of the internal structure of private law and do not readily map onto the functionalist's extrinsic goals. To the extent that functionalism ignores or dismisses these aspects, it fails to account for what is most characteristic of private law as a legal phenomenon.

Moreover, the favored goals of the functionalists are independent not only of private law but also of one another. For example, compensation and deterrence, the two standard goals ascribed to tort law, have no intrinsic connection: nothing about compensation as such justifies its limitation to those who are the victims of deterrable harms, just as nothing about deterrence as such justifies its limitation to acts that produce compensable injury. Understood from the standpoint of mutually independent goals, private law is a congeries of unharmonized and competing purposes.

In this book, I will argue that, despite its current popularity, the functionalist understanding of private law is mistaken. Private law, I will claim, is to be grasped only from within and not as the juridical manifestation of a set of extrinsic purposes. If we *must* express this intelligibility in terms of purpose, the only thing to be said is that the purpose of private law is to be private law.

So ingrained is the functionalism of contemporary legal scholarship that ascribing to private law the purpose of being itself is dismissed out of hand as a hopelessly unilluminating tautology.[6] In the dominant contemporary view, private law is—and can be nothing but—the legal manifestation of independently justifiable goals.

Nonetheless, this dismissal of the internal intelligibility of private law is surprising. It cannot be (one hopes) that the very idea of a phenomenon intelligible only in terms of itself is unfamiliar. Some of the most significant phenomena of human life—love or our most meaningful friendships, for instance—are intelligible in this way. We immediately recognize the absurdity of the suggestion that the point of love is to maximize efficiency by allowing for the experience of certain satisfactions while at the same time avoiding the transactions costs of repeated negotiation among the parties to the relationship.[7]

---

[6] Richard A. Posner, *The Problems of Jurisprudence*, 447 (1990); Richard A. Epstein, "The Utilitarian Foundations of Natural Law," 12 *Harvard Journal of Legal and Public Policy* 713 (1989); Owen Fiss, "Coda," 38 *University of Toronto Law Journal* 229 (1988).

[7] Posner, *Economic Analysis of Law*, 238–239.

The very terms of the analysis belie the nature of what is being analyzed. Explaining love in terms of extrinsic ends is necessarily a mistake, because love does not shine in our lives with the borrowed light of an extrinsic end. Love is its own end. My contention is that, in this respect, private law is just like love.

Moreover, it is only to contemporary ears (especially contemporary American ears) that the idea of the internal intelligibility of private law sounds strange. This idea has been standard in Western legal theory ever since the distinctive character of private law was first noticed by Aristotle. Among its subsequent proponents were Aquinas, Grotius, Kant, and Hegel. Indeed, so dominant has the idea of the private law's internal intelligibility been in the history of legal theory that one can fairly regard it as the classical understanding of private law. My intention in this book is to recall this understanding and to argue for its continuing significance.

1.3. The Assumptions of Functionalism

The functional approach to private law goes hand in hand with a number of widespread assumptions concerning law's place among the intellectual disciplines and its status as a justificatory enterprise. For my argument to be persuasive, these assumptions too will have to be reconsidered.

The first assumption is the denial that law is an autonomous body of learning.[8] Because the functionalist goals are justifiable independently and the law's purpose is to reflect them, the study of the law becomes parasitic on the study of the nonlegal disciplines (economics, political theory, and moral philosophy are currently the most popular) that might validate those goals. Hence the proliferation among academic lawyers of rich interdisciplinary interests in "Law and...," with the vital element in the pairing being invariably the nonlegal one. Law provides only the authoritative form into which the conclusions of nonlegal thinking are translated. The governing presupposition is that the content of law cannot be comprehended in and of itself, simply as law. Law is considered to have no meaning except that which it manages to leach from other disciplines and inquiries. Indeed, the capacity to funnel insights about law through alien concepts and

---

[8] For a description of the factors that have undermined the idea of legal autonomy in recent years, see Richard A. Posner, "The Decline of Law as an Autonomous Discipline: 1962–1987," 100 *Harvard Law Review* 761 (1987).

terminology is considered the mark of scholarly detachment and sophistication.

The second assumption underlying the current functionalism is that law and politics are inextricably mixed. Recourse to independently valid goals implies the nonexistence of a distinctively legal mode of justification. On this view, the considerations that count as reasons in the forum of law are no different from the considerations that count as reasons in the arena of politics. Controversy exists regarding the desirability or the feasibility of the various goals that might be proposed, but none of those goals or the arguments supporting them can claim a privileged position by being in some sense inherently legal. Justifications that affect the terms of social interaction can be good or bad, but they cannot be legal as opposed to political.

Of course, functionalists recognize that law contains its own terms and concepts. These, however, are regarded merely as the vehicles of the consequences they carry. One understands the law by discerning these consequences and assessing their desirability. The law's invocation of these concepts is a ritual,[9] a veil to be pierced by clear-headed analysis,[10] a practice encoded with functionalist principles,[11] or even a salutary obfuscation that itself has functional value.[12] The third assumption of the current functionalism, then, is that law's conceptualism is not to be taken seriously in its own right.

The fourth assumption is that no distinction exists between private and public law.[13] All law is public, in that the legal authorities of the state select the favored goals and inscribe them into a schedule of collectively approved aims. The various methods for elaborating the community's purposes—legislation, adjudication, administrative regulation, and so on—are merely different species of the generically single activity of translating goals into a legal reality. The assumption denies that private law is private in any significant sense. At most, private law is public law in disguise.[14]

These four assumptions are intertwined and mutually supporting.

---

[9] Jerome Frank, "What Courts Do In Fact," 26 *Illinois Law Review* 653 (1931).

[10] Felix S. Cohen, "Transcendental Nonsense and the Functional Approach," 35 *Columbia Law Review* 809 (1935).

[11] Richard A. Posner, *The Economic Structure of Tort Law*, 23 (1987).

[12] Guido Calabresi, "Concerning Cause and the Law of Torts: An Essay for Harry Kalven, Jr.," 43 *University of Chicago Law Review* 107 (1975).

[13] For discussion see Symposium on the Private/Public Distinction, 130 *University of Pennsylvania Law Review* 1289 (1982).

[14] Leon Green, "Tort Law Public Law in Disguise," 38 *Texas Law Review* 1, 258 (1959).

The study of law cannot be an autonomous discipline if its subject matter is not a distinctive normative enterprise. Similarly, the discounting of the law's characteristic concepts dissolves law both as an enterprise and as a discipline into whatever pertains to the formulation and assessment of independently justifiable purposes. This flattening of law in turn precludes the hiving off of private law from the collective pursuit of public goals.

In asserting that the sole purpose of private law is to be private law, I aim to undermine all these assumptions. I will argue that private law construes the litigating parties as immediately connected to each other. Interaction so conceived is categorically distinct from that of public law, which relates persons only indirectly through the collective goals determined by state authority. The different mechanisms for enunciating legal norms—adjudication and legislation—broadly reflect the different contours of these two modes of interaction. The autonomy of private law as a body of learning is a consequence of the distinctiveness of private law as a mode of interaction. To understand private law, we must take seriously its fundamental concepts, which, far from being surrogates for the operation of independently justifiable collective purposes, are the juridical markers of the immediate connection between the parties. Understood in this way, private law is a juridical, not a political, phenomenon. By thus jettisoning the functionalist assumptions we can return to the idea that private law is to be understood from within.

1.4. Understanding Private Law from Within

How can private law be understood from within? This question subdivides into two. What is private law? And how is its intelligibility internal?

1.4.1. *What Is Private Law?*

In one sense, the initial question "What is private law?" is premature. Because our aim is to understand what private law is, answering the question is the end—the telos, both the aspiration and the conclusion—of our exposition. The question thus invites us to look back over territory traversed.

In another sense, however, the question points to a journey anticipated. It goes to the identity of what we are attempting to understand.

Unless we have some answer—however blurred, dim, or inchoate—to this question, we will be unable to proceed.

In asking the question "What is private law?" I do not mean to suggest that private law is arcane. On the contrary, the question is meaningful only because private law is within the intellectual experience of any serious student of law. An inquiry into the nature of private law is not an exploration of uncharted territory, but a visit to the familiar landmarks of our legal world. Because we know, however inarticulately or provisionally, what private law is even before we explicitly confront the question, we can insist that the response be true to that knowledge.

The point of departure for theorizing about private law—as well as about anything else—is experience.[15] We can understand only that which is familiar to us. I raise the question "What is private law?" not to short-circuit the inquiry by stipulating a favored definition, but to direct us to our experience of the law, especially the experience of those who are lawyers. This experience allows us to recognize issues of private law and to participate in its characteristic discourse and reasoning. Whatever our difficulty in defining private law or resolving particular issues within it, we are aware of a body of law possessing such characteristics as an allegation of wrongdoing, a claim by one person against another, an injury, a demand for redress, a system of adjudication, a set of liability rules, a corpus of case law, and so on.

Within private law's massive complex of cases, doctrines, principles, concepts, procedures, policies, and standards, certain features have a special significance. These are the ones that are salient in our conception of private law, in the sense that their systematic absence would mean the disappearance of private law as a recognizable mode of ordering. So central are they that any plausible discussion of private law presupposes them or invokes them. At the level of practice, they are inescapably basic to the continuing elaboration of legal doctrine. At the level of theory, they are the features that must be explained or explained away, because an exposition that ignores them or does them violence runs the risk of being regarded as contrived or artificial or somehow amiss. These features characterize private law in the literal sense of providing the indicia of its distinctive character.

Both institutional and conceptual features have this special status. On the institutional side, private law involves an action by plaintiff

---

[15] Georg W. F. Hegel, *Hegel's Logic: Being Part One of the Encyclopedia of the Philosophical Sciences*, sect. 12 (1830) (William Wallace, trans., 3rd ed., 1975).

against defendant, a process of adjudication, a culmination of that process in a judgment that retroactively affirms the rights and duties of the parties, and an entitlement to specific relief or to damages for the violation of those rights or the breach of those duties. On the conceptual side, private law embodies a regime of correlative rights and duties that highlights, among other things, the centrality of the causation of harm and of the distinction between misfeasance and nonfeasance. For lawyers working within this system, these institutional and conceptual features are the stable points within which their thinking moves when engaged in the consideration of private law.

The apparent centrality of these features does not mean that they escape controversy. Legal argument or legal scholarship may call any of them into question. For instance, a court decision may disregard the convention of retroactive judgment by restricting its holding to its prospective effect, or economic analysis may assert the insignificance of the requirement of causation. Nonetheless, a lawyer confronted by these developments may well feel—even if unable to articulate the theoretical reasons for so feeling—that these are not normal (or even mistaken) elaborations of private law, but instead are fundamentally at odds with the nature of the entire enterprise. And private law may reflect this feeling by incorporating them, if at all, only for special occasions and with special justifications.

The ensemble of institutional and conceptual features I have listed serves to identify, at least in a preliminary way, the phenomenon of private law. They form, as it were, the skeleton of private law, the minimal characteristics without which lawyers would begin to lose their sense of private law as a distinctive mode of legal ordering. Unlike the functionalism of independent goals, the account offered in this book arises out of these features and makes them its focus. It thereby purports to contribute to an understanding of private law rather than of independent goals that private law may or may not forward.

Moreover, the features I have mentioned appear to be aspects of, and thus to point toward, the master feature characterizing private law: the direct connection between the particular plaintiff and the particular defendant. The institutional features elaborate the process of litigation and adjudication through which the plaintiff vindicates a claim directly against the defendant. The conceptual features, such as the requirement that the defendant have caused the plaintiff's injury, base that claim on what the defendant has done to the plaintiff. The presence of these features suggests that the central task of private law theory is to illuminate the directness of the connection between the parties.

When we put these two points together—functionalism's attention to independent goals rather than to the features of private law, and the directness of the connection between the parties to the private law relationship—we see why functionalism does not illuminate private law. Instead of relating the parties directly to each other, functionalism inquires into the goals that assessing damages against the defendant and awarding damages to the plaintiff might separately serve. Having bifurcated the parties' relationship, functionalist approaches cannot treat seriously the features that express the plaintiff's direct connection to the defendant.

A consequence of functionalism's academic dominance is that the very idea of direct connection has become unfamiliar. For if one assumes that law must promote independent purposes, what connections can there be except those that operate through such purposes? The apparatus of legal scholarship thus denies what our legal experience affirms. If we are to make sense of private law, we shall have to explore—indeed, resurrect from nonfunctionalist legal theory—the notion of direct connection. The structure of the parties' relationship is therefore a major theme of the chapters that follow.

1.4.2. Internal Intelligibility

The second question to be considered is "How is the intelligibility of private law internal?" To a certain extent, I already engaged this question when I identified private law by referring to its salient characteristics. I made this identification by ascertaining what is presupposed in the practice and discourse of private law. The standpoint for identifying private law was already internal to private law.

Furthermore, not only does an internal account orient itself to the features salient in legal experience, but it also understands those (and other) features as they are understood from within the law. This can be contrasted with functionalist analyses. For instance, a functionalist might construe the plaintiff's right of action as a mechanism for bribing someone to vindicate the collective interest in deterring the defendant's inefficient behavior. An internal account, by contrast, interprets that right of action simply as what it purports to be: the assertion of a right by the plaintiff in response to a wrong suffered at the hands of the defendant. Similarly, while a functionalist might regard causation as an indirect way of achieving market deterrence or some other extrinsic goal, an internal account treats causation as causation, that is, as a concept that represents the unidirectional sequence from action to effect. Whereas the functionalist might regard adjudication as a stylized process of legislative policy making, an internal account adheres to the lawyer's—indeed, the ordinary—sense that adjudication, unlike legislation, declares the rights of the parties, that considerations relevant to the public welfare can be inappropriate to a judicial setting, that in adjudication the substance of argument is intimately related to the process of presenting argument, that, in short, adjudication is not merely a more cramped form of legislation.

Moreover, an internal account respects the dynamism of private law, as understood from the standpoint of those who think about the law in its own terms. Several aspects of this dynamism are particularly significant. First, private law is a justificatory enterprise that articulates normative connections between controversies and their resolutions. Private law is not merely a compilation of the decisions that the legal authorities enforce on the litigants. Rather, for those who take the task of legal thinking upon themselves, the process of justification is at least as important as the results of individual adjudications. In any sophisticated legal system, private law is a collective wisdom—"fined and refined by an infinite number of Grave and Learned Men"[16]—that elaborates the grounds for regarding certain results as justified. The common law, where reasons for judgment are routinely attached to judicial decisions, provides a familiar example of the internal significance of justification.[17]

Second, private law values and tends toward its own coherence. In sophisticated legal systems, private law is not an aggregate of isolated and unrelated emanations of official power. Rather, private law strives to avoid contradiction, to smooth out inconsistencies, and to realize a self-adjusting harmony of principles, rules, and standards. The value that private law places on coherence indicates that the institutional and conceptual features I have listed, understood as lawyers understand them, are the interconnected aspects of a single complex of ideas that illuminates the continuing elaboration of legal doctrine.

---

[16] Thomas Hobbes, *A Dialogue between a Philosopher and a Student of the Common Laws of England*, 55 (Joseph Cropsey, ed., 1971).

[17] The point is equally if not more valid in the civil law tradition, where juristic activity in the form of scholarship or the *responsa jurisprudentium* is regarded as integral to legal enterprise, although separated from the exercise of official power and, consequently, from the direct production of legal results. See John H. Merryman, *The Civil Law Tradition*, 59–64 (1969); Fritz Schulz, *History of Roman Legal Science*, 49–59 (1946).

Third, coherence is an aspiration, not a permanent or inevitable achievement. Not every decision is a felicitous expression of the system's coherence. Particular holdings—even those that have spawned an extensive and ramified jurisprudence—may be mistaken to the extent that they do not adequately reflect the whole ensemble of institutional and conceptual features that must cohere if the law is truly to make sense. The law itself announces the possibility of its own erroneous resolution of particular controversies through dissents and overrulings. Moreover, the very presence in the common law of reasons for judgment is an invitation to take those reasons seriously *as* reasons, and therefore to entertain the possibility that they may be right or wrong, sound or unsound, adequate or inadequate. Thus to understand private law from the inside does not entail the acceptance of the entire corpus of holdings as if they were facts of nature. Internal to the process of law is the incremental transformation or reinterpretation or even the repudiation of specific decisions so as to make them conform to a wider pattern of coherence. In the classic phrase of common law lawyers, the law can work itself pure.[18]

An internal account deals with private law on the basis of the juristic understandings that shape it from within. Jurists share, if only implicitly, assumptions about the institutional and conceptual features that their activity presupposes, about the function these features play in their reasoning, and about the significance of coherence for the elaboration of a legal order. Shared understandings on such basic matters are indispensable to effective participation in juristic activity. Indeed, to participate in that activity is to be animated by those understandings.

The idea of coherence suggests a further aspect of internal intelligibility. Coherence implies integration within a unified structure. In such a structure the whole is greater than the sum of its parts, and the parts are intelligible through their mutual interconnectedness in the whole that they together constitute. If private law has the potential for coherence (as is assumed in its practice), its various features should be understandable through their relationship with one another and, thus, through the roles that each plays in the larger whole.

The notion of coherence, therefore, has a twofold significance for the internal intelligibility of private law. First, the striving for coherence is a characteristic of private law and is thus internal to it. Consequently, those who think about private law in its own terms must

---

[18] Omychund v. Barker, 26 Eng. Rep. 15, 23 (1744).

include the law's pervasive impulse toward coherence within their purview. Second, coherence has no external referent. Coherence signifies a mode of intelligibility that is internal to the relationship between the parts of an integrated whole. Thus not only does an internal approach to private law reflect the features of private law as comprehended from within, but it also regards those features from the standpoint of their mutual relationship within the integrated whole that they constitute. The understanding is internal with respect to its mode of operation, as well as with respect to the concepts and institutions of private law.

1.5. Private Law as a Self-Understanding Enterprise

This twofold conception of internal intelligibility—of an understanding that is internal both to private law and to itself—suggests that private law is simultaneously explanandum and explanans, both an object and a mode of understanding. As an object of understanding, private law presents a set of features that are the focus of intellectual effort. As a mode of understanding, private law is an internal ordering of the features that compose it. To sum up this integration of the activity of understanding with the matter to be understood, we may say that private law is a self-understanding enterprise. The concepts of private law are both the products and the channels of this self-understanding. Similarly, the issuing of reasons for judgment is private law's announcement of the terms of its understanding of itself in the context of particular controversies.

Private law's self-understanding has several aspects. First, as an *understanding*, private law is an engagement of thought. Law is in the first instance an exhibition of intelligence rather than a set of observed regularities or a display of monopolized power.[19] To grasp private law is to come to terms not merely with a series of results that arrange and rearrange the legal landscape in response to pressures operative within the organism of social life, but with the way in which a conceptual structure finds expression in the arguments of those who take the task of legal thinking upon themselves. To regard law in this light is to take seriously the ancient commitment of natural law theorizing to the possibility that law resides in the reason.

Second, as a *self*-understanding, private law is an exhibition of intelligence that operates through reflection on its own intelligibility. In

---

[19] On exhibitions of intelligence see Michael Oakeshott, *On Human Conduct*, 13 (1975).

resolving controversy private law refers to its own ensemble of concepts, doctrines, and institutions, determines the meaning of that
ensemble in specific situations, and attempts to maintain the mutual
coherence of the ensemble's components.

Third, as a self-understanding, private law embodies a dynamic
process. The law's aggregate of specific determinations does not per-
manently freeze the intelligibility of law to their contours. Being an
exhibition of human intelligence rather than of divine omniscience,
private law includes a self-critical dimension that manifests itself in
overrulings, dissents, juristic commentary, and other indicia of controversy. Moreover, because private law develops over time and in the
context of contingent situations, subsequent occurrences or the thinking of subsequent jurists may lead to fresh nuances in doctrine or to a
reevaluation of the coherence or plausibility of previously settled law.

Fourth, as the *law*'s self-understanding, this internal intelligibility is
systemic to the legal order rather than personal to individual jurists.
The point is not to ascribe to the law a super-intellect distinct from
the intellect of individual human beings. Rather, the attribution of
self-understanding to the law draws attention to the personal self-
effacement of those who participate in the elucidation of law from
within. What matters is the law as something to be understood, not
the lawyer or scholar or judge as a freelancing intellectual adventurer.
This is why at common law the reasons for judgment are not seen as
expressing the adjudicator's subjective intent, but are accorded an
objective and impersonal status that yields their author no privilege
with respect to their interpretation.[20] Of course, all understandings are
the activities of the individual minds that understand. But in orienting
their efforts to the law, these minds are themselves possessed by the
idea of that which they are trying to understand,[21] so that this idea is
not only the object of their attentions but the subject that animates
them to work toward its realization and to subordinate their person-
alities to its intelligible requirements. The understandings of jurists

[20] For a dramatic instance, see Mutual Life v. Evatt, [1971] 1 All Eng. Rep. 150 (P.C.),
where the Judicial Committee of the Privy Council, in the face of dissents by Lord Reid and
Lord Morris of Borth-y-Gest, adopted a restrictive interpretation of the opinions that Lord
Reid and Lord Morris had given in the leading case of Hedley, Byrne v. Heller, [1963] 2 All
Eng. Rep. 575 (H. L.).

[21] Samuel Taylor Coleridge, *On the Constitution of the Church and State according to the Idea
of Each*, 5 (John Barrell, ed., 1972).

count to the extent that they are not personal opinions but are expressions of what is demanded of law if it is to remain true to its own nature.

The idea that private law is a self-understanding enterprise directs our attention away from the supposed external purposes of private law to the internal conditions of this self-understanding. Thence arise the issues to be discussed in this book: By what method does one explicate the perspective that animates private law from within? What conceptual structure is presupposed when private law is regarded as a self-reflective and systemic engagement of thought? And having abandoned the standpoint of external purpose, what normative grounding, if any, can we claim for private law?

A satisfactory answer to these questions results in an account of private law that has the following advantages over its functionalist rivals. First, such an account is comprehensive because, unlike the functionalist approaches, it includes the self-understanding that regulates private law from within. Functionalist approaches have limited scope. They align external purposes merely with the results of cases and are indifferent to the specific juristic reasoning, doctrinal structure, and institutional process from which these results emerge. An internal approach, in contrast, considers this reasoning, structure, and process to be crucial indicia of the law's self-understanding. The account is as much an account of these as of the results of particular cases.

Moreover, an account that explicates the self-understanding of private law is decisively critical. Of course, any evaluative theory of private law, including a functionalist one, contains criteria by which it judges certain ideas to be mistaken. However, because functionalist criticism is based on external purposes, jurists working within private law can regard such criticism as irrelevant to their particular enterprise. In contrast, an account that flows from and captures the law's self-understanding assumes the perspective internal to juristic activity. Its strictures, therefore, cannot be evaded.

Finally, an internal account is nonreductive. Because legal concepts and institutions are indicia of the law's self-understanding, an internal account attempts to make sense of them on their own terms by allowing them to have the meaning they have in juristic thought. In contrast to functionalist approaches, it illuminates private law without effacing its juridical character or reducing legal thinking to an alien discipline or technique.

1.6. Law and...

A nonreductive understanding of private law does not imply that other disciplines cannot yield helpful insights. It is of course true that work in other disciplines might show that a particular legal development reflects the presence of specific historical factors, or has certain economic consequences, or fits into a particular pattern of social relationships. But these nonlegal perspectives assume theoretical interest only at the point of reductionism, when they become more ambitious and more exclusive, when their invocation implies the denial that legal material can be juridically understood, when one or another of these views of the cathedral claims primacy in the interpretation of what a cathedral is.[22] Then the presuppositions of invoking the other discipline become firm, specific, and open to analysis and objection.

The assertion that law is to be understood in terms of some other discipline seems to embody two premises, one about the nature of the chosen discipline and the other about the nature of explanation. The premise about the chosen discipline posits that the qualities of a specific discipline entitle it to rank as the primary or exclusive vehicle for the understanding of law. The premise about the nature of explanation, in contrast, posits that an explanation of something is and must always be in terms of something else. Under this premise a thing cannot be grasped except by an intellectual operation that transforms it into something different, so that understanding is conceived as a kind of intellectual digestion in which the juices and acids of the mind work the object presented to it into a matter of different composition and appearance.

The difficulty is that these premises cannot stand together. If explanation of something can only be in terms of something else, the explanation of law in terms of, say, economics or history might be justified, but economics or history could not claim primacy or exclusivity because, under the explanatory premise, their content would itself have to be explained in terms of something else. And so on, in infinite regress. The premise concerned with explanation cannot concede to any other discipline the self-sufficiency that it denies to law.

The other possibility is that the alien discipline, by the sheer force of its own illuminating power and without the aid of the explanatory

---

[22] For the image of the cathedral, see Guido Calabresi and A. Douglas Melamed, "Property Rules, Liability Rules, and Inalienability: One View of the Cathedral," 85 *Harvard Law Review* 1089 (1972).

premise, can account for what is significant in private law. There is, however, little reason for confidence in such an enterprise. The reduction of law to something else involves the sacrifice or the transformation of some element that is salient in the law's self-understanding. The consequent depreciation of the law and its self-understanding decreases the explanatory power of the substituted discipline and renders suspect the claim that the discipline is entitled to primacy by virtue of its sheer illuminating force.

In dismissing the autonomy of private law the methodology of contemporary legal scholarship is, accordingly, confronted with a dilemma. One understands something either through itself or through something else. If one understands something through something else, the self-understanding of private law is denied, but the infinite regress occasioned by this notion of understanding equally undermines every nonlegal mode of understanding private law. If, however, one understands something through itself, the law's self-understanding is possible, and it is sheer dogmatism to insist that other disciplines have, when applied to law, an intelligibility that law lacks on its own. The result is that one must either accede to the possibility that law can be understood through itself or deny the possibility that law can be understood at all. Perhaps it is hardly surprising that dissatisfaction with contemporary scholarship has caused exponents of "critical legal studies" to explore this latter skeptical alternative.

1.7. The Theory of Private Law

So far I have been emphasizing the internal character of private law in order to orient us toward an understanding that reflects that character. Before explicating this understanding in detail, I propose to introduce the three mutually reinforcing theses that constitute it and to indicate the conception of theory that it postulates.

The first thesis concerns the theoretical framework. An internal account of private law sets in opposition to contemporary functionalism the thesis that private law is immanently intelligible. Building on the jurist's understanding of private law as a distinctive and coherent ensemble of characteristic features, the thesis integrates the distinctiveness, the coherence, and the character of private law into a single theoretical approach. Underlying this integration is the notion that one understands a legal relationship through its unifying structure, or "form." Applied to private law, the thesis of immanent intelligibility is a version of legal formalism.

The second thesis identifies Aristotle's conception of corrective justice as the unifying structure that renders private law relationships immanently intelligible. Corrective justice is the pattern of justificatory coherence latent in the bipolar private law relationship of plaintiff to defendant. By abstractly schematizing this pattern, Aristotle made manifest the distinctive rationality of private law. And by decisively distinguishing corrective from distributive justice, Aristotle established the categorical difference between private law and other legal orderings.

The third thesis concerns the normativeness of corrective justice. Corrective justice is the justificatory structure that pertains to the immediate interaction of one free being with another. Its normative force derives from Kant's concept of right as the governing idea for relationships between free beings. For Kant, freedom itself implies juridical obligation. On this view, the doctrines, concepts, and institutions of private law are normative inasmuch as they make a legal reality out of relations of corrective justice.

The idea of private law lies in the synthesis of these three theses. Each of them highlights a different aspect of the possible coherence of private law. Coherence bespeaks a unifying structure. Formalism goes to the relevance of understanding the private law relationship through its structure; corrective justice is the specification of its structure; and Kantian right supplies the moral standpoint immanent in its structure.

The theory of private law presented through the elaboration of these three theses is intimately related to private law itself. An internal understanding of private law reaches corrective justice and the Kantian concept of right by reflecting on the juristic experience of private law and on the presuppositions of that experience. One starts with the ensemble of institutional and conceptual features salient in juristic experience. One then works back to the justificatory framework presupposed in that ensemble, all the while preserving the tendency toward coherence that characterizes both theorizing in general and private law in particular. This process of regression leads to the category of corrective justice, which represents the structure of the relationship between parties at private law. A further regression to the normative presuppositions of this structure leads to the Kantian concept of right. Thus corrective justice and Kantian right are the arch-concepts by which one must conceptualize the features of private law if they are to constitute a coherent normative ensemble.

The relationship between private law and its theory can be formulated as a difference between what is explicit and what is implicit. In one sense, the theory is implicit in the functioning of private law. Because they are categories of legal theory rather than ingredients of positive law, corrective justice and Kantian right are not themselves on the lips of judges. But even though these theoretical categories do not figure explicitly in the discourse of private law, they are implicit in it as a coherent justificatory enterprise, in that they provide its unifying structure and its normative idea. They are as present to private law as the principles of logic are to intelligible speech. Private law makes corrective justice and Kantian right explicit by actualizing them in doctrines, concepts, and institutions that coherently fit together.

In another sense, legal theory renders explicit the philosophical categories that are implicit in private law. Legal theory takes these categories as the specific materials of its investigation. It seeks to elucidate their morphology, their interconnection, and the extent to which they represent viable notions of moral rationality. Whereas private law makes corrective justice and Kantian right explicit as determinants of legal ordering, legal theory makes them explicit as objects of philosophical inquiry.

Of course the closeness of the connection between the theory of private law and private law as a legal reality must be more than a theoretical postulate. Readers are entitled to wonder how this closeness manifests itself in legal doctrine. It is one thing to claim that corrective justice and Kantian right are implicit in a sophisticated system of private law. It is another thing to show how this relationship of implicit to explicit bears on specific legal controversies.

Although my approach applies to the entire domain of liability (tort, contract, and unjust enrichment), my most extended discussion will be of the treatment of accidental injuries in the common law of torts.[23] Because the negligent defendant's culpability seems morally detachable from the fortuity of injury, liability for negligence poses a particularly severe challenge to the stringent notion of coherence that I shall be developing. If formalism illuminates negligence law, it presumably illuminates less problematic bases of liability as well. At any rate, the prevalent academic assumption that crucial doctrines of negligence law—the standard of care and proximate cause, for instance—are explicable only in functionalist terms should dispel the suspicion that I have chosen to defend the internal approach on the legal terrain that contemporary scholars would initially regard as most favorable to it.

---

[23] See below, Chapters 6 and 7.

Thus the argument of this book proceeds from law to theory and back to law. At issue are two broad questions: What theoretical ideas must be implicit in the legal materials, if those materials are to be coherent? And how do the doctrines of private law reflect those ideas? The movement is a circle of thought that feeds upon its own unfolding theoretical explicitness: from the salient features of private law, to the immediate juristic understanding of those features, to the unifying justificatory structure implicit in that understanding, to the explicit elucidation of that structure and of its normative standpoint, to the consideration of the conformity to that structure of a particular set of private law relationships.

My basic contention, then, is that private law relationships have a unifying structure. This structure is internal in the two senses suggested above, that it is implicit in the salient features of private law and that it is intelligible without external referent as a harmony of parts making up a coherent whole. Because private law attempts to elaborate doctrines expressive of its own potential coherence, the structure is also a regulative idea. This is why the purpose of private law is simply to be private law.

2

Legal Formalism

2.1. Introduction

So far I have drawn attention to the internal dimension of private law and to the challenge that it poses to the dominant academic assumptions. In this chapter I want to elucidate the theory appropriate for understanding this internal dimension. The theory goes under the currently discredited name of legal formalism.

Legal formalism leads to an internal understanding of private law by bringing together the ideas of character, kind, and unity. Character refers to the features of private law that are salient in juristic experience. Kind suggests that private law is a distinct phenomenon, categorically different from other modes of legal ordering. And unity is necessary to elucidate the nature of coherence in legal ordering. My contention is that the conjunction of these ideas under the banner of legal formalism constitutes a single integrated approach to legal understanding.

In contemporary academic discussion, "formalism" is a term of opprobrium.[1] Accordingly, there is little familiarity with its vocabulary, conceptual apparatus, and philosophical tradition. Formalism is like a heresy driven underground, whose tenets must be surmised from the derogatory comments of its detractors. Everyone knows that legal formalism asserts the distinction of law and politics. The curiosity of this distinction makes formalism seem at best a pathetic escape from the social relevance of law, and at worst a vicious camouflage of the realities of power. One would not guess that formalism, properly

---

[1] "[T]he name 'formalism' ... seems to me, at least in general use, to be little more than a loosely employed term of abuse." A. W. B. Simpson, "Legal Iconoclasts and Legal Ideals," 58 *Cincinnati Law Review* 819, at 835 (1990).

understood and stripped of the encrustations of hostile polemics, embodies a profound and inescapable truth about law's inner coherence. This truth is the theme of the present chapter.

The most illuminating recent treatment of legal formalism appears in Roberto Unger's influential critique.[2] In Unger's account, three considerations underlie the formalist's differentiation of law from politics. First, formalism asserts the possibility of "a method of legal justification that can be clearly contrasted to open-ended disputes about the basic terms of social life."[3] This method of justification consists in a mode of rationality—"a restrained, relatively apolitical method of analysis"[4]—that is different in kind from the less determinate rationality of political and ideological contest. Second, the distinctive rationality of law is immanent in the legal material on which it operates. Formalist doctrine is characterized by the working out of the implications of law from a standpoint internal to law. Unger accordingly defines legal analysis as a conceptual practice that works from within a collective tradition of institutionally defined materials.[5] Finally, formalism presupposes that the authoritative legal materials "display, though always imperfectly, an intelligible moral order."[6] Formalism relies on some guiding vision about human association that supplies the normative theory sanctifying the tradition as a whole and yet allows some of the received understandings and decisions in it to be rejected as mistaken.

Formalism can accordingly be summed up as proffering the possibility of an "immanent moral rationality."[7] Each term in this phrase corresponds to one of the three features in Unger's description. The first feature, that law has a distinctive rationality, expresses the formalist conception of law negatively through a contrast with political justification. The second, the immanent operation of legal rationality, characterizes law's distinctiveness affirmatively through the claim that

---

[2] Roberto Unger, "The Critical Legal Studies Movement," 96 *Harvard Law Review* 561, 563–576 (1983).

[3] Id. at 564.

[4] Id. at 565.

[5] Id.

[6] Id. In Unger's terminology this feature is a characteristic of objectivism rather than formalism. Unger seems to distinguish between formalism and objectivism only because "[t]he modern lawyer may wish to keep his formalism while avoiding objectivist assumptions." Id. Since Unger himself considers (correctly in my view) such a distinction to be untenable, we may regard objectivism as an aspect of formalism.

[7] Id. at 571.

the content of law is elaborated from within. The third asserts the moral dimension of this rationality, ascribing normative force to its application.

The only observation that needs to be added to Unger's account is that formalism is an integrative notion.[8] The rationality, immanence, and normativeness that, in the formalist view, characterize law are not disjointed attributes contingently combined, but mutually connected aspects of a single complex. For the formalist, law is not merely rational *and* immanent *and* normative. Rather, it has each of these qualities only insofar as it has the other two. Its rationality consists in being immanent in and normative for legal relationships; its immanence reflects its understanding of itself as a locus of normative rationality; and its normativeness is a function of its success in embodying in its doctrines and institutions the rationality immanent in them. Formalism postulates not merely the joint presence of the features to which Unger perceptively refers, but their mutual dependence and interrelationship in a single approach to legal understanding.

2.2. Formalist Method

The basic unit of formalist analysis is the legal relationship. Law connects one person to another through the totality of cases, rules, standards, doctrines, principles, concepts, and processes that come into play when a legal claim is asserted. For example, if the claim is for breach of contract, the legal relationship of the parties is defined by the doctrines and concepts of contract law and by its accompanying procedures of adjudication. Or if the claim concerns a nonconsensual harm, the relationship is made up of the norms, concepts, and processes of tort law.

Formalism looks at these relationships as juridical phenomena. I use the word "juridical" in its etymological sense to refer to that which is "declaratory of *jus*" and which therefore transcends the merely pos-

---

[8] A noteworthy feature of Unger's account of formalism is that he expressly refuses to equate formalism with "the search for a method of deduction from a gapless system of rules." Id. at 564. His characterization of formalism thus differs from the one that appeared in his own earlier work—see Roberto Unger, *Knowledge and Politics*, 92 (1975)—and in the work of others—see, e.g., Duncan Kennedy, "Legal Formality," 2 *Journal of Legal Studies* 351 (1973); Frederick Schauer, "Formalism," 97 *Yale Law Journal* 509 (1988). Unger's account now includes the invocation of all impersonal formulations of legal content, including principles that do not deductively yield determinate conclusions. The relation between formalism and indeterminacy is discussed below in section 8.4.

ited aspect of law as *lex*. The juridical is the legal seen from the standpoint not of its status in positive law but of its intelligibility within an internally coherent normative ensemble. *Qua* juridical, a relationship can be understood in a specifically legal way that is not exhausted by the positivist inquiry into the relationship's legal existence or validity. While it is true that positive law is crucial to identifying the doctrines and processes that constitute the private law relationship, my concern is with that relationship not as a construct of positive law, but as the locus of (in Unger's words) "an immanent moral rationality."

To explicate the juridicial quality of legal relationships, formalism focuses on their internal structure. The formalist wants to comprehend how the components of a legal relationship stand to one another and to the totality that they together form. Is a legal relationship an aggregate of autonomous elements, contingently juxtaposed, connected to one another only like so many grains in a heap of sand? Or are these elements the interdependent constituents of an internally coherent whole?

At the core of formalism lies the priority of the formal over the substantive. Formalism does not directly assess the substantive merit of particular legal determinations. Instead, it first elucidates a legal relationship's internal principle of organization. Only in the light of this formal principle does it then evaluate considerations of substance.

From this attention to the formal arises the formalist differentiation of law from politics. Those who assert the inevitably political nature of law see politics as a direct engagement with the substantive merits or demerits of particular legal arrangements. The formalist, while not denying that legal arrangements have political antecedents and effects, nonetheless holds that the specifically juridical aspect of those arrangements reflects formal considerations that are in some significant sense anterior to judgments about what is substantively desirable.

2.3. Classical Formalism

Legal formalism makes the notion of form central to the understanding of juridical relationships. What, precisely, do we mean by form?

From the beginning of the Western philosophical tradition, the idea of form has been regarded as crucial to intelligibility.[9] In classical

---

[9] For the leading modern treatment of Aristotle's notion of form, see Joseph Owens, *The Doctrine of Being in the Aristotelian "Metaphysics,"* 307–399 (3rd ed., 1978). Twentieth-century legal philosophers who have paid attention to the significance of form are Giorgio del

Greek thought, form defines the nature of something. To seek the intelligibility of something is to inquire into *what* the something is. This search for "whatness" presupposes that the something is a *this* and not a *that*—that it is determinate and thus distinguishable from other things and from the chaos of unintelligible indeterminacy that its identification as a something denies. The principle that makes something what it is and differentiates it from what it is not, is the thing's form.

The classical notion of form has been conveniently summarized and illustrated as follows:

Form is the principle which constitutes not only the identity of an object with other objects of the same kind, but the unity which enables it to be regarded as itself a single object. Thus the form of a table is that essence which is comprehended in its definition, and is, in this case, equivalent to its end or purpose. This form is not only identical in all tables, but is the principle of unity in each. It is that which so orders the indeterminate multiplicity of the sensible "matter" that the various sensible qualities cohere together to constitute a single object. This particular colour, those particular tactual qualities of hardness and smoothness, have in their own nature no affinity with one another. They "belong together" only in so far as the form, plan or design of a table demands the compresence of them all, and so links them one with another that the resulting unit can be designated by a singular noun. No object is possible or conceivable except as such a union of form with matter; and of these two form is universal and intelligible, matter is particular and sensible.[10]

This description of form points to three interrelated aspects. First, to understand something through its form is to regard that thing as having a certain character. This character is the ensemble of characteristics that allows us to define something as the sort of thing it is. The specification of the characteristics that go to a thing's form is not

Vecchio, *The Formal Bases of Law,* 68–80 (John Lisle, trans., 1921); Michael Oakeshott, *On Human Conduct,* 3–8 (1975) (understanding in terms of ideal character); and Rudolf Stammler, *The Theory of Justice,* 167–169 (Isaac Husik, trans., 1925). Emilio Betti has defined form as "an homogeneous structure in which a number of perceptible elements are related to one another and which is suitable for preserving the character of the mind that created it or that is embodied in it." Emilio Betti, "Hermeneutics as the General Methodology of the Geisteswissenschaften," in *Contemporary Hermeneutics,* 54 (Josef Bleicher, ed., 1980).

[10] M. B. Foster, *The Political Philosophies of Plato and Hegel,* 13 (1935).

an exhaustive recapitulation of all of a thing's individuating attributes; that would be as unilluminating as a detailed map drawn to actual scale that reproduced the topography it was supposed to outline. Rather, the exercise demands a selection of those attributes so decisive of the thing's character that they can truly be said to *characterize* it. Elucidation of the thing's form therefore entails differentiating between the attributes that are definitive of the thing and those that are merely incidental.[11] Accordingly, in inquiring after form we can ask, "[W]hat elements of a conception are for other constituents of the same conception logically determining, in the sense that they cannot be left out of account, if one is not to lose the entire mental representation which is directly under discussion...?"[12] Through reference to the ensemble of characteristics that give a thing its character, we comprehend the thing in question as what it is; in classical terminology, we grasp its nature or essence. And conversely, if its character eludes us, we cannot be said to have understood it at all.

Second, form is a means of classification. The presence of form makes something not only the thing that it is but also classifiable with other things of the same kind. Because specifying an ensemble of characteristics involves distinguishing the essential from the inessential qualities, form signifies not the thing's fully individuated particularity, but the general class under which it falls. Form goes to species as well as to essence.

Third, form is a principle of unity. Form is the abstracted representation of what connects the essential attributes to one another, so that together they determine the thing's character. The thing that has a form is a single structured entity, characterized by the ensemble of

---

[11] The differentiation is illustrated by Aquinas: "[T]he essence or nature includes only what falls within the definition of the species; as humanity includes all that falls within the definition of man, for it is by this that man is man, and it is this that humanity signifies, that, namely, whereby man is man. Now individual matter, with all the individuating accidents, does not fall within the definition of the species. For this particular flesh, these bones, this blackness or whiteness, etc., do not fall within the definition of a man. Therefore this flesh, these bones, and the accidental qualities designating this particular matter, are not included in humanity; and yet they are included in the reality which is a man. Hence, the reality which is a man has something in it that humanity does not have. Consequently, humanity and a man are not wholly identical, but humanity is taken to mean the formal part of a man, because the principles whereby a thing is defined function as the formal constituent in relation to individuating matter." Thomas Aquinas, *Summa Theologica*, I, Q. 3, Art. 3, in *Introduction to St. Thomas Aquinas*, 29 (Anton C. Pegis, ed., 1948).

[12] Rudolf Stammler, "Fundamental Tendencies in Modern Jurisprudence" (pts. 1 and 2), 21 *Michigan Law Review* 862, 883 (1922–23).

attributes that make it what it is. Form is thus the idea that elucidates the thing's organization as a unified entity.

To summarize this classical notion: form exhibits character, kind, and unity as the three aspects of intelligibility. In the formalist understanding, character, kind, and unity are interconnected. Character is the set of characteristics that constitutes something as a unified entity classifiable with other entities of the same kind.

The example of the table adduced in the quoted passage illustrates these aspects of formal intelligibility. The form of a table is the design that guides the artisan to impart to the chosen material a set of attributes (elevation, flatness, hardness, smoothness, and so on) that make something a table. In the classical understanding of form, the representation present to the artisan's mind—what the quoted passage terms "the form, plan, or design of the table"—is the principle that organizes these attributes into the single thing known as a table. The set of properties that embodies this form is what makes something a table. Accordingly, the form of a table is present in all tables and enables us to classify them *as* tables.

2.4. Form in Juridical Relationships

The legal formalist understands juridical relations in the light of this venerable notion of form. The form of a juridical relationship is the principle of unity that gives the relationship its character and renders it classifiable with juridical relationships that have the same character, and distinguishable from juridical relationships that have a different character.

Each of the three aspects of formal intelligibility—character, kind, and unity—is applicable to juridical relationships. The character of a juridical relationship is given by the ensemble of features that are salient in our conception of the relationship as the embodiment of a distinct mode of ordering. In the case of private law, these features include the direct linking of plaintiff and defendant institutionally through litigation and adjudication and doctrinally through causation and the other appurtenances of correlative right and duty. If these legal markers of the link between plaintiff and defendant were systematically absent, relationships of private law would cease to exist.

The presence of these characterizing features distinguishes private law from other kinds of legal ordering, thereby enabling the relationships of private law to be classified together. The classification of juridical relationships reflects the lawyer's awareness that different modes of ordering have different sets of legal features. A difference in character bespeaks a difference in kind.

The unity of a juridical relationship lies in its coherence. In the formalist view, a juridically intelligible relationship does not consist in an aggregate of conceptually disjoined or inconsistent elements that, like pebbles in a pile, happen to be juxtaposed. Rather, the relationship forms a normative unit, each feature of which expresses the unifying principle that pervades the entire relationship and that makes it a coherent juridical phenomenon.

Among the three aspects of formal intelligibility, the aspect of unity is paramount. Just as the form of the table brings together the qualities that characterize tables as a class of objects, so in a juridical relationship the principle of the relationship's unity determines its character and classification. The principle of unity states the terms under which certain legal features coalesce in a single juridical relationship. It thus shapes the relationship's character by excluding from it features that do not coherently interconnect. Moreover, different kinds of juridical relationships have features that are not only different but differently organized, so that the various kinds of unity applicable to juridical relationships serve a classificatory function. Indeed, on the formalist view, the contrast between private law and other legal orderings rests on the different principles of unity evinced by the various kinds of legal relationships.[13]

2.5. The Role of Coherence

In explaining form as the combination of character, kind, and unity, I made use of the illustration of the table. I want now to register an important caveat about this illustration. Although they both involve character, kind, and unity, the formal understanding of juridical relationships differs significantly from the formal understanding of tables and other natural and artifactual objects. The features that determine the character of objects are predicates that describe physical attributes. In contrast, the features that determine the character of juridical relationships are legal concepts, doctrines, principles, and institutional arrangements.

A different conception of unity applies to the attributes of tables than applies to the features of a juridical relationship. A table brings together a group of predicates that, as the quoted passage says, "have

---

[13] See below, Chapter 3.

in their own nature no affinity with one another."[14] The table may be hard, smooth, and elevated, but hardness has in itself nothing to do with smoothness, nor smoothness with height. These otherwise diverse properties come together in a single object "only in so far as the form...demands the compresence of them all."[15] Although coexisting in the table, the properties as such are indifferent to one another.[16]

A more stringent conception of unity applies to juridical relationships, especially to those of private law. As I have noted, private law values its own internal coherence. The coherence of a private law relationship refers to more than the compresence of a number of otherwise independent features. If a private law relationship is to be coherent, the features of that relationship cannot subsist in a mutual indifference that disconnects the elements of the plaintiff's claim from one another and from their litigational and adjudicative environment. Instead, coherence points to the existence of some sort of internal connection between the various features that cohere. For a juridical relationship to be coherent, its component features must come together not through the operation of something beyond them that brings them together but because they are conceptually connected in such a way that, in some sense still to be explained, they intrinsically belong together.

The role of coherence should obviate two possible misconceptions of the formalist position. First, one might suppose that, by directing us toward the distinctive characteristics of a juridical relationship, the formalist's reference to character and class is an invitation to essentialism. On an essentialist view, an entity has certain of its properties essentially, in the sense that it could not fail to have those properties;[17] if it did so fail, it would not be the entity we initially thought it was. The entity's essential properties supply the ultimate measure for understanding what the entity is. Considered in essentialist terms, a juridical relationship would be an entity having certain essential properties that together constitute the criterion of the relationship's intelligibility.

Seeing legal formalism as a version of essentialism involves ignoring the primacy of unity over character and kind. It is true that the char-

---

[14]   See above, note 10.

[15]   Id.

[16]   See Georg W. F. Hegel, *The Phenomenology of Spirit*, chap. 2 (Arnold V. Miller, trans., 1977) (discussing the difficulty of locating the principle of unity among the various properties of a physical object).

[17]   Michael A. Slote, *Metaphysics and Essence*, 1 (1974).

acter of a juridical relationship is contained in the set of features that are salient in our conception of the relationship as the embodiment of a distinct mode of ordering; by referring to that combination of features, accordingly, juristic experience allows us to identify the kind of relationship that we are seeking to understand. A given list of features, however, is not the ultimate criterion of juridical intelligibility. The features are relevant to intelligibility only on the assumption that a sophisticated legal system values its own coherence and that therefore the features that juristic experience regards as salient reflect the system's attempts to achieve coherence. Those attempts may, even in the law's self-understanding, be unsuccessful, incomplete, defective, or mistaken.[18] If, however, the salient features completely defied coherent ordering (if, for instance, we could not see in them even the inchoate glimmerings of a coherent justificatory enterprise), we would be unable to understand them as juridical phenomena. The characteristics of a legal relationship are juridically intelligible only from the standpoint of their possible coherence. For the legal formalist, then, the truly operative criterion is not the presence of the features but their mutual coherence.

The second misconception is that formalism is concerned with the meaning or the use of words like "private law" and "tort law." Under this misconception, questions like "What is private law?" or "What is tort law?" are queries not into the salient features of private law and tort law, but into the entitlement to use the words "private law" and "tort law." The formalist specification of the character of private law or of tort law is seen as an attempt to determine proper semantic meaning or linguistic usage. The upshot is that features of positive law that do not satisfy the formalist strictures are not really what is meant by "private law" or "tort law"—a conclusion that, even if it were at all important, might be confirmed or refuted simply by canvassing the appropriate community of language users.

Legal formalism, however, is not a semantic or lexicographical project. Its concern is with the intelligibility of juridical relationships, not with what those various relationships might be called. It is true that the English language groups certain juridical relationships under the term "tort law," so that those words provide access to the juridical phenomena to which they refer. Nonetheless, the formalist theme is the intelligibility of those phenomena, not the usage of the words. Even if we happened to call that grouping of juridical relationships by a

---

[18] See above, section 1.4.2.

different name or had no general name for it but a number of separately labeled liability fields (occupiers' liability, products liability, and
so on) that featured the conjunction of certain doctrines and institutions, the formalist's interest in the coherence of juridical relationships
would be unaffected.

2.6. The Nature of Coherence

The reference to coherence raises many questions. What is it, precisely,
that must cohere with what? What makes the relationship among these
things, whatever they are, one of coherence? Why is coherence important to private law? In short, what conception of coherence is operative in private law and how is that conception itself to be explicated?

In this section I first set out in fairly abstract terms what the coherence of private law relationships entails, and I then turn to a specific
illustration from tort law. In the next section, I discuss why coherence
so conceived is a requirement of both the normativeness and the intelligibility of private law. In both sections I emphasize the close linkage
between the notion of coherence and the notion of justification.

2.6.1. Coherence and Unity

In the law's self-understanding, private law is a justificatory enterprise.
The relationship between the parties is not merely an inert datum of
positive law, but an expression of—or at least an attempt to express—
justified terms of interaction. Coherence must be understood in the light
of this justificatory dimension. For a private law relationship to be coherent, the consideration that justifies any feature of that relationship must
cohere with the considerations that justify every other feature of it.
Coherence is the interlocking into a single integrated justification of all
the justificatory considerations that pertain to a juridical relationship.

Tort law, for instance, connects the plaintiff to the defendant
through an institutional procedure (the plaintiff-defendant lawsuit)
and through an ensemble of doctrines and concepts (cause, fault, duty,
remoteness, and so on). We can inquire into the justification for any
of the relationship's features: Why does the procedure link a specific
plaintiff to a specific defendant? Why is the causation of injury generally a precondition of liability? Why does fault in an action for negligence consist in the breach of an objective rather than a subjective

standard of care? Why is the defendant, if liable, obligated to pay precisely what the plaintiff is entitled to receive? The relationship between the parties to a tort action is coherent if the answers to all these questions cohere. And the presence of any feature unsupportable by a justificatory consideration that coheres with the considerations justifying the other features renders the relationship as a whole incoherent to that extent.

Two points about this conception of coherence are worth noting. The first concerns what has to cohere. In the formalist approach to private law, coherence applies to the considerations that justify the various features composing a private law relationship. These features are the concepts, doctrines, and institutional arrangements that come into play on the assertion of a legal claim. The relationship between the parties is a coherent one to the extent that its features cohere, and its features cohere to the extent that the considerations that justify them do.

The second point concerns the meaning and operation of coherence. By insisting that the justificatory considerations interlock into a single integrated justification, the formalist puts forward a particularly demanding conception of coherence. Coherence goes beyond mutual consistency or noncontradiction to the underlying unity of the elements that cohere. Of course considerations that are inconsistent or contradictory do not cohere, but coherence is more than the absence of inconsistency or contradiction. Features can be consistent or noncontradictory because they exist indifferent to one another on separate epistemological planes, as do hardness and elevation in the example of the table. Consistency and noncontradiction might accordingly attest only to the fundamental discreteness rather than to the unity of the elements to which they apply. In contrast, the features of a juridical relationship cohere when their justifications not merely coexist in the relationship but form an integrated justificatory ensemble.

The idea of coherence has as its counterpart the idea of the unity of the aspects that cohere. One might think that the requirement of unity is satisfied by the very fact that the features participate in a single legal relationship, for does not singleness itself signify some kind of unity? One can distinguish, however, two ways to conceive of a unity.[19]

---

[19] The nature of unity was much discussed among medieval Jewish philosophers, who were concerned to vindicate the unity of God. My outline of the two kinds of ordering follows the distinction between accidental and true unity in the eleventh- or twelfth-century work of Bachya ibn Paquda. See Rabbi Bachya Ben Joseph ibn Paquda, *Duties of the Heart*, vol. 2, 90–92 (Moses Hyamson, trans., 1962).

In the first way, the aspects that are united are intelligible only through the integrated whole that they form as an ensemble. Every aspect contributes to the meaning of the whole, and the whole gives meaning to its constituent aspects. Since the whole is greater than the sum of its parts, each of the parts can be grasped only through comprehending its interconnection with the others and, thus, the relative position of each part in the whole that all the parts together constitute. Every aspect conditions and is simultaneously conditioned by the others, so that to refer to one is to presuppose the relevance of the rest. The aspects belong together and are unintelligible in isolation. Their unity is intrinsic to them.

In the second way, the aspects are independent of one another and fully comprehensible in isolation. When placed together, the aspects form an aggregate, a sum of individually intelligible items. Their conjunction in a single phenomenon arises not from an internal necessity of their own intelligible natures but from a separate and extrinsic operation upon them. They are atomistic elements heaped together like grains of sand in a single sandpile. Their unity is accidental.

The difference between these two conceptions of unity is that intrinsic unity presents a coherent ordering of its constitutive aspects whereas accidental unity does not. An intrinsic unity is an intimate community in which every constituent is implicated in every other constituent; an accidental unity is a loose confederacy of autonomous elements. The constituents of an intrinsic unity are the reciprocally reinforcing articulations of the single idea that runs through the phenomenon as a whole; the constituents of an accidental unity are the mutually independent factors that all happen to be present in the phenomenon.

If a legal relationship embodies an intrinsic unity, the considerations that justify the various features of that relationship do not play their justificatory role in isolation from one another. What connects the features so that they form a single juridical relationship is that their justifications dovetail into a single justification that pervades the entire relationship.

If, however, a legal relationship embodies an accidental unity, its various features come together because positive law happens to bring them together or because a single designation (for example, "tort law") happens to apply to them in combination. The relationship between the considerations that justify these features is not intrinsic to their justificatory function but rather reflects the fact that they apply to a legal space conventionally regarded as common to them all. The features of the relationship are linked because of the contingencies of positive law or linguistic usage.

Intrinsic and accidental conceptions of unity yield different understandings of the role of positive law. In a relationship whose features are intrinsically unified, the role of positive law is to make explicit—and thus give authoritative public recognition to—the justificatory connection already implicit in the relation between the features. For an accidental unity, however, positive law is the external force that combines (or chooses not to combine) features whose justifications are otherwise unconnected. Put in terms of legal process, positive law functions adjudicatively for intrinsically unified relationships and legislatively for accidentally unified ones.

Coherence, accordingly, signifies the intrinsic unity of the features that cohere. Unless the justificatory momentum of one feature carries over to the others, the relationship as a whole does not hold together. Conversely, if the consideration that justifies one feature of a legal relationship is independent of the consideration that justifies any other, the relationship is incoherent to that extent.

This conception of coherence as involving a single integrated justification has a particular consequence for the relationships of private law. As noted earlier, the salient characteristic of these relationships is the doctrinal and institutional linking of plaintiff and defendant. If this linkage is coherent, it will be supported by a single justification that embraces the two parties in their mutual connection. Because the relationship is between two particular parties, neither more nor less, the justification for the relationship must extend up to but not beyond those two parties. The justification should be neither more expansive by embracing parties outside the relationship nor more restrictive by applying to one of the parties but not to the other.

The reason for requiring the justification of a private law relationship to be coterminous with the relationship is that coherence is incompatible with the presence of independent justificatory considerations. If the normative force of the justification is overinclusive because it embraces additional parties, we need, *ex hypothesi*, a second justificatory consideration to restrict its application to the plaintiff and the defendant. Similarly, if the normative force of the justification is underinclusive because it applies to only one of the parties, we need a second consideration that applies to the other. Neither the absence nor the presence of the second consideration is satisfactory. If the second consideration is absent, then the relationship as such, that is, the specific nexus of plaintiff and defendant, has not been justified.

And if it is present, then the overall justification is composed of mutually independent elements, so that the justification for the specific nexus is incoherent.

2.6.2. The Example of Loss-Spreading

Let me turn from these abstract formulations to a specific example. Consider the following statement from a foundational case of American products liability. In arguing that the manufacturer of a bottle that exploded ought to be liable even without fault, Justice Traynor noted that "[t]he cost of an injury and the loss of health and time may be an overwhelming misfortune to the person injured, and a needless one, for the risk of injury can be insured by the manufacturer and distributed among the public as a cost of doing business."[20]

This sentence encapsulates a constant theme of contemporary tort analysis: the best resolution of the plaintiff's tragedy is to dissipate the effect of injury through the defendant's insurance, thereby shifting the loss from the one person massively affected to a large group whose members would share—and therefore be less sensitive to—the burden. The solution envisages both an end and a means. The end is the spreading of loss among people and over time, in the belief that a large number of small deprivations is easier to bear than a single large one. The means is the channeling of liability through insurance arrangements, so that the group among which the cost of injury is dissipated is the pool of insured persons who have insured against that kind of loss.

The reference to insurance introduces an incoherence into the tort relationship. As a justification for holding an injurer liable, the insurance rationale is overinclusive. On the insurance rationale the purpose of the plaintiff's lawsuit is to secure access to the insurance fund to which the defendant has contributed. The idea of distributing injury losses through insurance, however, does not justify singling out for liability the particular party who caused the injury. The rationale would apply against any member of the insurance pool—indeed, against any member of *any* liability insurance pool. The insurance rationale is overinclusive in that it justifies the liability not of the injurer in particular, but of anyone (including the injurer) for whom liability triggers the payment of insurance.

---

[20] Escola v. Coca-Cola Bottling Co., 24 Cal. 2d 453, 462; 150 P. 2d 436, 441 (1944) (Traynor, J., concurring).

Of course tort law (even as developed by Justice Traynor) does not actually allow the plaintiff to recover from any person with liability insurance. In tort law the juridical relationship is between the victim and the perpetrator of the injury. Tort law effectively curtails the operation of the insurance rationale by making the causation of injury to the plaintiff a prerequisite to the defendant's liability.

The consideration that justifies the requirement of causation is independent of the insurance rationale. From the standpoint of insurance as a device for the spreading of losses, the fact that the defendant has caused the plaintiff's injury is no reason to hold the defendant, rather than some other insured person, liable. Conversely, from the stand-point of causation, the lack of insurance is no reason to exclude the defendant from liability. Causation and insurance are heterogeneous factors, the former dealing with the occurrence of injury, the latter with the alleviation of its effects. The consideration (whatever it is) that justifies the causation requirement must focus on the sequence from the defendant's action to the plaintiff's injury; that sequence has nothing to do with insurance as a mechanism for loss-spreading.

Because causation and insurance are independent of each other, a private law relationship that combines them is incoherent. The justificatory considerations that each represents do not lock into a single integrated justification. They come together in the tort relationship not because their justificatory significance makes them intrinsically complementary, but because positive law, as embodied in the pronouncements of Justice Traynor, brings them together in an accidental unity.

The incoherence exemplified in this sentence from Justice Traynor's judgment applies not only to liability insurance as a means of loss-spreading, but to the very idea of using tort law to spread losses. As a goal of tort law, loss-spreading is dramatically overinclusive. The idea that money should be exacted from some for the benefit of others in order to spread the burden of a catastrophic loss as lightly and as widely as possible is as pertinent to a nontortious injury as to a tortious one. Moreover, the principle of the diminishing marginal utility on which loss-spreading rests should lead not to the adjudication of tortious claims but to social insurance of accident losses and, more generally, to a redistribution of wealth through progressive taxation.[21] Loss-spreading thus overshoots both the doctrines and the institutions that connect the tort plaintiff to the tort defendant.

---

[21] Guido Calabresi, *The Costs of Accidents*, 39–45 (1970).

The problem with loss-spreading and other versions of the goal of compensation is that they focus exclusively on the victim of injury without implicating its perpetrator. Behind the identification of compensation as a goal of tort law is the need created in the victim by the very fact of injury. This need, however, is unaffected by the way the injury was produced. The goal of compensation does not in itself embrace the tortfeasor.

If compensation is to be a goal of tort law, it must be supplemented by the introduction of a second goal that focuses on the action of the defendant. A goal frequently invoked for this purpose is deterrence,[22] whereby the prospect of tort liability is supposed to discourage the potential tortfeasor from the commission of a wrong. When taken together compensation and deterrence encompass both poles of the tort relationship: deterrence operates on actors by providing incentives to avoid acts that might cause harm, and compensation focuses on the injuries suffered by the victim.

Invoking these goals makes the tort relationship incoherent, because the goals are independent of each other. If compensation is justified at all, it is justified even for injuries that cannot be deterred. Similarly, if deterrence is justified, it is justified regardless of whether injury occurs. Nothing about the justificatory consideration expressed by the goal of compensation limits its operation to injuries that the injurer should be deterred from causing. And nothing about the justificatory consideration expressed by the goal of deterrence limits its operation to acts that cause compensable injury. The two goals do not coalesce into a single integrated justification.

2.7. Why Coherence Matters

I must now confront a crucial question. Even allowing that a relationship that combines mutually independent considerations is incoherent, why does coherence matter? In this section I propose two interrelated answers. First, because coherence is essential for justification, the coherence of the private law relationship is indispensable to private law's being a justificatory enterprise. Second, only from the perspective of its possible coherence can we make sense of the nexus between a particular plaintiff and defendant. Thus coherence is a presupposition both of the justificatory nature and of the intelligibility of private law.

---

[22] Or punishment. The structure of the argument that follows is not affected by the identity of the defendant-oriented goal.

2.7.1. Coherence and Justification

The first answer to the question "Why does coherence matter?" is this: coherence matters because justification matters. The private law relationship is not merely an emanation of official power; it is a mode of moral association that attaches decisive importance to the justification of the norms that constitute it. Coherence is important for private law relationships because it is indispensable to justification.

The necessity for coherence arises from the nature of justification. A justification justifies: it has normative authority with respect to the material to which it applies. The point of adducing a justification is to allow that authority to govern whatever falls within its scope. Thus if a justification is to function as a justification, it must be permitted, as it were, to expand into the space that it naturally fills. Consequently, a justification sets its own limit. For an extrinsic factor to cut the justification short is normatively arbitrary.

An incoherent private law relationship is arbitrary in precisely this way. The features of such a relationship are supported by justificatory considerations that are independent of—and thus extrinsic to—one another. Yet because these considerations are situated within the same relationship, they are mutually limiting. Instead of applying to the full extent of its normative reach, each justificatory consideration truncates the others. None of them plays a truly justificatory role.

The loss-spreading example illustrates the point. Whether we look at the use of liability insurance as a means of loss-spreading or at the loss-spreading principle itself or at the coexistence of compensation and deterrence, we see the arbitrariness of combining independent justificatory considerations. Housed within the relationship of victim and injurer, the idea of loss-spreading both impedes and is impeded by a competing consideration.

Consider, first, the effect of the causation requirement on the operation of the insurance rationale. Once we accept the plausibility of allowing injured plaintiffs to tap into the defendant's liability insurance, the defendant, if insured, should be held liable regardless of his or her role in causing the injury. The normative appeal of the idea that loss is more easily borne when distributed among the participants in an insurance pool is unaffected by the identification of the injurer. From the standpoint of the insurance rationale, the defendant's causal role is an arbitrary factor, no more relevant a reason for limiting loss-spreading than is the color of the defendant's hair. By insisting on a link between injury and cause, the law frustrates the accomplishment of loss-spreading whenever the injurer happens to have insufficient insurance.

Even without the mechanism of liability insurance, loss-spreading can be achieved only haphazardly through tort law. Tort law encases loss-spreading in an ill-fitting framework of doctrine and procedure. The idea of loss-spreading, that the cost of injuries should be distributed among the largest possible number, is as applicable to nontortious injuries as it is to tortious ones. Moreover, the procedure appropriate to this idea is not the adjudication of individual tort claims, but a legislated levy on the entire citizen body to spread the costs of accidents as thinly and as broadly as possible. Doctrinally and procedurally, tort law arbitrarily curtails loss-spreading by preventing it from extending to the limits of its justificatory authority.

The same difficulty presents itself when the tort relationship is understood as a combination of compensation and deterrence. From the standpoint of deterrence, tort damages operate excessively on some defendants and insufficiently on others. On the one hand, the damage award reflects the severity of the injury suffered by the plaintiff, even though the defendant might have been deterred by the prospect of a lower penalty or might have required the incentive of a higher one. On the other hand, the deterrent falls only upon those who actually cause injury, thus passing over wrongdoers whose actions fortuitously do not result in harm. Similarly, the plaintiff receives compensation only when the law fails to deter the defendant, even though the plaintiff's need for compensation does not vary with the rationality of the deterrence. Tort damages tie compensation to deterrence in a way that frustrates the full achievement of either. As justificatory considerations operating within the same relationship, compensation and deterrence are mutually limiting.[23]

The treatment of the tort relationship as a compound of independent and mutually limiting considerations means that the justificatory authority of these considerations is not taken seriously. Because compensation and deterrence limit each other, neither fills the space to which its justificatory status entitles it. If compensation is a worthwhile goal, why not compensate regardless of how the injury is produced? If the justificatory force of deterrence is powerful enough to

---

[23] As Bruce Berner observes, "Thus, the initially alluring fact that under the Tort Model each dollar of compensation is a dollar of punishment and vice versa has an incurable downside—*compensation and punishment are mutually limiting.*" Bruce G. Berner, "Fourth Amendment Enforcement Models: Analysis and Proposal," 16 *Valparaiso University Law Review* 215, 242 (1982) (emphasis in original).

limit compensation, why is its operation triggered only by the occurrence of a compensable injury? It seems strange that the working of deterrence should depend on a consideration—the presence of an occasion for compensation—that deterrence itself limits, just as it is strange that compensation should operate only when conjoined to deterrence, which compensation similarly limits.

Two alternatives lie open if we wish to pursue the possibility of justifying the private law relationship by reference to such independent goals as compensation and deterrence. One is to postulate that the existence of legal relationships resting on mutually limiting justifications in fact serves some comprehensive justificatory purpose, such as the maximization of utility. Perhaps, when viewed from a suitably broad perspective, relationships that amalgamate imperfectly achieved goals are preferable to a more coherently organized system of law. The fact that the goals are fortuitously combined in a single relationship, however, undermines the plausibility of this alternative. Can one seriously believe that deterrence and compensation are optimally combined when the incidence and amount of the deterrence are set by the fortuity of the plaintiff's injury, and when the occurrence of compensation for the injured is determined by the need to deter potential injurers? That would be a coincidence of Panglossian proportion.

The other alternative is to decry the moral arbitrariness of private law so understood. Recognition of this arbitrariness, for instance, has led some scholars to propose the abolition of tort law. These scholars argue that tort law, understood as a mixture of compensation and deterrence, is a double lottery. It is a lottery for plaintiffs, because instead of treating alike victims who suffer like harms, it makes their entitlement to compensation depend upon the happenstance of the defendant's faulty conduct. At the same time, it is a lottery for defendants, because the existence and extent of their liability depends on the fortuitous nature of the resulting harm.[24]

Those who criticize tort law on these grounds argue that instead of having a mode of ordering that entrenches the purposeless mutual interference of different goals, we should translate each goal into the legal ordering appropriate to its particular requirements. We would then have one set of institutions that dealt with deterrence and another

---

[24] Terence G. Ison, *The Forensic Lottery* (1967); Marc A. Franklin, "Replacing the Negligence Lottery: Compensation and Selective Reimbursement," 53 *Virginia Law Review* 774 (1967); Stephen D. Sugarman, "Doing Away with Tort Law," 73 *California Law Review* 555 (1985).

that dealt with compensation. Whatever mutual restrictions were necessary (for example, not setting compensation so high that deterrence suffers) would be dealt with on the merits rather than remitted to the haphazard operation of tort law. Thus tort law would be replaced by administrative or compensatory regimes that more rationally reflect the justificatory considerations that it incoherently combines.

This argument for the abolition of tort law accurately reflects the moral arbitrariness of incoherent legal relationships. Private law is normatively inadequate if it is understood in terms of independent goals. Such goals are mutually frustrating. Each of them is limited not by the boundaries to which its justificatory authority entitles it, but by the competing presence in the same legal relationship of different goals. In this mixing of justifications, no single one of them occupies the entire area to which it applies. Thus none of them in fact functions as a justification. The consequence of incoherence is that private law ceases to be a justificatory enterprise.

2.7.2. Coherence and Intelligibility

In considering why coherence matters, I have so far concentrated on coherence as a justificatory necessity. I now turn to the role of coherence in rendering private law intelligible.

Because private law is itself a justificatory phenomenon, the issues of justification and intelligibility are closely related. As a justificatory necessity, coherence is what private law values and tends toward to the extent that it takes the project of justification seriously. Their potential coherence therefore supplies the internal standpoint from which to understand the doctrines, concepts, and institutional processes of private law.

The assumption behind this emphasis on coherence is not that the juridical relationships of positive law are in fact always coherent. Whether (or to what extent) they are is a separate issue. Rather, the point is that the justificatory nature of juridical relationships makes coherence their implicit organizing principle. Accordingly, a legal system that takes the justificatory enterprise seriously attempts to develop its doctrines and institutions so as to reflect the requirements of coherence. Coherence is thus a virtue immanent in such a system, so that one makes sense of its relationships by seeing them as exemplifications of that virtue. The operative premise is not that the legal relationships under a specific regime of positive law are actually coherent, but that coherence is the standard for whatever juridical intelligibility those relationships have.[25]

For the private law relationship, intelligibility and coherence have one overriding focus: the direct nexus between the plaintiff and the defendant. Private law's adjudicative process, doctrinal structure, and remedial apparatus all reflect the parties' direct connection. One cannot understand private law's linking of this particular plaintiff and defendant by thinking in terms of considerations that pertain independently to each of the parties and thus leave unexplained the relationship between them. The relationship as such is intelligible only if we can understand it through considerations that, being themselves relational, tie the parties to each other in a coherent whole.

For example, the analysis of tort law in terms of deterrence and compensation fails to make sense of the relationship between the parties. Each goal applies to one of the parties (compensation to the plaintiff and deterrence to the defendant), but neither supplies a reason for linking the parties to each other. Nor do they, being independent, supply this reason when combined. There may be good reason for compensating injured persons and for deterring injurious acts, but there is no reason to connect a particular application of deterrence with a particular award of compensation.

Of course, what links the parties is the particular accident. That accident, however, does not cause the compensation rationale and the insurance rationale to converge on a particular tort relationship. From a deterrence standpoint, the accident is irrelevant, since the moral force of deterrence applies regardless of whether harm materializes. From a compensation standpoint, the accident does not morally differentiate this injured person from other injured persons who also have claims under the compensation rationale. Thus neither rationale singles out the particular accident through which the law might link the particular plaintiff to the particular defendant.

To understand the relationship between the parties, we need a set of considerations that embraces plaintiff and defendant in a single movement of thought. The accident must therefore be seen as the locus

---

[25] Law's justificatory character makes the remarks of Northrop Frye about poetry even more apposite to legal relationships: "'Every poem must necessarily be a perfect unity,' says Blake: this, as the wording implies, is not a statement of fact about all existing poems, but a statement of the hypothesis which every reader adopts in first trying to comprehend even the most chaotic poem ever written." Northrop Frye, *Anatomy of Criticism: Four Essays*, 77 (1957).

of justificatory considerations that apply simultaneously to both injurer and victim. This desideratum can be satisfied only if the factors pertinent to the moral situation of both parties interlock in a single justification that is coterminous with the parties' relationship. The relationship can then be understood as a unity whose components cohere.

Thus the need to account for private law's linking of plaintiff and defendant makes relevant the distinction, mentioned in section 2.6, between accidental and intrinsic unity. In an intrinsic unity, the nexus between the parties reflects justificatory considerations that are coherent when combined. We can therefore account for the linking of the parties by pointing to the integrated justification that such linking achieves. If, on the other hand, the relationship is conceived as an accidental unity, the joinder of the parties must be attributed not to a justificatory necessity but to the juridically unexplained operation of convention or positive law. Once it has been hacked into discrete segments that can no longer be coherently reassembled, the relationship between the parties becomes unintelligible. And so do the concepts, doctrines, and processes that are the legal manifestations of that relationship.

The formalist claim, then, is that private law is intelligible to the extent that the doctrinal and institutional features linking plaintiff to defendant can be seen as a coherent set. For the formalist, the exploration of this coherence—its morphology, its normative grounding, its consequence for determining liability rules, and so on—is central to understanding what a private law relationship is. And such a relationship differs in kind from other legal relationships because it differs both in its salient features and in its internally unifying structure.

Accordingly, the postulate of coherence implicates all three aspects of juridical form: unity, character, and kind. First, as the principle of a juridical relationship's unity, coherence is crucial both to the relationship's character and to its kind. Second, in a sophisticated legal system the features that define the character of a juridical relationship are the markers of the law's striving to achieve coherence. Third, juridical relationships of the same kind exemplify a mode of ordering in which the same principle of unity is operative. To understand a relationship of private law, therefore, one must understand how the characteristic features of the relationship come together to form the kind of relationship that they do. Unity, character, and kind are thus the interconnected aspects of a single approach to juridical intelligibility.

2.8. The Formalism of Coherence

Later, in the last chapter, I will discuss in some detail the formalist claim that private law is apolitical. Here, though, I want briefly to indicate the bearing of coherence on that claim.

In the formalist understanding of private law, coherence has a criterial function. By this I mean that the unity in a juridical relationship provides the standpoint from which to assess both the justificatory standing of any feature in the relationship and the intelligibility of the relationship as a whole. No feature has a significance that is independent of its interplay with the other features. It is not the presence or absence of this or that desirable feature that is decisive for the assessment of a juridical relationship, but the extent to which all of its features cohere.

The role of coherence is what keeps private law, according to the formalist understanding of it, separate from politics. One way of being apolitical is by avoiding judgments about the desirability of particular legal arrangements. The formalist insistence on coherence in legal justification is apolitical in precisely this way. In the formalist view, the central question for private law is not whether a given exercise of state power is desirable on its merits, but whether the justificatory consideration that supports it coheres with the considerations that support the other features of the relationship. An argument of coherence does not affirm the goodness of any feature of a legal relationship; it only affirms the connection between that feature and other features. Thus the formalist's emphasis on coherence bears out Unger's observation that formalism postulates the possibility of distinguishing between legal and political rationality.

To return to my illustration, the adverse judgment that formalism passes on the goals of compensation and deterrence in tort law is not due to an antipathy toward these goals considered on their own. Formalism is unconcerned with the substantive merit of particular justifications; all that formalism demands is that justifications animating private law live up to the coherence required of their justificatory status. Accordingly, questions about the undesirable incentive effects of compensation or about the soundness of the theory (on which the loss-spreading version of compensation is based) of the decreasing marginal utility of money play no role in the formalist rejection of compensation as a goal of tort law. That goal is shunned in the tort context for the company it keeps, not for what it is. If compensation were conjoined to doctrinal and institutional features that reflected the same justificatory impulse (for instance, coverage of nontortious injuries and an apparatus for administering a scheme of social insurance), the demands of formalism would be fully met.

Accordingly, legal formalism is not a political position. In opposing ideas like loss-spreading through tort law, the formalist is not a libertarian who stands against the use of state machinery to transfer wealth from those who have it to those whose need for it is more pressing. Nor is the formalist's insistence on the possibility of a coherent tort law an argument that tort law should be preferred to a general social insurance scheme that embodies loss-spreading or some other compensatory principle. What is paramount to the formalist is not the substantive desirability of any legal arrangement, but the coherence of the justificatory considerations that support its component features.

2.9. Some Contemporary Theories

In the formalist approach to juridical intelligibility, the ideas of unity, character, and kind come together. For private law, the coherent linking of plaintiff and defendant lies at the heart of the formalism. Such linking intrinsically unifies the private law relationship, determines the doctrines, concepts, and processes that characterize private law, and establishes private law as a distinctive kind of legal ordering.

Here I propose to illuminate the formalist approach by contrasting it with other contemporary discussions of private law. My aim is neither to survey the now vast theoretical literature on private law nor to treat particular theories in detail, but rather to illustrate how the failure to recognize the overriding significance of the plaintiff-defendant link undermines the plausibility of some well-considered accounts. For this purpose, I focus broadly on economic analysis and on two supposedly noninstrumentalist treatments. And in the transition from the former to the latter, I make some observations about the meaning of noninstrumentalism in the context of private law theory.

2.9.1. Economic Analysis

Economic analysis takes the promotion of economic efficiency to be the aim of law. The basic claim of economic analysis is that a defendant should be liable for failing to guard against an accident only when the cost of precautions is less than the probable cost of the accident. Thus from the economic standpoint, the liability rules of private law provide incentives for cost-justified precautions. Ambitious claims have been made on behalf of this mode of analysis: economic ideas have been said to reveal the "inner nature"[26] and "implicit logic"[27] of the common law and to constitute the "true grounds"[28] of judicial decisions.

Three properties of economic analysis undermine the plausibility of these claims. First, economic analysis treats the parties as subject to separate incentives, without linking the plaintiff and the defendant in a unified juridical relationship. The inducing of cost-justified precautions supports taking money from the defendant "[b]ut that damages are paid to the *plaintiff* is, from the economic standpoint, a detail."[29] The plaintiff's receipt of the damage award reflects a separate group of incentives (such as the need to induce enforcement of the norm and to prevent prospective victims from preempting the precautions incumbent on actors)[30] that do not entail taking the money from the actual defendant. Both parties are thereby involved in the damage award, but for separate reasons. Efficiency might as easily be served by two different funds, one that receives tort fines from inefficient actors and another that disburses the indicated inducements to victims. Instead of linking each party to the other, economic analysis construes the presence of both as a consequence of combining incentives that are independently applicable to each.

Second, economic analysis operates independently of the doctrines, concepts, and institutions that characterize private law. While economists applaud legal results that coincide with efficiency, their framework does not respect the law's characteristic features on their own terms. The economists "dispense with" or regard as "alien"[31] even so

---

[26] Richard A. Posner, *The Problems of Jurisprudence*, 361 (1990).

[27] Richard A. Posner, *Economic Analysis of Law*, 229–233 (3rd ed., 1986).

[28] Id. at 15.

[29] Posner, *Economic Analysis of Law*, 143 (2nd ed., 1977) (emphasis in original).

[30] Posner, *Economic Analysis of Law*, 176 (3rd ed., 1986).

[31] William M. Landes and Richard A. Posner, *The Economic Structure of Tort Law*, 229 (1987) ("the idea of causation can largely be dispensed with in an economic analysis of torts"); William A. Landes and Richard A. Posner, "Causation in Tort Law: An Economic Approach," 12 *Journal of Legal Studies* 109, at 134 (1983) ("In so analyzing the causation cases we are admittedly far from the language and concepts with which the courts analyze these cases"); Guido Calabresi, "Concerning Cause and the Law of Torts: An Essay for Harry Kalven, Jr.," 43 *University of Chicago Law Review* 69, 105 (1975) ("the alien language of causation"). For detailed criticisms of the economists' treatment of causation, see Richard W. Wright, "Actual Causation vs.

central a feature as causation: because both parties might have taken precautions, the task is to determine not whether the defendant caused the plaintiff's injury, but which of them could have avoided the accident more cheaply.

Third, economic analysis ignores the distinctiveness of private law as a mode of legal ordering. From the economic standpoint, private law is to be understood as a judicially created and enforced regime for the taxation and regulation of inefficient activity. Courts act as administrative tribunals that set norms for efficient behavior and exact fines when those norms are breached. The plaintiff's function in initiating a lawsuit is not to secure redress for wrongful injury but to claim a bounty for prosecuting inefficient economic activity. Economic analysis thus submerges the private nature of tort law in a public law of economic regulation.

Instead of illuminating private law, economic analysis breaks apart its relationships, effaces its characteristic features, and submerges its private nature. Despite the claim that "the structure of the common law...is economic in character,"[32] structure is precisely what economic analysis ignores. The economic analysts are not so much concerned with understanding private law as with assessing the degree to which its rules coincide with what efficiency demands. Far from being the focus of their attention, private law is merely the foreign language into which economic discourse has somehow been translated.[33]

2.9.2. Instrumentalism and Noninstrumentalism

Scholars of private law sometimes distinguish between instrumentalist and noninstrumentalist theories. Instrumentalist theories view private law as a means of forwarding the community's aggregate welfare through a strategy of maximization often expressed in economic terms. Noninstrumentalist theories view private law as a collection of moral norms that respect the primacy of the individual. The preceding critique of economic analysis readily discloses the opposition of for-

---

Probabilistic Linkage: The Bane of Economic Analysis," 14 *Journal of Legal Studies* 435 (1985).

[32] Landes and Posner, *The Economic Structure of Tort Law*, 302. For an analysis of implications of wealth maximization for the structure of tort law, see Jules L. Coleman, "The Structure of Tort Law," 97 *Yale Law Journal* 1233 (1988).

[33] For the characterization of law as the translation of economic principle, see Landes and Posner, *The Economic Structure of Tort Law*, 23; Posner, *The Problems of Jurisprudence*, 361.

malism to instrumentalist theories. Before considering specific noninstrumentalist accounts, however, I want to point out that even noninstrumental moral ideas that are external to private law are as unsatisfactory as instrumentalist ones.

Instrumentalist approaches, such as economic analysis, are particularly vulnerable to the criticism that they fail to reflect the unity, character, and distinctiveness of the private law relationship. There are many reasons for this vulnerability. First, instrumentalist approaches regard private law as a means of forwarding the aggregate interests, however construed, of everyone in the community; instrumentalism can, therefore, hardly be expected to be sensitive to the direct nexus of plaintiff to defendant. Second, because instrumentalist goals implicate the collective welfare, they naturally lead to construing private law not as a distinctive moral ordering but as a variety of public regulation. Third, instrumentalist thinking often invokes mutually independent goals, and so is not likely to lead to intrinsically unified private law relationships. And finally, instrumentalism substitutes its own vocabulary for private law's apparently moral notions of reasonableness, fault, cause, duty, and so on.

These observations indicate that a noninstrumentalist approach, which speaks the language of morality and focuses on individuals as ends in themselves, is more promising. Such an approach offers the prospect of understanding private law as a mode of ordering with its own integrity, rather than as a device for forwarding collective interests.

However, we cannot achieve an adequate understanding of private law merely by shifting from the discourse of economics to the discourse of a noninstrumental morality. The economic approach has the defect of operating outside the law's self-understanding. Now if we substitute moral for economic argument, we may be exchanging one external viewpoint for another without making contact with the internal standpoint of the law's self-understanding. Moral argument, no less than economic argument, can be external to the law's self-understanding, and it is this externality of standpoint generally, not the particular externality of economics, that is problematic. Moral argument itself has no preferred status for private law except as it participates in a legally immanent intelligibility.

To have proper recourse to noninstrumental morality, we must appreciate what it is that renders an account of private law instrumentalist. An instrumentalist account understands private law as a means to something else, whereas a noninstrumentalist account construes law as being internally intelligible and thus requiring no reference to purposes external to itself. Whether an account of private law is noninstrumentalist is determined not by moral theory or by preconceptions about the ingredients of noninstrumentalism (the irrelevance of judgments about collective welfare, for instance), but by the account's connection to private law. Even an account that uses such notoriously noninstrumental conceptions as individual fairness and the Kantian idea of persons as ends in themselves is instrumental if it does not reflect the character, kind, and unity of the private law relationship. For the upshot of such an account is that private law serves as a means for the achieving of a purpose—even a morally noninstrumental purpose—that is alien to its own nature.

Accordingly, to understand private law noninstrumentally, we cannot start with morality—even noninstrumental morality—and consider law merely a means of implementing it. Rather, the moral notions must themselves reflect the character of private law as a distinctive and coherent mode of ordering. Moral inquiry can be directed toward a wide variety of issues (motive, virtues of character, discrete acts, human interactions, and so on), whereas we seek the morality specifically appropriate to private law. Even if we isolate the realm of moral duties as particularly relevant, there is no ground for assuming that legal duties are the collectively imposed counterparts of prior moral ones. There is, indeed, a significant difference between moral duties and the duties of private law: whereas moral duties restrict or direct a person's action, the duties of private law have the additional feature of being correlative to the rights of others. Unless we take account of this additional feature, we will be treating private law—paradoxically—merely as a means to a noninstrumental morality.

Two examples, one from contract theory and the other from tort theory, illustrate the pitfalls involved in importing noninstrumental moral ideas into the theory of private law.

2.9.3. Contract as Promise

In his book *Contract as Promise*, Charles Fried argues that one can locate the underlying and unifying structure of contract law in the morality of promising. In affirming that promise is a "quintessentially individualist ground of obligation,"[34] Fried repudiates the idea that contractual standards "are ineluctably collective in origin and thus

---

[34] Charles Fried, *Contract as Promise*, 5 (1981).

readily turned to collective ends."[35] Furthermore, his invocation of the morality of promising stands opposed to the reduction of contract law to social policies such as wealth maximization and economic efficiency.[36] Relying on Kant, Fried claims that the idea of contract as promise expresses the liberal notion of the right, which enshrines the self's capacity to determine its own conception of the good.[37] The enforcement of contracts is a way of respecting the self's capacity to determine, and to take responsibility for, the good it chooses. And because the choosing self is not instantaneous but is extended in time, to respect the self's choices is to respect their persistence over time. Through the law of contract, we take the promisor seriously as a person.[38]

Fried's account, with its appeal to Kant, its emphasis on individual rights, and its aversion both to collective interests and to economic analysis, has an unmistakably noninstrumentalist coloration. Nonetheless, his tying of contract law to the morally obligatory nature of one's promises is problematic. The fact, if it is a fact, that promises create moral obligations does not mean that those obligations should be given legal form. Moreover, even if it were accepted that law, as a reflex of morality, should enforce whatever obligations are disclosed by moral argument, a link with the law of contracts would still remain to be forged. The wrongfulness of breaking one's promise can receive legal expression in other ways besides the enforceability of contracts—through the application of criminal sanctions, for instance, or of private law remedies in tort or restitution. Contract law not only imposes an obligation on the promisor but grants a correlative right to the promisee to whom the obligation is owed. In law, the requirement that promises be kept takes a certain shape that embraces the plaintiff's right as well as the defendant's duty and that finds legal expression in such doctrines as offer and acceptance, consideration, and the entitlement to expectation damages. A moral argument that does not illuminate this shape is inadequate.

In this light, consider one of Peter Benson's criticisms of Fried's argument about promissory obligation.

[T]he argument does not establish that the promisee has a right *against the promisor* to the promised performance: holding

---

[35] Id.
[36] Id.
[37] Id. at 9, 20, 132.
[38] Id. at 20.

the promisor to his or her conception of the good can be intelligibly viewed as requiring merely internal self-consistency on his or her part— and not as vindicating another's right that is correlative to the promisor's duty in the external relation between the parties. In other words, the argument does not go so far as to explain a duty that is *owed* to another as a matter of justice, in contrast to a duty of fidelity or self-consistency that, though it may *relate* to another, is required only as a part of virtue.[39]

Benson's point is that even if the morality of promising grounds an obligation to adhere to one's promise, it provides no basis for contract law as such. In contract, obligation is relational: not only must the contractually bound defendant perform the promised act, but that performance is owed to a particular plaintiff. The persistence of the self over time, however, is morally relevant only to the promisor; it supplies the promisee with no right to insist on performance.

With its one-sided reference to the promisor, Fried's theory of contract as promise does not include both poles of the contractual relationship. Even if the temporal extension of the self provides grounds for a promissory obligation, there is no reason for the obligation to take a contractual form. The promisee's right is not the consequence of the moral reasoning that supports the obligation, but is added on to it in a separate operation. Contract is implicitly conceived as a mechanism for enforcing an obligation that is morally complete without it.

The result is that Fried's supposedly noninstrumental view of contract not only fails to make contract law intelligible in its own terms; it also transforms contract law into an instrument for coercing the moral virtue of the promisor. Fried's account of promise is noninstrumental, but the moral argument at the basis of that account focuses on the promisor without assigning a role to the promisee. Contract law supervenes on the promise with the promisee's power to enforce it. This power is not derived from the moral argument that makes promises obligatory. Contract law is thus merely a means of enforcing an obligation that arises independently of it. Although Fried's conception of promise is noninstrumental, his conception of contract law is not.[40]

---

[39] Peter Benson, "Abstract Right and the Possibility of a Nondistributive Conception of Contract: Hegel and Contemporary Contract Theory," 10 *Cardozo Law Review* 1077, at 1116 (1989).

[40] In Kantian terms, Fried's theory postulates the external enforcement through law of an obligation that is solely internal. See below, section 4.4.

Benson's criticism can be expressed in terms of the formalist strictures concerning coherence and intelligibility. Fried's elucidation of promissory obligation posits a justificatory consideration that is underinclusive in that it operates on the defendant alone. Having thus separated the defendant from the plaintiff, Fried's account does not faithfully reflect the character and unity of their juridical relationship. With respect to the promissory obligation, we are entitled to ask what gives the plaintiff, of all people, the right to its performance. Reference to the extension of the promising self through time cannot answer this question. And without an answer, the relationship remains unintelligible. Because of his sundering of the defendant from the plaintiff, Fried's account faces problems similar to those confronting expressly instrumentalist understandings.

2.9.4. *The Fairness of Excuses*

The second example is George Fletcher's account of tort law.[41] Fletcher's treatment of the contrasting themes of fairness and utility is an eloquent plea not to regard tort law as a medium for accident insurance or as a mechanism for maximizing social utility. In Fletcher's view, tort law is a repository of noninstrumental norms of individual fairness.

A key aspect of Fletcher's theory is the role he ascribes to excuses. The existence of excusing conditions, such as compulsion and unavoidable ignorance, raises a distinct issue of fairness to the defendant. Because anyone similarly situated would have acted as the defendant did, "[t]o find that an act is excused is in effect to say that there is no rational, fair basis for distinguishing between the party causing harm and other people."[42] Excuses are "expressions of compassion for human failings in time of stress."[43] Excusing is not an exercise in the assessment of social consequences, but a perception of the moral equivalence between an act under exigent circumstances and no act at all.[44]

Both in substance and in idiom, Fletcher's analysis prescinds from instrumental judgments about collective welfare. Its substantive focus is on the nature of the defendant's act in its circumstances and, con

---

[41] George P. Fletcher, "Fairness and Utility in Tort Theory," 85 *Harvard Law Review* 537 (1972).

[42] Id. at 541.

[43] Id. at 553.

[44] Id. at 552.

sequently, on the fairness of liability to the defendant as an individual. Its idiom is the language of moral discourse rather than of economics or social science.

The difficulty is that, as with Fried's promises, the moral significance of Fletcher's excuses is one-sided. Excuses deal with the defendant in isolation from the plaintiff. What matters is the relationship between the defendant's act and the defendant's excusing conditions of compulsion or ignorance. To excuse the defendant, however, is to let the loss lie where it has fallen, on the plaintiff. The question that arises is why moral considerations that are relevant only to the actor should affect the legal position of the victim at all. In order to be liable in tort, the defendant need not be adjudged morally evil. Even if excuses are germane to judgments about the actor's character or moral blameworthiness, why specifically do they excuse the actor from liability to the plaintiff?

The difficulty is aggravated by the place that excuses have in legal argument. Excuses excuse from something. They occupy a second stage in legal argument because they presuppose the liability that would obtain in their absence. If applicable to tort law, the excuse would supervene on an already existing cause of action to frustrate the plaintiff's entitlement to recover for the wrongful harm done by the defendant. What we now need—and what Fletcher does not provide—is an account not of why the excuse mitigates the defendant's blameworthiness generally, but why it neutralizes the plaintiff's right specifically. Why should the probability that most people in the defendant's position would have committed the same wrong lead to the cancellation of a particular plaintiff's right? Why does the fact that the defendant has wronged the plaintiff not suffice to single the defendant out as the party who must make good the plaintiff's damage? Even if the excusing condition moves *us* to compassion, on what grounds does our compassion operate at the *plaintiff's* expense?

Fletcher's ascription of a noninstrumental morality to excuses does not mean that their incorporation into tort law makes tort law noninstrumental. A noninstrumental account of tort law must noninstrumentally relate the plaintiff's right to the defendant's liability. Fletcher's account sacrifices the plaintiff's right—on grounds not pertinent to that right—in order to satisfy moral considerations that are unilaterally directed to the defendant. If we allow excuses for Fletcher's reasons, we are either obliging the victim to be compassionate to the wrongful injurer or we are exercising collective generosity with the plaintiff's right.

Like Fried, Fletcher postulates a justificatory consideration that applies to the defendant independently of the plaintiff. His account leaves us wondering why the moral force of an excusing condition that pertains solely to the defendant's act (and seems therefore morally irrelevant to the plaintiff) should operate at the expense of the plaintiff's right. His approach to excuses severs the defendant's moral position from the plaintiff's entitlement, and thus precludes conceiving of the plaintiff–defendant relationship as an intrinsic unity. Yet unless the relationship is so conceived, we cannot make sense of the characteristic feature of private law, that liability simultaneously affects the legal position of both parties.[45]

These observations about Fletcher's excuses and Fried's promises are not intended to dispute the pertinence of noninstrumentalist accounts of private law. On the contrary, to understand private law, we need a purified noninstrumentalism. Infusing law with noninstrumental morality is insufficient unless that morality reflects and captures the special character of private law. Accordingly, a truly noninstrumentalist account construes private law not as the servant even of a noninstrumental morality, but as a coherent and distinctive mode of legal ordering that is intelligible in its own terms.

With these strictures in mind, I now turn to Aristotle's account of corrective justice as the form of private law. For by integrating the defendant's act and the plaintiff's claim, Aristotle's account renders the private law relationship intelligible as a distinctive and coherent justificatory phenomenon.

---

[45] For a conception of excuse that avoids the difficulties of Fletcher's position, see below, section 4.3.4.

3

Corrective Justice

3.1. Introduction

Aristotle's account of corrective justice[1] is the earliest—and in many respects, still the definitive—description of the form of the private law relationship. By Aristotle's day the rectification of injury through the recognition and enforcement of one party's claim against the other was a familiar phenomenon. Aristotle, however, was the first to point to the distinctive features of this process: its bipolarity, its constrained standards of relevance, and its relationship to adjudication. His treatment of corrective justice reveals both what unites the private law relationship and what sets private law apart from other kinds of ordering. In the history of legal philosophy, private law is Aristotle's discovery.

Aristotle observed that what we would now call private law has a special structure of its own. Justice is effected by the direct transfer of resources from one party to the other.[2] The resources transferred simultaneously represent the plaintiff's wrongful injury and the defendant's wrongful act. Corrective justice thus treats the wrong, and the transfer of resources that undoes it, as a single nexus of activity and passivity where actor and victim are defined in relation to each other.

Implicit in Aristotle's inquiry is the basic question of private law: what entitles a specific plaintiff to sue and recover from a specific

---

[1] Aristotle, *Nicomachean Ethics*, V, 4 (Martin Ostwald, trans., 1962).

[2] Aristotle is particularly interested in the structure of the relationship for which the award of damages (or the equivalent specific relief) is a rational response to the commission of the wrong. Since what matters is the conceptual structure of the relationship between the actor and the victim, his analysis does not require that a wrong actually has taken place or that damages actually have been awarded. His remarks are therefore as applicable to an injunction that prospectively restrains a wrong as to damages that retrospectively repair a wrong.

defendant? Aristotle realized that the answer to this question lies in the elucidation of the intrinsic unity of the plaintiff-defendant relationship. Only if the plaintiff and the defendant are linked in a single and coherent justificatory structure can one make sense of the practice of transferring resources directly from the defeated defendant to the victorious plaintiff. In his treatment of corrective justice, Aristotle sets out the most general representation of that structure.

Because he is primarily concerned with structure rather than substance, Aristotle's account of corrective justice is sparse and formal. Aristotle presents corrective justice in mathematical terms, as an equality between the two parties to a bipolar transaction. He contrasts corrective justice with distributive justice, conceived mathematically as a proportion in which each participant's share is relative to whatever criterion governs the distribution. Thus the difference between these two forms of justice is a difference between the mathematical operations that reflect their respective structures.

In this chapter I deal both with what is significant and with what is problematic in Aristotle's account. I begin by recapitulating Aristotle's position in a way that makes its formalism salient. Because the hallmark of this formalism is Aristotle's mathematization of justice, I shall have to give particular consideration to why Aristotle portrays corrective justice as a specific mathematical operation and what he thereby achieves. Then I shall argue, in response to modern criticism of Aristotle, that despite its abstraction from particular prescriptions, Aristotle's formalism is by no means empty. Aristotle's attention to structure enables us to appreciate both the internal coherence of the private law relationship and the categorical difference between private law and other legal orderings. For this reason his account constitutes a decisive contribution to the theory of private law.

Despite his achievement, however, Aristotle's exposition, like all great pioneer efforts, is seriously incomplete. Aristotle presents corrective justice as a transactional equality, but he does not tell us what the equality is an equality of. This omission is serious, because corrective justice remains opaque to the extent that the equality that lies at its heart is unexplained. However, the omission is also understandable, since the very formalism of corrective justice presupposes a formal equality that has become the object of serious reflection only in the last few centuries. Indeed, the measure of Aristotle's achievement is that his relentless striving to make sense of legal relationships led him to a correct understanding of private law that defied explication in terms of his own ethics.

In the final section of this chapter I attempt to fill in the lacuna in Aristotle's account by connecting corrective justice to Kant's legal philosophy. If my argument is correct, the equality of corrective justice is the abstract equality of free purposive beings under the Kantian concept of right. On this interpretation, the bipolar structure of corrective justice represents a regime of correlative right and duty, with the disturbance of equality in Aristotle's account being the defendant's wrongful infringement of the plaintiff's rights. Aristotle's account of corrective justice thus coalesces with the Kantian right in a single approach to the understanding of private law. Consideration of Aristotle's omission leads to Kant's legal philosophy, the subject of Chapter 4.

3.2. Aristotle's Account of Justice

3.2.1. Justice as Mean

To a modern reader the most remarkable feature of Aristotle's account is that he presents corrective and distributive justice as different mathematical operations. Justice involves the achievement of *to ison*, which in Greek signifies both fairness and equality. In Aristotle's account, fairness as a norm is inseparable from equality as a mathematical function.

Aristotle's conception of corrective and distributive justice as mathematical operations arises from his general treatment of ethics. For Aristotle, ethics is the study of virtues considered as excellences of character. Just as nothing can felicitously be added to or taken from an excellent work, so excellence of character involves the absence of both excess and deficiency.[3] Aristotle analyzes virtues as intermediate states, or means, that lie between vices that are deficiencies or excesses relative to that mean. Courage, for instance, lies between the deficiency of cowardice and the excess of recklessness. Similarly, temperance lies between profligacy and insensibility, generosity between prodigality and stinginess, gentleness between irascibility and apathy, wittiness between buffoonery and boorishness, and so on.

Aristotle begins his account of justice by asking how justice fits into the analysis of virtue as a mean.[4] The difficulty is that justice has a

---

[3] *Nicomachean Ethics*, II, 6.

[4] Aristotle opens *Nicomachean Ethics* V by remarking that "concerning justice and injustice we must investigate what sort of acts they are about, what sort of mean justice is, and intermediate to what does the just lie." *Nicomachean Ethics*, 1129a3.

[handwritten: So B if the, of I do wrong then I am worthe I X value and that value has to be returned to those I have wrong?,]

CORRECTIVE JUSTICE 59

different orientation than do other virtues. While other virtues are excellences of character internal to the virtuous person, justice is directed "towards another" *(pros allon)*.[5] Its reference is not internal but external; it looks not to the perfection of one's moral being but to the terms of one's interaction with others.[6] Whereas virtue is one's own good, "justice seems to be the good of someone else."[7] Given this external focus, how can justice be a mean? *[handwritten: ah.]*   *[handwritten: ✓ I agree I think]*

One answer is that the external focus changes nothing. Even virtues that are primarily concerned with character have external effects. To use Aristotle's examples, the coward who deserts in battle and the rake who commits adultery[8] not only evince defects of character but cause harm to others. The virtues come within the purview of justice once they are regarded from an interpersonal point of view.[9] Justice so conceived is virtue practiced toward others. Because adding the external perspective of justice does not change the nature of virtue, the analysis in terms of means is unaffected. Here, justice is coextensive with virtue.

This, however, is not the entire answer. Aristotle recognizes that not all issues of justice involve external effects of character. The other-directedness of justice figures also in controversies concerning one's holdings—wealth, honor, and security are Aristotle's examples.[10] An excess or deficiency in one's holdings can be unjust quite apart from any vice of character.[11] Indeed, being deprived of one's due is not the exhibition of a dispositional vice at all, but the suffering of a wrong.

---

[5] Id. at 1129b27, 1130a4, 1130a13.

[6] Aquinas comments on the opening sentence of *Nicomachean Ethics* that "the virtues and vices discussed before are concerned with the passions, for there we consider in what way a man may be internally influenced by reason of the passions; but we do not consider what is externally done, except as something secondary, inasmuch as external operations originate from internal passions. However, in treating justice and injustice we direct our principal attention to what a man does externally; how he is influenced internally we consider only as a by-product according as he is helped or hindered in the (external) operation." Thomas Aquinas, *Commentary on the Nicomachean Ethics*, vol. 1, 384 (C. I. Litzinger, trans., 1964).

[7] *Nicomachean Ethics*, 1130a2. Aristotle's use of this phrase is provocative: it is the description of justice given by the immoral Thrasymachus in Plato, *Republic*, 343c (Allan Bloom, trans., 1968).

[8] *Nicomachean Ethics*, 1129b20.

[9] Id. at 1130a12.

[10] Id. at 1130b2. Aristotle's term for justice in holdings is "partial justice," in distinction to the "perfection" and "completeness" that he ascribes to the justice that is coextensive with virtue. *Nicomachean Ethics*, 1130a14, 1129b26–1130a1, 1130a9. The term "justice in holdings" is not completely felicitous. See below, note 57.

[11] Id. at 1130a15–1130a27.

Judgments of excess and deficiency about vices differ from judgments of excess and deficiency about unjust holdings. Judgments about vices compare the actual and ideal qualities of a single person. A reckless person, for instance, exhibits too much (and a coward too little) of the emotion which, if exhibited in proper measure, would make that very person courageous. Excess or deficiency in holdings, however, is interpersonal. The holdings of any one person can be termed "excessive" only in relation to the holdings of another. Whereas the excess and deficiency of vice is compared to a dispositional mean, the excess or deficiency of an unjust holding is relative to the holdings or the actions of others.

To capture the relativeness of one's holdings to the holdings or actions of someone else, Aristotle identifies equality as the mean of justice in holdings.[12] On the one hand, equality is a relational concept, because something is equal, not to itself, but only to something else.[13] On the other hand, equality is a mean because it lies between the unjust excess of having too much compared with another and the unjust deficiency of having too little.[14] Equality thereby serves as the mean applicable to the pure other-directedness of justice in holdings.

Thus although Aristotle sees both justice in holdings and the justice that is coextensive with virtue as other-directed, he draws a distinction between them. In the justice that is coextensive with virtue, equality plays no role: the external standpoint is merely grafted on to a virtue already intelligible in terms of a single person. In contrast, equality is the defining feature of justice in holdings, because justice in holdings is intrinsically other-directed.

Aristotle's account of justice in holdings assimilates three ideas: justice, equality, and the mean. Aristotle encapsulates the function of these ideas in his remark that "*qua* mean, [justice] is between certain things (these are the more and the less); *qua* equal, it links two; *qua* just, it applies to certain persons."[15] The last member of this triptych defines the domain of justice: because justice is other-directed, the just applies to the relationship among persons, rather than to a person considered singly. The middle member sums up the formal principle

[12] In so doing, Aristotle puts to theoretical use the common Greek notion that justice is a matter of *to ison*, an expression that denotes both fairness and equality. See *Nicomachean Ethics*, 1131a10–1131a14.

[13] *Nicomachean Ethics*, 1131a15; see Thomas Aquinas, *Summa Theologiae*, II-II, 58, 2 (T. Gilby, trans., 1975).

[14] *Nicomachean Ethics*, 1133b33.

[15] Id. at 1131a17–1131a18. By "two" Aristotle means "at least two," as is clear from the previous sentence.

that organizes this domain: equality represents the baseline for deter- *(handwritten margin note)* mining whether one has, compared with another, too much or too little. The first member distinguishes justice from injustice: justice is a mean that is intermediate between the injustices that consist in having more or having less than one's equal share.

Aristotle's identification of justice in holdings with equality does not imply that everyone's holdings ought to be the same in quantity or value. His point is formal. Like equality, justice in holdings orders the relationship between distinct entities; like equality, justice in holdings is disturbed by excess or shortfall. In maintaining that in every just arrangement the parties are equals, Aristotle is not committed to any particular set of holdings or to any particular criterion of equality. Equality is merely a way of representing the norm that injustice violates. *(handwritten: I guess it can be relative,)*

3.2.2. Distributive and Corrective Justice

The idea of equality allows Aristotle to describe justice in holdings as mathematical operations. Justice functions for holdings as equality functions for mathematical terms. In mathematics, equality relates one term to another through an equal sign. The specific arrangement of the terms on either side of an equal sign, however, depends on the mathematical operation being performed. Just as different mathematical operations link various elements in different ways, so justice in holdings has different ways of ordering the relations among persons. *(handwritten: OK)* Aristotle calls these different modes of ordering the "forms"[16] of justice.

Justice in holdings assumes two contrasting forms: distributive justice and corrective justice. Each of these forms regulates holdings *(handwritten: OK)* through a different mathematical operation. Injustice consists in having more or less than the equal allotment due under one or the other of these mathematical operations.

In introducing the two forms of justice, Aristotle remarks that distributive justice occurs "in distributions" and corrective justice occurs *(handwritten: sure)* "in transactions."[17] "Distributions" and "transactions" are general terms that refer to all the particular manifestations of the two forms of justice. A transaction is an interaction regulated in conformity to corrective justice. Similarly, a distribution is an arrangement that has

---

[16] Id. at 1130b31, 1131b27.
[17] Id. at 1131a1, 1131b25, 1131b31.

the structure of distributive justice. Distributive and corrective justice are "in" distributions and transactions as the modes of ordering implicit in these arrangements.

Distributive justice divides a benefit or burden in accordance with some criterion. An exercise of distributive justice consists of three elements: the benefit or burden being distributed, the persons among whom it is distributed, and the criterion according to which it is distributed. The criterion determines the parties' comparative merit for a particular distribution. The greater a particular party's merit under the criterion of distribution, the larger the party's share in the thing being distributed. Thus distributive justice corresponds to a mathematical operation in which a series of equal ratios align comparative shares with comparative merit. Aristotle explains this operation in the following passage, in which A and B represent the parties to the distribution, and c and d their relative shares:

Consequently, the just is something proportionate... Proportion is equality of ratios and involves at least four terms. The just, too, involves at least four terms, and the ratio [between the terms of one pair] is equal [to that between the terms of the other], for persons and things are similarly distributed. Therefore, $A:B = c:d$ and, by alternation, $A:c = B:d$.... Consequently, the combination of term [person] A with term [share] c and of term [person] B with term [share] d is just.[18]

Distributive justice, in other words, consists in an equality of ratios.[19]

In contrast, corrective justice features an equality of quantities.[20] It focuses on a quantity that represents what rightfully belongs to one party but is now wrongly possessed by another party and therefore must be shifted back to its rightful owner. Corrective justice embraces quantitative equality in two ways. First, because one party has what belongs to the other party, the actor's gain is equal to the victim's loss.[21] Second, what the parties would have held had the wrong not occurred provides the baseline from which the gain and the loss are computed. That baseline, accordingly, functions as the mean of equality for this form of justice. Of course this equality is a notional

---

[18] Id. at 1131a29–1131b10. The words enclosed by square brackets are clarifications that Martin Ostwald has inserted in the text of his translation.

[19] Aristotle terms this kind of equality "geometrical." Id. at 1131b13.

[20] Aristotle terms this kind of equality "arithmetical." Id. at 1132a30.

[21] Aristotle notes the difficulty of conceiving of personal injuries in this way. Id. at 1132a10. For a discussion and proposed resolution of the difficulty, see Chapter 5.

one. Equality consists in persons' having what belongs to them.[22] The parties do not have the same quantity of holdings, but they are equal as the owners of whatever they do have. This equality is a mean because the parties have neither more nor less than what is theirs.

These two aspects of quantitative equality are interconnected. The quantitative equality of gain and loss is the basis for the simultaneous annulment of both in corrective justice. There would be no point, however, in concentrating on this quantitative equality unless the annulment vindicated equality in some sense. For if the initial sets of holdings embodied only an inequality, the subsequent gain by one party at the expense of another, to the extent that it mitigated the initial inequality, would itself be just. Thus attention to the equality of gain and loss in corrective justice presupposes the notional equality of initial holdings, and the annulment of those gains and losses affirms that initial equality.

A violation of corrective justice involves one party's gain at the other's expense. As compared with the mean of initial equality, the actor now has too much and the victim too little. Because the actor has gained what the victim has lost, equality is not restored merely by removing the actor's gain (which would still leave the victim with a shortfall) or by restoring the victim's loss (which would still leave the actor with an excess). Rather, corrective justice requires the actor to restore to the victim the amount representing the actor's self-enrichment at the victim's expense.[23]

3.3. The Bipolarity of Corrective Justice

Presenting corrective justice as a quantitative equality captures the basic feature of private law: a particular plaintiff sues a particular defendant. Unjust gain and loss are not mutually independent changes in the parties' holdings; if they were, the loss and the gain could be restored by two independent operations. But because the plaintiff has lost what the defendant has gained, a single liability links the particular person who gained to the particular person who lost.

Without some conception such as Aristotle's, private law's linking of the particular parties becomes a mystery. For Aristotle, the defendant's gain at the plaintiff's expense justifies simultaneously diminishing the defendant's resources and augmenting the plaintiff's. In con-

---

[22] Id. at 1132a28–1132a29.
[23] Id. at 1132a32–1132b5.

trast, to reject Aristotle is to postulate that the reason for taking resources from the defendant is not the same as the reason for giving resources to the plaintiff. But then, how could reasons separately applicable to the two parties justify directly *linking* the two parties? And even if a set of reasons embraced both parties, how could such reasons exclude others, so as to enable *this* plaintiff to recover from *this* defendant? Once plaintiff and defendant are separated, the reason for diminishing the defendant's resources will connect the defendant not to the plaintiff but to other persons to whom that reason applies, without justifying the plaintiff's singling out the defendant. Similarly, the reason for increasing the plaintiff's resources will connect the plaintiff to others who are similarly circumstanced, without providing a reason for holding the defendant liable to the particular plaintiff.[24]

In Aristotle's account of corrective justice, quantitative equality pairs one party with another. Corrective justice treats the defendant's unjust gain as correlative to the plaintiff's unjust loss. The disturbance of the equality connects two, and only two, persons. The injustice that corrective justice corrects is essentially bipolar.

The bipolarity of corrective justice is also evident in its conception of interaction. Aristotle repeatedly describes the two parties to corrective justice as being active and passive with respect to each other. Corrective justice looks to "whether one has committed and the other has suffered injustice, and if the one has harmed and the other been harmed."[25] The injustice of battery and murder, for instance (in Aristotle's words, "when one has hit and the other has been hit, and when one has killed and the other has been killed"), lies in the fact that "the doing and the suffering have been unequally divided."[26] Just as when

---

[24] Assume, for example, that tort liability combines the rationale of deterrence for careless defendants and compensation for injured plaintiffs. Deterrence would be applicable to all those who are careless, even if their carelessness did not result in injury to the plaintiff, and there would be no reason for the plaintiff to recover from one careless person rather than another. Similarly, compensation would be justified for all who are as disabled as the plaintiff, so that there would be no reason for any particular disabled person to recover from his or her injurer. On the impossibility of making sense of the plaintiff-defendant relationship through considerations, such as deterrence and compensation, that apply independently to each party and others similarly situated, see above, section 2.7.2.

[25] *Nicomachean Ethics*, 1132a5–1132a6.

[26] Id. at 1132a8–1 32a9. The language of division *(dieiretai)* does not imply distribution *(nome* or *dianome)*. Aquinas explains Aristotle's reference to unjust division as follows: "[T]his division of action and passion brings about inequality because the assailant and the murderer have more of what is esteemed good, inasmuch as they have done their own will and so seem as it were to have gained. But the man who is

the equality of corrective justice is disturbed, one person's gain necessarily entails another's loss, so the doing of injury by one entails the suffering of injury by another. The correlativity of gain and loss supervenes on the correlativity of one person's doing and another's suffering harm.

The bipolarity of corrective justice also fashions the remedy, that is, the rectification, that corrective justice accomplishes. The rectification responds to—indeed corresponds to—the injustice that is being rectified. Because the defendant has realized a gain correlative to the plaintiff's loss, the correction entails a loss to the defendant that is simultaneously a correlative gain to the plaintiff. In this way the rectification reverses the unjust act by undoing the excess and the deficiency that constitute the injustice.

The agent of this rectification is the judge. Aristotle connects adjudication to the bipolarity of corrective justice by deriving the word for judge *(dikastes)* from *dicha*, split in two.[27] Aristotle compares the judge to a geometer. We are to imagine a line divided into unequal segments. The judge is like one who reestablishes the midpoint of the line, thereby reattaching to the smaller segment the amount by which the larger segment exceeds the half.[28] By splitting the line into two equal parts, the judge vindicates quantitative equality. "For when the whole has been divided into two *(dicha)*, then people say they have what belongs to them when they take equal parts."[29] This fanciful etymology draws attention to the regulative function of quantitative equality. A controversy in corrective justice involves an allegation that the defendant has disturbed the equality pertaining to transactions. The parties to the dispute "have recourse to the judge. To go to the judge is to go to justice; for the judge means to be justice ensouled."[30] For Aristotle, the judge is the living representative of the quantitative equality between the parties.

Thus the bipolar nature of corrective justice has many aspects. Corrective justice embraces: a bipolar conception of interaction that relates the doer of harm to the sufferer of that harm; a bipolar conception of injustice as a violation of quantitative equality; a bipolar

wounded or murdered has more of evil insofar as he is deprived against his will of well-being or life, and so he seems, as it were, to have suffered loss." Aquinas, *Commentary on the Nicomachean Ethics*, vol. 1, 411.

[27] *Nicomachean Ethics*, 1132a30–1132a32.
[28] Id. at 1132a21–1132a32.
[29] Id. at 1132a27–1132a29.
[30] Id. at 1132a22.

conception of damage as a loss by the plaintiff correlative to the defendant's gain; a bipolar conception of the adjudicative process as a vindication of the quantitative equality of the litigants; and a bipolar conception of the remedy as the annulment of the parties' correlative gain and loss.

3.4. Kelsen's Critique

What does Aristotle's treatment of justice in holdings as two different mathematical operations achieve? At first blush, the assimilation of justice to mathematics appears to be an inconsequential conceit: merely evidence of the stylishness of mathematics in the philosophical discourse of the ancient Greeks. At best, Aristotle's account of justice seems an exercise in pointless elegance; at worst, a sham that presents metaphors as solutions.

This indeed was Hans Kelsen's view. In a well-known critique,[31] Kelsen argued that Aristotle merely stated in an elaborate and tortuous way the tautology that justice consists in rendering to each his due. What is required, according to Kelsen, is a mechanism for determining what *is* each person's due, and this Aristotle does not provide. This failure on Aristotle's part was inevitable, Kelsen claimed, because the formula "to each his own" is a tautology devoid of specific content.

This criticism exploits the fact that the corrective justice and the distributive justice of Aristotle's account are formal categories, not substantive prescriptions. Aristotle's outline of distributive justice, for example, does not present an ideally just set of arrangements against which all distributions can be measured. His representation of distributive justice as an equality of proportions under a criterion of merit suggests neither the relevant indicia of equality nor the optimal criterion of merit. As Kelsen rightly remarks, given the inevitable existence of differences of age, sex, wealth, and so on, "[t]he decisive question for social equality is: Which differences are relevant? To this question Aristotle's mathematical formula of distributive justice has no answer."[32] And as for the criterion, Aristotle himself notes that different political philosophies are committed to different conceptions of merit. "Everyone agrees," Aristotle observes, "that in distributions the just shares must be given on the basis of what one deserves, though not everyone would name the same criterion of deserving: democrats

---

[31] Hans Kelsen, *What Is Justice?* 125–136 (1957).
[32] Id. at 127.

say it is free birth, oligarchs that it is wealth or noble birth, and aristocrats that it is excellence."[33]

Aristotle's description of corrective justice is similarly devoid of specifics. None of the issues that preoccupy modern scholars of private law—the standard of liability in tort law, the measure of damages in contract law, and the definition of causation, for example—receives any attention. Instead, Aristotle presses the obvious point that, because a defendant who has taken something from a plaintiff has a comparative excess of twice the amount taken, the initial equilibrium is restored when the defendant returns to the plaintiff the amount taken. For Kelsen, restoring a quantity "is no solution to the problem of just return...[i]t is only another way of presenting the problem."[34]

One can expand Kelsen's criticism to include Aristotle's failure to value one form over the other. Modern thinkers often assert the superiority of one of the forms of justice. Sometimes the issue is localized to a given set of problems, as when one advocates that the regulation of personal injury through the corrective justice system of tort law be replaced by a distributive system of social insurance.[35] Sometimes the issue is more general, as when one claims for corrective justice a moral force so strong that it leaves no room for an independent notion of distributive justice.[36] Aristotle offers no assistance in these controversies. He presents the two forms and contrasts the mathematical operations that each embodies, but he gives no grounds for preferring one over the other.

Although these criticisms accurately point to Aristotle's omissions, they are nonetheless misguided. The strength of Aristotle's treatment of justice lies precisely in the differentiation between corrective and distributive justice. Even if, as Kelsen argues, each of the forms taken separately is tautologous, this does not mean that Aristotle's account as a whole is tautologous. The two forms of justice may be reducible to the empty formula "to each his own," but the emptiness is not the same for both. Corrective and distributive justice both require that every person be given his or her due, but what is due under corrective justice is due correctively and not distributively, and what is due under distributive justice is due distributively and not correctively.[37] Even if

---

[33] *Nicomachean Ethics*, 1131a25.

[34] Kelsen, *What Is Justice?* 130.

[35] E.g., Marc A. Franklin, "Replacing the Negligence Lottery: Compensation and Selective Reimbursement," 53 *Virginia Law Review* 774 (1967); Stephen D. Sugarman, "Doing Away with Tort Law," 73 *California Law Review* 555 (1985).

[36] E.g., Robert Nozick, *Anarchy, State, and Utopia*, 149–160 (1974).

[37] Aquinas, *Summa Theologiae*, II-II, Q. 61, Art. 1, ad 5.

empty, each form of justice has its own emptiness and not the other's. The tautology that Kelsen alleges is itself qualified by Aristotle's distinction between corrective and distributive justice.

Kelsen says that a form of justice is a "way of presenting the problem of just return," and he criticizes Aristotle for not offering a solution. But before criticizing the absence of a solution, we should explore Aristotle's formulation of the problem. For without a correct formulation of the problem, no solution will be adequate; and, conversely, the formulation of the problem presumably imposes a certain structure on the solution and is, therefore, the first step in its discovery. Indeed, one consequence of Aristotle's account is to cast doubt on Kelsen's own reference to "*the* problem of just return." For by dividing justice into corrective and distributive, Aristotle indicates the existence of *two* different problems of just return.

Although Aristotle presents no specific content for the forms of justice, the forms (as I shall now argue) are nevertheless decisive for whatever content one might consider. These forms are structures for coherent justification. Accordingly, even without offering solutions Aristotle contributes fundamentally to our understanding of problems of just return.

3.5. The Forms as Classifications

To see the significance of the forms of justice, we must first understand how they further Aristotle's insight that justice is other-directed. Since Aristotle views justice as the domain of external relationships, the external perspective obtains both for justice in holdings and for the justice that is coextensive with virtue. But whereas the justice that is coextensive with virtue adds an external standpoint to the internal phenomenon of character, justice in holdings deals with inherently external relationships. Dividing justice in holdings into corrective and distributive justice is a way of classifying those relationships. What kind of classification is it?

Broadly speaking, classification of external relationships can be either empirical or conceptual. Empirical classification observes the physical or social world upon which justice operates, and cuts that world into different slices. One might, for instance, divide the realm of justice according to legally significant effects. For example, if the occurrence of physical injury were such an effect, one would group together the various ways (tort law, insurance contracts, safety regulation, state welfare provisions, public compensation schemes, and so on) in which the law involves others, directly or indirectly, in the handling of someone's injury. Or one might divide the empirical world on the basis of the different causes of legally significant effects. (The Talmudic law of torts, for example, begins by classifying tortious injuries under paradigm causes, such as oxen, pits, and fires.)[38] Or one might base the classification on the different roles of the interacting persons (corporate directors, insurance agents, the manufacturers of products, and so forth) and on the legal incidents that attach to each of these roles.

In contrast, a conceptual classification of external relationships looks at the different ways in which one can conceive of the operations of justice. The focus is not on the empirical world that makes up the subject matter for the operations of justice, but on the structure of the operations. Conceptual classification does not work in an empirical vacuum that ignores effects or causes or social roles; the point is rather that the empirical factors do not themselves function as organizing principles. What matters is how the constituent elements of the external relationships of justice stand toward one another. The issue that animates a conceptual classification is: how can one understand the relationships of justice as relationships?

Aristotle's classification is conceptual. Having identified the subject matter of justice in holdings as the relationship of one person to another through their respective holdings, he examines the different dynamics possible among the constituent elements of such relationships. His focus is not on persons and holdings as the discrete elements connected, but on the different forms of the connection. Given that justice in holdings has the external focus of direction (as Aristotle puts it) "toward another," he explicates the possible meanings of "toward."

This conceptualism is evident in the abstractness of Aristotle's presentation. He works with the broadest possible conceptions of the components of justice in holdings, namely, the persons entitled to the holdings and the holdings to which they are entitled. Further particularization of persons or holdings is irrelevant, because conceptual differences in kinds of relationship do not vary with who specifically holds what. He combines persons and holdings in a correspondingly broad way, because the more abstractly he can portray the operations of justice, the more salient he can render the conceptual differences between the kinds of external relationship. Accordingly, he formu-

---

[38] *Babylonian Talmud, Baba Kamma* 2a (I. Epstein, trans., 1935).

lates the operations of justice in language so abstract that they assume the shape of operations of mathematics.

Because Aristotle's classification is conceptual rather than empirical, corrective justice and distributive justice differ in structure, not subject matter.[39] Neither corrective nor distributive justice lays exclusive claim to a certain slice of the empirical world. Both forms of justice have as their subject matter the things and events that figure in external relations among persons; they differ in the structure of the operation that each performs upon those things and events. Just as proportions and quantities can both apply to any numbers,[40] so either of the forms of justice can apply to any external incident.

To take a modern example, the legal regime of personal injuries can be organized either correctively or distributively. Correctively, my striking you is a tort committed by me against you, and my payment to you of damages will restore the equality disturbed by my wrong. Distributively, the same incident activates a compensation scheme that shifts resources among members of a pool of contributors and recipients in accordance with a distributive criterion. From the standpoint of Aristotle's analysis, nothing about a personal injury as such consigns it to the domain of a particular form of justice. The differentiation between corrective and distributive justice lies not in the different subject matters to which they apply, but in the differently structured operation that each performs on a subject matter available to both.

Corrective and distributive justice reflect two different conceptions of interaction. In corrective justice the interaction of the parties is

---

[39] Aquinas makes this point specifically in *Summa Theologiae*, II-II, Q. 61, Art. 3.

[40] Aquinas, in fact, explains the difference between the two mathematical operations by showing how the same numbers (6 and 4) can figure in each: "He [Aristotle] says first that the just thing that exists in transactions agrees somewhat with the just thing directing distributions in this—that the just thing is equal, and the unjust thing, unequal. But they differ in the fact that the equal in commutative justice is not observed according to that proportionality, viz., geometrical, which was observed in distributive justice, but according to arithmetical proportionality which is observed according to equality of quantity, and not according to equality of proportion as in geometry. By arithmetical proportionality six is a mean between eight and four, because it is in excess of the one and exceeds the other by two. But there is not the same proportion on the one side and the other, for six is to four in a ratio of three to two while eight is to six in a ratio of four to three. On the contrary by geometrical proportionality the mean is exceeded and exceeds according to the same proportion but not according to the same quantity. In this way six is a mean between nine and four, since from both sides there is a three to two ratio. But there is not the same quantity, for nine exceeds six by three and six exceeds four by two." Aquinas, *Commentary on the Nicomachean Ethics*, vol. I, 410.

immediate; in distributive justice it is mediated through a distributive arrangement. Corrective justice joins the parties directly, through the harm that one of them inflicts on the other. Aristotle represents this immediacy in mathematical terms by identifying the victim's loss with the injurer's gain. In distributive justice, by contrast, the parties interact not directly but through the medium of a distributive scheme. Instead of linking one specific party to another, distributive justice links all parties to the benefit or the burden that they jointly share.

Corresponding to the distinction between immediate and mediated interaction are two different structures of injustice. An unjust advantage in a distributive context is an overdrawing of a common resource that diminishes the benefit available to the other participants in the distribution. Such overdrawing, however, affects any one of those other participants only derivatively: they receive less individually because there is less for all to share. Under corrective justice, by contrast, the wrongdoer directly diminishes the holdings of the sufferer, so that a single operation enriches the former at the expense of the latter. Under corrective justice, unlike distributive justice, the injustice immediately implicates a specific victim.

By presenting the forms of justice mathematically, Aristotle formalizes the distinction between immediate and mediated interaction, thereby allowing the implications of that distinction to emerge with particular clarity. The contrast between proportional and quantitative equality guarantees the categorical nature of the distinction between the corresponding forms of justice. The two forms of justice are no more reducible to each other than are the two kinds of equality. The difference in their mathematical representations shows that each form of justice is independent of the other and has its own integrity.

The contrast between the equalization of quantities in corrective justice and the equalization of proportions in distributive justice is especially evident in the number of parties that each can embrace. Because the transfer of a single quantity increases one amount at the expense of another, it can occur only between two amounts. Accordingly, the form of justice that Aristotle describes as an equalization of quantities is restricted to two parties at a time, with each interacting pair being treated discretely. In contrast, a series of equal proportions can be continued infinitely. Aristotle's mathematical representation of distributive justice mirrors the open-endedness of the number of parties that can participate in a distribution. Whereas the addition of parties in corrective justice is inconsistent with its structure, the addition of parties in distributive justice merely decreases the size of each person's share in the subject matter of the distribution.[41]

Moreover, the contrast between the two mathematical operations certifies that the two forms of justice cannot be integrated into a broader form. No single mathematical operation combines proportionate and quantitative equality, because no single mathematical operation can have both a restricted and an open-ended number of terms. Similarly, there is no overarching form of justice into which corrective and distributive justice can be dissolved.[42]

The categorical distinctiveness of the two forms of justice and the absence of any overarching form that might unite them mean that corrective and distributive justice are comprehensive and fundamental modes of ordering external relationships. They are comprehensive because they map justice in holdings through the barest and most inclusive abstractions: persons, holdings, immediate interaction, and mediated interaction. They are fundamental because there are no larger conceptions of interaction that embrace these mutually irreducible forms.

3.6. The Juridical Significance of the Forms

What does the contrast between corrective and distributive justice signify for the functioning of a legal system? The answer to this question lies in considering the forms of justice as modes of *ordering*.

Corrective and distributive justice are modes of ordering because they represent the different ways in which external relationships can be coherent. Coherence signifies a unified conceptual structure, the constituents of which express a single idea. Justice in holdings necessarily involves a plurality of elements, namely, the interacting parties and their holdings. Aristotle's forms of justice are two ways of organizing these elements into integrated wholes.

In distributive justice, the criterion of distribution expresses the

---

[41] To be sure, certain distributions involve no more than two parties. That, however, is merely a contingent feature of those particular distributions, rather than an essential quality of distributions as such. In contrast, bipolarity is a defining characteristic of transactions under corrective justice. See above, section 3.3.

[42] Even if we formulate corrective justice in distributive terms ("to each of these two litigants in accordance with the corrective criterion of liability"), we do not eradicate the conceptual difference between corrective and distributive justice or employ some overarching form that integrates them. In this formulation distributive justice does no work, but merely supervenes verbally upon the still independent functioning of corrective justice.

group's collective unity. The criterion is the principle that relates the persons to their holdings and to one another. It represents the purpose common to the parties *qua* participants in the distribution. The holding of shares pursuant to that criterion is the concrete manifestation of the governing criterion. Thus the criterion is what renders the distribution a single structured arrangement, rather than a random collection, of goods and persons.

In corrective justice, however, the unity of the plaintiff-defendant relationship lies in the very correlativity of doing and suffering harm. In Aristotle's language of gain and loss, the gain that consists in doing is also a loss that consists in suffering. Corrective justice construes the doing and the suffering of harm as the active and the passive aspects that together constitute a single unit of juridical significance. When the defendant harms the plaintiff, neither the doing nor the suffering counts independently of the other. The doing of harm is significant only because of the suffering that is correlative to it, and vice versa. The doing and the suffering are, for purposes of corrective justice, not two separate events but the two correlative aspects of a single event.

Corrective and distributive justice provide the most abstract representations of the unity of justificatory considerations. If these considerations elaborate what the doer of harm owes to the sufferer of harm, they have the shape of corrective justice; if they point to the desirability of dividing a benefit or burden among a group, they have the shape of distributive justice. Thus the two forms of justice are structures of justificatory coherence: the terms "corrective" and "distributive" apply to an external relationship by applying to the type of justification that supports that relationship.[43]

Because corrective and distributive justice are the categorically different and mutually irreducible patterns of justificatory coherence, it follows that a single external relationship cannot coherently partake of both. Aristotle's contrast of corrective and distributive justice does not determine whether the law should treat an incident correctively or distributively. But if the law is to be coherent, any given relationship cannot rest on a *combination* of corrective and distributive justifications. When a corrective justification is mixed with a distributive one, each necessarily undermines the justificatory force of the other, and the relationship cannot manifest either unifying structure.

This conclusion has far-reaching consequences for private law. To

---

[43] Robert Nozick, *Anarchy, State, and Utopia*, 27 (1974) ("the term 'redistributive' applies to the types of reasons for an arrangement rather than to an arrangement itself").

the extent that private law relationships are characteristically bipolar, their coherence is a matter of corrective justice. The bipolarity of corrective justice is evident in the lawsuit, which takes the form of an action by the plaintiff against the defendant for harm that the plaintiff has suffered at the hands of the defendant. Similarly, the concepts and many of the principal doctrines of the common law—for example, offer and acceptance, consideration, unconscionability, and expectation damages in contract law,[44] and causation, fault, and compensatory damages in tort law[45]—reflect the bipolarity of private law relationships. Inasmuch as such relationships are coherent, the justificatory considerations that underlie them have the structure of corrective justice. And if courts are to maintain this coherence, their reasoning about these relationships will also have to adhere to the contours of corrective justice.

Conversely, the introduction of distributive considerations renders these relationships incoherent. Admixing distributive considerations into the corrective framework of private law precludes the relationship from attaining the coherence of either corrective or distributive justice. It precludes the former because it introduces considerations that are alien to the immediate interaction of doer and sufferer. It precludes the latter because the bipolarity of private law institutions and concepts truncates the natural reach of distributive principles. And it precludes a coherent mixture of the two because no such mixture is possible within a single legal relationship.

To illustrate this point, consider again the example, discussed in Chapter 2, of spreading losses through tort law, and recall that the justificatory considerations that underlie causation and loss-spreading frustrate each other, because they do not form a single interlocking justification. Expressed in the terms of Aristotle's analysis, the difficulty is that the introduction of loss-spreading into tort law mixes corrective and distributive justice. The principle that accident losses should be distributed so as to minimize their felt impact has the proportional structure of distributive justice—it mandates the sharing of burdens in accordance with a criterion. Its use in tort law, however, fails to achieve distributive justice, because continuing the proportion by applying the principle to everyone within its reach is inconsistent with its being channeled through the doer and sufferer of a single harm. Conversely, since the issue of how the loss is ultimately spread

---

[44] See below, section 5.6.2.
[45] See below, Chapter 6.

is not germane to the relationship of doing and suffering as such (indeed the best conduit for loss-spreading might be some third party), the orienting of tort law toward loss-spreading cannot adequately actualize corrective justice. The combination of elements from both forms of justice ensures that neither form is achieved. And since coherence consists in having a legal relationship reflect one of the forms of justice, loss-spreading as a tort doctrine is incoherent.

The problem with combining corrective and distributive justice within a single relationship is that distributive justice splits asunder what corrective justice joins together. Corrective justice involves the intrinsic unity of the doer and the sufferer of the same harm. A distributive criterion disassembles this unity by selecting a feature morally relevant to only one of the parties to the transaction. It then groups that party with other persons to whom that feature applies and who therefore should also be subject to the burden or the benefit to be distributed. Thus the distributive criterion has a vitality of its own that is not confined to the transaction whose unity it has decomposed. Rather, it floats free to cover all the persons who fall under its independent sway.

Aristotle's account of corrective and distributive justice outlines the modes of ordering that inform legal arrangements. As Kelsen observes, Aristotle does not specify the content of justice. This formalism, however, is not a defect. Aristotle's assimilation of the forms of justice to different mathematical operations demonstrates that the forms are categorically different and mutually irreducible. Thereby they represent the contrasting structures of justification that underlie the coherence of external relationships.

3.7. Corrective Justice as Form

Corrective justice is the form of the private law relationship. As shown in Chapter 2, form involves the integration of three aspects: unity, kind, and character. Corrective justice embraces these three aspects as they apply to the private law relationship.

The correlativity of gains and losses is a way of representing the unity of the private law relationship. Because they are correlative, a gain cannot be considered independently of a loss. When mapped onto the private law relationship, this correlativity ties the parties to each other. Corrective justice thus treats the plaintiff-defendant relationship as a single normative unit.

Corrective justice also defines a distinct kind of legal relationship.

The equalization of correlative gain and loss is a categorically different operation from equalization within a series of proportions. Only in an interaction of two parties can gain and loss be correlative to each other; no such limitation applies to the sharing of burdens and benefits under distributive justice. Corrective justice thus constitutes a distinctive justificatory structure that informs the bipolar relationships of private law.

Finally, corrective justice reflects the character of private law. The most distinctive feature of private law, expressed both in its procedures and in its doctrines, is the bipolarity of the relationship between the parties. By representing this bipolarity through correlative gains and losses, corrective justice singles out a particular plaintiff and a particular defendant and makes the duties of one correlative to the rights of the other.

Corrective justice brings together the aspects of unity, class, and character in a single approach to legal intelligibility. It is because the correlative gain and loss represent a distinctive unity that the structure of corrective justice differs from that of distributive justice. Conversely, the categorical difference between corrective and distributive justice means that the introduction of distributive considerations into corrective justice not only blurs separate categories but brings incoherence to the plaintiff-defendant relationship. Moreover, open-ended distributive considerations are incompatible with the bipolar link between the parties that characterizes the doctrines and institutions of private law. Thus under corrective justice, unity, kind, and character are the mutually reinforcing aspects of a formal understanding of private law.

3.8. The Problem of Equality in Corrective Justice

There is, however, a troubling lacuna in Aristotle's explication of corrective justice. Aristotle's corrective justice presupposes the equality of the two parties to a transaction.[46] The problem is: in what respect are the parties equal?

This question is fundamental. Corrective justice serves a normative function: a transaction is required, on pain of rectification, to conform to its contours. Because Aristotle conceptualizes violations of corrective justice as disturbances of the equality between the parties, he rests the entire normative weight of corrective justice on that equality. Con-

---

[46] *Nicomachean Ethics*, 1132a2–1132a5.

sequently, we cannot understand the normative character of corrective justice until we elucidate the normative significance of its equality.

The closest Aristotle comes to addressing the problem is in an important but very obscure passage, just after he introduces corrective justice by contrasting its quantitative equality with the proportional equality of distributive justice. He remarks: "Whether a worthy person has taken something from an unworthy person or vice versa, makes no difference nor whether a worthy or a worthless person has committed adultery; but the law looks to the difference in the harm alone, and it treats them as equals, if the one commits and the other suffers injustice, and if the one has inflicted harm and the other has suffered harm."[47] This sentence describes the equality of corrective justice first in terms of what does not matter and then in terms of what does. The parts of the sentence on either side of the semicolon formulate the identical point negatively and positively. We must understand each side in a way that harmonizes with the other.

The first part of the sentence formulates the equality of corrective justice negatively, by pointing to a consideration that corrective justice excludes. The passage's context (the contrast with distributive justice) and content (the distinction between worth and harm) enable us to supply the reason that moral or social worth is irrelevant to corrective justice. Such worth (or lack of it) is a quality of persons as individuals; it is not, in and of itself, part of a process through which the worthy (or unworthy) person does a particular harm or wrong to someone else. To factor moral or social worth into justice in holdings, one must link persons to one another not through the correlativity of doing and suffering harm but through a comparison of the degree to which they each have such worth. This comparison could serve as a criterion under the proportional equality of distributive justice ("To each according to his or her worth"), but it could not constitute the purely bipolar link reflected in the quantitative equality of corrective justice. The immediate interaction of corrective justice allows no place for considering the various degrees to which the individuals have qualities that might be the basis of a mediating proportion under distributive justice.

Aristotle here is implicitly suggesting a distinction between the forms of justice that goes beyond this specific illustration: Whereas the proportional equality of distributive justice involves comparing the parties by reference to some criterion, the equality of corrective justice

---

[47] Id. at 1132a2–1132a6.

excludes *all* comparative assessments. Corrective justice is therefore as unmindful of the parties' comparative wealth or need, for example, as it is of their comparative virtues or social positions.

The second part of the sentence, which highlights the significance of harm, formulates the equality of corrective justice positively. Equality in corrective justice does not reside in what one is in comparison to another, but in what the one has done to the other. As Aristotle elsewhere notes, the logic of correlativity implies equality, because in the correlativity of doing and suffering harm, anything predicated of the doer can equally be predicated of the sufferer.[48] Corrective justice puts this logic to normative use by construing the immediate interaction as itself expressing (or if wrongful or harmful, disturbing) the just equality between the parties, which, for its part, exists in and through such interaction.

The question therefore remains: how are a normative equality and the possibility of its violation implicit in the correlativity of doing and suffering? To this Aristotle provides no answer. Nonetheless, he says enough to eliminate one initially plausible possibility.

One might suppose that although corrective justice is concerned with immediate interactions, the equality toward which it works is the proportional equality of distributive justice. Corrective justice presupposes the existence of entitlements, which, presumably, are the creation not of corrective justice itself but of distributive justice. On this view, the function of corrective justice is to preserve a given distribution of wealth.[49] Accordingly, the equality presupposed in transactions is the proportional equality of distributive justice.

This answer is unsatisfactory. At this point Aristotle is explaining how corrective equality *differs* from distributive equality. Corrective justice cannot, therefore, be merely a reassertion of the distributive equality disturbed by the defendant's action. In dismissing the rele-

---

[48] Aristotle, *Rhetoric,* II, 1397a23: "Another topic is derived from correlatives. If to have done rightly or justly may be predicated of one, then to have suffered similarly may be predicated of the other. Similarly with ordering and executing an order. As Diomedon the tax-contractor said about the taxes, 'If selling them is not disgraceful for you, buying them is not disgraceful for us.' And if rightly or justly can be predicated of the sufferer, it can equally be predicated of the doer, and if of the doer, then also of the sufferer."

[49] For this picture, see James Gordley, "Equality in Exchange," 69 *California Law Review* 1587 (1981). For other criticisms of Gordley, see Peter Benson, "Abstract Right and the Possibility of a Nondistributive Conception of Contract: Hegel and Contemporary Contract Theory," 10 *Cardozo Law Review* 1077 at 1194–1195 (1989).

vance of distributive criteria and claiming that doing and suffering has its own kind of equality, Aristotle affirms that the equality of corrective justice is implicit in the transaction as such, not in the distributive shares with which the parties enter the transaction.

The suggestion that the equality that defines corrective justice is that of the antecedent distribution is suspect for several reasons. First, the suggestion collapses the two forms of justice. Instead of their being the separate categories that Aristotle expressly postulates,[50] corrective justice becomes a species of distributive justice. Moreover, on this view a judge always has reason, at least in principle,[51] to consider the justice or injustice of the underlying distribution and to allow the Robin Hood defense, that an apparently wrongful taking has produced a more just distribution. This defense is inconsistent not only with the universal practice of private law, but, more specifically, with Aristotle's evident exclusion from corrective justice of comparisons (including, as I argued above, comparisons of wealth or need, which would usually be necessary to decide whether a distribution is just). Furthermore, if one deals with this difficulty by assuming that corrective justice operates only when the distribution is just, one is left with the problem of explaining why Aristotle should single out transactional disturbances of distributive justice. The arrangements of distributive justice can be upset in any number of ways—gifts from one participant to another, the destruction of someone's share through natural catastrophe, the growth of the pool through accession or birth, the diminishing of the pool through death or departure, and so on. The enrichment of one person at the expense of another is in some ways the least problematic of these, since the readjustment can be localized to the two parties. Finally, once one conceives of corrective justice in this way, transactional injustice would not be a wrong directly done to the sufferer. The inequality would consist not in something that the defendant has done to the plaintiff, but in the defendant's having more and the plaintiff less than each's fair share of the distribution. One could rectify this inequality in two separate steps, by giving something to the plaintiff and taking something from the defendant. Entitling the plaintiff to a direct transfer from the defendant would have the merely contingent advantage of administrative economy rather than provide the mark of a conceptually distinct structure of justice.

---

[50] *Nicomachean Ethics*, 1130b31–1131a1, 1131b25.
[51] I add this qualifying phrase to exclude administrative reasons not relevant to the theoretical point at issue.

Of course corrective justice presupposes the existence of entitlements. One cannot infer from this, however, that distributive justice provides the standpoint of equality for corrective justice. As an autonomous form of justice, corrective justice operates on entitlements without addressing the justice of the underlying distribution. The differing equalities of the two forms of justice represent the different structures of justification that apply to distributions and transactions. Even if corrective justice works against a distributive background, it accepts the distribution as given and does not incorporate the justification of the distribution into its own structure. Therefore, the existence of a distribution in no way implies that the equality of corrective justice is identical to the equality embodied in the distribution.

How, then, are we to make sense of Aristotle's assertion that "the law treats [the parties] as equals"? They cannot rightly be treated as equals unless they are equal in some relevant respect. What conception of the parties would put them on an equal footing?

Aristotle, unfortunately, cannot help us unravel the mystery that his account of corrective justice presents. The object of Aristotle's ethics generally is to elucidate the excellences of character that mark proper human functioning. Corrective justice, where "it makes no difference whether a worthy person has deprived an unworthy person or vice versa,"[52] obviously stands apart from Aristotle's general concerns. By ignoring considerations of worthiness, corrective justice abstracts from the considerations that pertain to Aristotle's rich and full notion of the good.

A comment by Aquinas indicates the extent of the impasse. "The law treats [the parties] as equals," he notes, quoting Aristotle's statement, but then he adds, "however much they may be unequal."[53] This formulation contains a paradox. The point of justice in holdings is to treat equals equally. The contradictoriness of treating unequals equally would disqualify corrective justice as a coherent justificatory structure. Aquinas, as it were, pauses on Aristotle's expression "as equals" and interprets it as stating something that is contrary to fact. So understood, private law is nothing more than an elaborate fiction.

3.9. From Corrective Justice to Kantian Right

Despite its compactness, the crucial sentence in Aristotle's text suggests the framework for a solution. The sentence formulates the dis-

---

[52] Id. at 1132a2.
[53] Aquinas, *Commentary on the Nicomachean Ethics*, vol. 1, 411.

tinctiveness of corrective justice in three ways: (1) corrective justice prescinds from considerations such as social rank and moral character ("whether a worthy person has taken something from an unworthy person or vice versa makes no difference"); (2) it regards the transacting parties as equals ("the law treats them as equals"); and (3) it focuses on the immediate relationship of doer to sufferer ("the law looks to the difference in the harm alone . . . if the one has inflicted and the other has suffered harm"). Accordingly, three ideas come together in corrective justice: the abstraction from such particulars as social status and moral character, the equality of the parties, and the sheer correlativity of doing and suffering.

In corrective justice these three ideas are intimately connected. Equality and the abstraction from particulars go hand in hand, because particulars are factors that might differentiate individuals and make them unequal. Similarly, abstraction from particulars and the sheer correlativity of doing and suffering go together, because when doing and suffering are each considered solely in relation to the other, the qualities particular to the doer or to the sufferer as individuals are irrelevant. Equality and the sheer correlativity of doing and suffering also go together, because the correlative elements are the active and passive poles of a single transaction, so that whatever applies to the doer applies equally to the sufferer. The three ideas thus form an integrated conception in which the immediate relation of doer and sufferer expresses an equality that consists in abstracting from the parties' particularities.

The solution, then, to the problem posed by Aristotle's reference to equality lies in an account that integrates that equality with corrective justice's abstraction from particularity and with the correlativity of doing and suffering. Only Kant's exposition of the concept of right, aside from subsequent treatments that incorporate its insights, provides such an account.[54] Kant understood right as the juridical manifestation of self-determining agency. The fundamental feature of this agency is the agent's capacity to abstract from—and thus not to be determined by—the particular circumstances of his or her situation.

---

[54] Many of the points developed here and subsequently in Kantian terms could also be expressed in Hegelian ones. See Ernest J. Weinrib, "Right and Advantage in Private Law," 10 *Cardozo Law Review* 1283 (1989). For a different view of the relationship between the Kantian and Hegelian approaches to private law, see Alan S. Brudner, "Hegel and the Crisis of Private Law," 10 *Cardozo Law Review* 949 (1989). For an exchange on the issue, see Ernest J. Weinrib, "Professor Brudner's Crisis," 11 *Cardozo Law Review* 549 (1990), and Alan S. Brudner, "Professor Weinrib's Coherence," 11 *Cardozo Law Review* 553 (1990).

Inasmuch as this capacity is a defining feature of self-determining agency, all self-determining agents are equal with respect to it. In Kantian legal theory private law governs the interaction of doer and sufferer on terms that respect their moral status as self-determining agents.

The three ideas found in Aristotle's crucial sentence each have Kantian counterparts. First, the abstraction from particulars corresponds to what Kant termed "negative freedom," the capacity of the agent to rise above the givenness of inclination and circumstance.[55] Second, the equality of the parties corresponds to the irrelevance for the normative dimension in agency of the particular features—desires, endowments, circumstances, and so on—that might distinguish one agent from another and that therefore might form the basis of comparing them and judging them unequal. Third, the sheer correlativity of doing and suffering corresponds to Kant's treatment of doing and suffering as a single normative sequence in which, regardless of the particularities of doer and sufferer, the doing must be capable of morally coexisting with the suffering that it causes.

Accordingly, the equality of corrective justice acquires its normative force from Kantian right. Indeed, one might describe corrective justice in Kantian terms as the point of view from which noumenal selves see each other,[56] that is, as the ordering of immediate interactions that self-determining agents would recognize as expressive of their natures. Such agents are duty-bound to interact with each other on terms appropriate to their equal status. Implicit in corrective justice's relationship of doer and sufferer are the obligations incumbent in Kantian legal theory on free beings under moral laws.[57]

From his observation of the regulation of contract and delict by the law of his day, Aristotle brilliantly outlined the justificatory structure

---

[55] Immanuel Kant, *The Metaphysics of Morals*, 42 [213], 52 [226] (Mary Gregor, trans., 1991). Georg W. F. Hegel, *Philosophy of Right*, sect. 5 (T. M. Knox, trans., 1952), formulates the same idea when he notes that the first moment of the will "involves the dissipation of every restriction and every content either immediately presented by nature, by needs, desires, and impulses, or given and determined by any means whatever."

[56] John Rawls characterizes the original position as "the point of view from which noumenal selves see the world." John Rawls, *A Theory of Justice*, 255 (1971).

[57] Kant, *Metaphysics of Morals*, 56 [230]. Corrective justice therefore deals with the immediate interaction of free beings as they express their freedom. It is a part of "justice in holdings" only if one understands "holdings" to include not only the plaintiff's entitlements but also the defendant's freedom to act. See above, note 10.

that characterizes what we would today call private law. In doing this, he rightly saw that distributional considerations and dispositional virtue were irrelevant to this structure's distinctive equality. His account invites us to ask: what kind of equality can inform private law without regard to considerations of distribution or virtue? Inasmuch as corrective justice disregards everything whose justificatory significance derives from its possible role in distributive justice, all that remains as the subject matter of this equality is the capacity to abstract from one's particular situation that is the minimal condition of every exercise of agency.

In Kant's legal philosophy, the conception of agency presupposed in corrective justice becomes the deliberate focus of analysis. Kant attempts to demonstrate how corrective justice arises from the structure of self-determining agency. His argument moves from agency as the ground of right to private law as a consequence of that ground.

The differences between the Kantian and the Aristotelian accounts of private law are expository, not substantive. Kant treats from the standpoint of self-determining agency what Aristotle describes as a structure of interaction. With interaction as his starting point, Aristotle elucidates the other-directedness of justice and links the parties through the notion of equality. Kant, in contrast, starts with agency and shows its necessary embodiment in a juridical order of abstractly equal agents. Aristotle's account of corrective justice and the Kantian account of right move over the same ground but from different directions.

The convergence of corrective justice and Kantian right bridges the oft-asserted chasm between ancient and modern conceptions of law. The trite contrast between the rich particularity of Aristotelian good and the impoverished starkness of Kantian right does not apply to private law. Nor is it invariably true that in the classical tradition "to be a man is to fill a set of roles each of which had its own point and purpose: member of a family, citizen, soldier, philosopher, servant of God," whereas in modernity "man is thought of as an individual prior to and independent of all roles."[58] Inasmuch as Aristotle's corrective justice is concerned with the sheer correlativity of doing and suffering, it presupposes a conception of the person that abstracts from role. Aristotle's account of corrective justice is inchoately Kantian.

---

[58] Alasdair MacIntyre, *After Virtue*, 59 (2nd ed., 1984).

4

Kantian Right

4.1. Introduction

In this chapter I situate corrective justice within Kant's philosophy of right. For Kant as for Aristotle, corrective justice is the justificatory structure that pertains to the immediate interaction of doer and sufferer. Kant, however, differs from Aristotle in presenting corrective justice not as an isolated category but as part of a ramified legal philosophy. His treatment therefore enables us to see the place of corrective justice within its family of associated concepts.

These concepts extend both backward to corrective justice's normative presuppositions and forward to its legal consequences. On the one hand, Kant locates the conceptual roots of corrective justice in the free purposiveness of self-determining activity. He thereby connects corrective justice to his obscure but powerful analysis of the process of willing. The equality of corrective justice turns out, as I have noted, to be the equality of free wills in their impingements on one another. In the Kantian view, such equality is normative because it reflects the normativeness intrinsic to all self-determining activity.

On the other hand, Kant connects corrective justice to the institutions of a functioning legal order. Aristotle himself had noted that disputants in corrective justice have recourse to the judge, "justice ensouled." The involvement of the judge means that corrective justice, although it deals with the interaction of two parties, involves an impartial and disinterested third party in assessing and enforcing the legal consequences of that interaction. In Kantian legal theory, the presence of the judge is not merely a phenomenologically observed element of private law but is conceptually necessitated by the mutual externality of the interacting agents. Corrective justice is thus part of a complex of ideas that includes the publicness of legal ordering. Kant terms the institutional operation of corrective justice "public law," referring thereby not to an instrumentalist amelioration of the collective good but to the legally authoritative framework for the norms arising as a matter of right.

Kant's legal philosophy traces the conceptual development of law from its origins in free purposive activity to its maturation in a system of public law. Corrective justice is literally central to this development, because it bridges the transition from will to institutions. When considered together with its associated components, corrective justice forms a totality that governs the external relationships of self-determining agents. That totality is the subject of this chapter.

Crucial to Kant's account of law is the role of coherence. Like Aristotle, Kant understands the transactional relationship as a normative unit. This relationship, however, is only one locus for the coherence of private law. Coherence also characterizes the entire complex of notions within which the transactional relationship is situated. Law, from its origin in the will to its manifestation in public institutions, is a unity that integrates its various parts into a whole.

"Idea of reason" is the phrase with which Kant refers to this integration. Consider, for example, his account of the transition from the provisional enjoyment of rights in a state of nature to the juridical condition of civil society. Kant ascribes this transition to an original contract in which people give up their inborn external freedom in order immediately to receive it back secure and undiminished as members of a lawful commonwealth.[1] Because this original contract is not a fact of history, the bindingness of law does not depend on the historical evidence for the existence of such a contract or on the process by which people have succeeded to these contractual rights and obligations.[2] Nor is it a response to the fact that a regime of lawful coercion is needed to repress the violence to which people are prone in its absence.[3] Rather, the original contract "is in fact merely an *idea* of reason, which nonetheless has undoubted practical reality; for it can oblige every legislator to frame his laws in such a way that they could

---

[1] Immanuel Kant, *The Metaphysics of Morals* 127 [315–316] (Mary Gregor, trans., 1991).

[2] Immanuel Kant, "On the Common Saying: 'This May Be True in Theory, but It Does Not Apply in Practice,'" in Kant, *Political Writings,* 79 (Hans Reiss, ed., 2nd ed., 1991).

[3] See Kant, *Metaphysics of Morals,* 123 [312].

have been produced by the united will of the whole nation, and to regard each subject, in so far as he can claim citizenship, as if he had consented within the general Will."[4]

The characterization of the contract as "an idea of reason" is thematic. Within the Kantian system generally, the phrase signifies an integrated totality of parts. Kant applies it, or variants of it, to a number of different elements in his legal philosophy: to the original contract, to property, to the sovereign, to relations between states, to the general will.[5] All these instances, if they are truly ideas of reason *in pari materia*, partake of a conceptual unity that integrates them into one comprehensive idea of reason. Before specifying the interrelationships among various aspects of this broader unity, I shall use the term "legality" to designate the whole ensemble of components constituting this inclusive idea of reason.

Legality, when conceived in Kantian terms as an idea of reason, is the articulated unity applicable to the external relationships of freely willing beings. This unity connects the various doctrines and institutions of law to a conception of volition. Kant sees law not as a harmony of *interests*, but as a distinctive community of *concepts* within whose regulative structure every free will can pursue whatever interests it has.

In this chapter I am concerned with three aspects of this notion of legality. First, I explore the significance of regarding legality as "an idea of reason which nonetheless has undoubted practical reality." This phrase refers to the presuppositions about agency and normativeness that underlie the equality of corrective justice. Like the corrective justice that derives from it, Kant's conception of the will is notoriously formal, inasmuch as Kant construes freedom through a process of abstraction from particular ends. In this chapter I show the connection between this notion of willing and the concept of right that figures in private law.

Second, I trace how a coherent and functioning system of private law emerges from the exiguous structure of the Kantian will. My discussion at this point focuses on Kant's reinterpretation of the Roman jurist Ulpian's three precepts of right: to live honorably, to injure no one, and to give each person his due. Kant treats these precepts as representing different aspects in the conceptualization of legality.

---

[4] "On the Common Saying: 'This May Be True in Theory, but It Does Not Apply in Practice,'" 79.

[5] Kant, *Metaphysics of Morals*, 73 [251], 120 [306], 124 [312], 127 [315], 134 [323], 146 [338], 151 [344], 177 [372].

Between them they embrace the possibility of coherent juridical relationships, the actuality of the transactions of corrective justice, and the normative necessity of legal institutions.

Third, I discuss the distinctive nature of legality as a normative enterprise. Kant elucidates what we now term the priority of the right over the good;[6] he divides morality into law and ethics, with law being the conceptually anterior field. In Kant's view the relationships of private law are morally intelligible independently of ethical considerations. Kant therefore would repudiate the accounts of private law that adduce justifications that he would regard as ethical only.[7] Accordingly, in the final section of this chapter I deal with the basis in Kant's thought for his exclusion of the ethical from the legal.

4.2. Legality as an Idea of Reason

Let me return to Kant's mention of "an idea of reason, which nonetheless has undoubted practical reality; for it can oblige every legislator…" This sentence gives rise to four questions. First, what is an idea of reason? Second, what is the meaning of the assertion that the reality of this idea is *practical?* Third, why does this idea have a reality that obliges lawmakers? Fourth, how can legality be such an idea?

4.2.1. An Idea of Reason

According to Kant, the function of reason is to order concepts so as to give them the greatest possible unity combined with the widest possible application.[8] In the absence of reason, concepts would occupy discrete territories, "isolated from one another, separated, as it were, by an empty intervening space,"[9] and their totality would be merely the aggregate that they all happen to form in combination. The systematizing function of reason enables them to be construed as parts of a whole in which each part conditions, and is simultaneously conditioned by, the other parts. Since this whole can be articulated into

---

[6] John Rawls, *Political Liberalism,* 173 (1993).
[7] Fried's thesis of contract as promise is an example; see above, section 2.9.3.
[8] Immanuel Kant, *Critique of Pure Reason,* A644/B672 (Norman Kemp Smith, trans., 1929).
[9] Id. at A659/B687; Kant, *Metaphysics of Morals,* 45 [218] (gapless subdivision as the proof of the completeness and the continuity of a system); 102 [284] (logical division within a genuine system contrasted with empirical division that "leaves it uncertain whether there are not additional members that would be needed to fill out the entire sphere of the concept divided").

its parts, it is not a single and indivisible unit. Conversely, being recip-rocally connected in terms of the unity in which they all partake, the parts are themselves not individually self-sufficient. The business of reason is thus to systematize concepts as parts of such an articulated unity.[10]

An idea of reason is an ordering principle by which reason unifies a group of diverse concepts.[11] The systematic unity that reason introduces presupposes something through which various concepts are related, the focus, as it were, upon which all the conceptual lines converge. This point of intersection represents the wholeness of the parts taken together, and it determines for every part its position and relation to the other parts. Such a uni-fying idea is necessary for the concepts to be related to one another and not merely juxtaposed and contingently aggregated under a single rubric.

4.2.2. A Practical Idea of Reason

Reason can operate upon different types of concepts. Some of these concepts relate to what is given to us in the empirical world, while others relate to what we bring into being through an operation of will. In the present context, only the second type of concept—in the realm of what Kant calls practical reason—is relevant.[12]

For Kant, the term "practical" has a special significance:

By "the practical," I mean everything that is possible through freedom.... A will is purely *animal (arbitrium brutum),* which cannot be determined save through sen-suous impulses, that is, *pathologically.* A will which can be determined independ-ently of sensuous impulses, and therefore through motives which are represented

---

[10] Kant notes that reason deals with the whole as an organized unity *(articulatio),* not as an aggregate *(coacervatio).* See Kant, *Critique of Pure Reason,* A833/B861.

[11] On ideas of reason, see Kant, *Critique of Pure Reason,* A311/B367–A320/B377, A643/B671–A669/B697, A834/B862–A836/B864. Kant considers ideas of reason to be principles that regulate scientific inquiry. For example, "in psychology, under the guidance of inner experience, [we] connect all the appearances, all the actions and receptivity of our mind, as if the mind were a simple substance which persists with personal identity (in this life at least) while its states, to which those of the body belong only as outer conditions, are in continual change." Id. at A672/B700. For a brief catalogue of Kantian "ideas," see Alfred C. Ewing, *A Short Commentary on Kant's Critique of Pure Reason,* 245–263 (1938).

[12] For Kant's sharp distinction between the theoretical and the practical, see *Critique of Pure Reason,* Bix–x; Immanuel Kant, *Critique of Judgement,* 3–8 [167–170] (Werner S. Pluhar, trans., 1987).

only by reason, is entitled *freewill (arbitrium liberum),* and everything which is bound up with this will, whether as ground or as consequence, is entitled *practical.*[13]

Thus the practical reality of the idea of reason refers to Kant's conception of the will as free.

Freedom of the will is for Kant what most sharply distinguishes purposive activity from the passivity of a sequence of efficient causes. Purposiveness involves a relationship of a peculiar sort between the purposive being and the object toward which this being acts. Crucial to the understanding of this relationship is the role of mental representations. A being is purposive insofar as it translates a representation of the object of its desire into reality.[14] As a process of actualizing a representation, purposive activity differs from the efficient causation of nature. In efficient causation the effect always follows the cause, but in purposive activity the effect, because it is antecedently represented in the mind of the purposive being who strives to give it life, is also the cause of its own coming into being.[15] Purposiveness can therefore be termed a causality of concepts.[16]

Purposive activity is always the effort to achieve the determinate end, which is the content of the mental representation. Whether purposive activity is or is not free depends on the way in which this end can be related to the capacity for purposiveness. Purposive action is *not free* when the mental representation of a particular end cannot be compared with (and revised in favor of) a different mental represen-

---

[13] Kant, *Critique of Pure Reason,* A800/B828–A802/B830 (footnote omitted) (emphasis in original).

[14] Kant, *Metaphysics of Morals,* 40 [211]; Immanuel Kant, *Critique of Practical Reason,* 9 [9], note 7 (Lewis White Beck, trans., 1976). In discussing purposiveness in terms of a representation or concept, Kant is not providing a physiological explanation of purposive activity, much less a criterion of whether a given act (e.g., one done under provocation or while the actor is drunk) is purposive. Rather, he is subjecting purposiveness to a conceptual analysis whose essential point is that in purposive activity, action is linked to an end through thought. The representation is of an end that the actor aims to accomplish, and Kant's parallel definition of an end is "the *object* of free choice, the representation of which determines it to an action (by which the object is brought about)." Kant, *Metaphysics of Morals,* 189 [384]; see id. at 186 [381]. The nature of the physiological mechanism of human cognition is a feature of the world given to us and therefore a matter of theoretical, not practical, reason.

[15] Kant, *Critique of Judgement,* 251 [372].

[16] See id. at 64–65 [220], 252 [373]; Kant, *Critique of Practical Reason,* 49 [48], 76 [74]. In connection with the free will, Kant terms the causality of concepts a causality of reason. See, e.g., *Critique of Pure Reason,* A803/B831; *Critique of Practical Reason,* 69 [67].

tation. Such action—which Kant terms animal will—is determined by sensuous inclination.[17]

For purposive action to be *free*, it must have the capacity to abstract from the immediacy of inclination, to reflect upon the content of the mental representation, and spontaneously to substitute one representation for another. Here purposiveness as a causality of concepts spontaneously and freely initiates a series of effects: the purposive being—although *affected* by inclination, which can suggest a content for action—is not *determined* by inclination and is therefore not in the coercive grip of any particular representation or object of desire. Since this mode of purposiveness is initially conceived through its contrast with sensuous determination rather than through any positive feature of its own, Kant characterizes it as freedom in its negative aspect. The term he attaches to this aspect of freedom is *freie Willkür* (free choice), and he associates it with human—as contrasted with animal—willing.[18]

Now if inclination does not determine free activity, then what does determine it? Kant's answer is that such activity can be self-determining. This means that the determining ground of free activity is not the *content* of any particular purpose—this would be the pathological determination of sensuous impulse—but the very *form* of purposiveness as a causality of concepts.[19] Purposiveness is most truly itself when its nature as a causality of concepts determines the particular concept to be actualized. Then the principle on which the purposive being chooses to act is one which is capable of functioning as a prin-

[17] Kant, *Metaphysics of Morals*, 42 [213]. In this and in the following paragraph of the text, I draw on Peter Benson's discussion in "External Freedom according to Kant," 87 *Columbia Law Review* 559, at 570 (1987).

[18] Kant, *Metaphysics of Morals*, 42 [213–214]. Again, Kant's argument is not empirical. What matters is the distinction between purposive activity and free purposive activity, not the anthropological or zoological correctness of ascribing the former to animals and the latter to humans. Kant is elsewhere explicit that the categorical imperative that emerges from his analysis of the will cannot be derived from the particular constitution of human nature, that it holds for all rational beings, and that it can be a law for humans only inasmuch as they are rational. See, for example, Immanuel Kant, *Foundations of the Metaphysics of Morals*, 33 [415–416] (Lewis White Beck, trans., 1969). Kant also repeatedly affirms that we cannot have theoretical knowledge of our own freedom. See, e.g., *Critique of Practical Reason*, 4 [4]; *Metaphysics of Morals*, 48 [221].

[19] Kant, *Critique of Practical Reason*, 26 [27] (when the content of the will is taken away, all that remains to determine the will is the causality of concepts or, as Kant phrases it, the "mere form of giving universal law"); Kant, *Foundations of the Metaphysics of Morals*, 82 [462] ("the form, the practical law of universal validity of maxims").

ciple valid for all purposive beings whatever their particular inclinations. Such a principle would determine choice by virtue of the ability to universalize and not by virtue of the particular content of the choice. The most general expression of this formalism is the categorical imperative: "Act upon a maxim that can also hold as a universal law,"[20] which entails at a minimum that one's reason for acting be capable of being conceived in universal terms without contradiction. Accordingly, purposive activity has a rational dimension; freedom consists in the capacity of purposive activity to be determined by its own rational nature.[21] This mode of determination is what Kant calls practical reason, or *Wille*, which is the positive aspect of freedom.[22]

Kant's conception of freedom of the will is thus comprised of two aspects: free choice *(freie Willkür)* as independence from determination by sensuous impulse, and practical reason *(Wille)* as the determining ground of purposive activity.[23] These two aspects of freedom are conceptually related as the negative and positive counterparts of each other. Once free choice is seen as independence from the arbitrariness of determination by the will's *content*, practical reason as the *form* of purposive activity must be presupposed as the will's determining ground. Practical reason is the fullest expression of the rationality inherent in purposiveness as a causality of concepts. Free choice and practical reason can both be defined in terms of each other: free choice is the capacity for determination by practical reason rather than by inclination, and practical reason is free choice determining itself as a causality of concepts. Neither free choice nor practical reason is intelligible independently of the other, and their integrated operation marks out the range of the "practical" as Kant uses the term.

Practical reason accordingly assesses particular acts from the abstract and formal standpoint of the causality of concepts through which free choice is determinable. This formality reflects the notion that purposiveness is presupposed in all particular purposive acts. Determination by causality of concepts does not mean that action is

---

[20] Kant, *Metaphysics of Morals,* 51 [224]. (By "maxim" Kant means a "rule that the agent himself makes his principle on subjective grounds." Id.)

[21] Kant, *Critique of Practical Reason,* 32 [82] (in passing judgment on the lawfulness of their action, men's reason "in every action holds up the maxim of the will to the pure will, i.e., to itself regarded as a priori practical").

[22] Kant, *Metaphysics of Morals,* 42 [213], 52 [226].

[23] On the relationship between free choice *(freie Willkür)* and practical reason *(Wille)*, see Lewis White Beck, "Kant's Two Conceptions of the Will in Their Political Context," in *Studies in the Philosophy of Kant,* 215 (1965); Lewis White Beck, *A Commentary on Kant's Critique of Practical Reason,* 198–202 (1960).

without content or that purposive activity is transformed into contemplation. All purposive activity is the effort to bring *something* into actuality, but this content is only the raw material, and not the determining ground, of free choice.[24] When purposive activity is free, the purposive being is linked to its particular purpose by a rational operation and not by the imposition of sensuous impulse. Action thus regarded stands in unqualified contrast to the passivity of things caught in a chain of efficient causes.

The free will can now be identified as the point on which everything practical (in Kant's sense), including law, converges. If one starts with the notion of legality, which I have defined as the whole ensemble of legal components constituting an inclusive idea of reason, and works backward to the precondition of such a notion, and further backward to the precondition of that precondition, and so on, one should ultimately arrive at the free will with its negative aspect of freedom from determination by sensuous impulse and its positive aspect of practical reason.

4.2.3. The Normative Force of a Practical Idea of Reason

Why is this practical idea of reason a reality that can oblige every legislator?[25] For Kant, legality as an idea of reason provides the archetype for bringing the juridical organization of humanity ever nearer to its greatest possible perfection,[26] and he thereby claims for it a normative significance. What justifies this claim?

That legality is an idea of reason means that Kant does not have much latitude in answering this question. An idea of reason is the articulated unity of parts in a conceptual whole. If legality originally lacks normative significance, so that such significance must subsequently be imported from outside, the unity of the idea of reason would be imperiled. Legality and normativeness would share in the same discourse, but without being interconnected as parts of an integrated conceptual system. Accordingly, the normative aspect of

---

[24] Kant, *Critique of Practical Reason,* 35 [34].

[25] On the argument presented here, lawmakers are obliged to make the positive law an expression of the idea of reason, and such positive law is obligatory for citizens. Kant's views on the obligation of citizens when positive law fails to express the idea of reason raise notorious problems of interpretation. For recent discussions, see Howard Williams, *Kant's Political Philosophy,* 198–214 (1983); Terry Hopton, "Kant's Two Theories of Law," 3 *History of Political Thought* 51 (1982); Leslie Mulholland, *Kant's System of Rights,* 337–346 (1990).

[26] Kant, *Critique of Pure Reason,* A316/B373.

legality cannot be thought of as something initially independent that is grafted onto law. The unity of the idea of reason requires that normativeness be *inherent* in the idea of legality. This, indeed, is Kant's solution.

Ascribing to legality an inherently normative nature arises from Kant's account of free choice. Legality as an idea of reason is "practical" in Kant's sense of being grounded in the notion of purposive activity. As the determining ground of free choice, practical reason provides norms. However, practical reason does not impose any demands on free choice from without; it merely makes explicit the normativeness implicit in purposiveness as a spontaneous causality of concepts. The meaning of normativeness is precisely the determination of free choice in accordance with its own nature. Therefore one cannot intelligibly ask what additional consideration gives the demands of practical reason a normative significance: they are normative inasmuch as they are the requirements of practical reason.

Kant expresses this conclusion in the language of necessity. To think of something as the cause of something else is to postulate a necessary connection between the two. In efficient causation, for instance, the effect necessarily follows its cause. Although the causality of concepts is a mode of causation different from efficient causation, it nonetheless has its corresponding notion of necessity: it is a conceptual necessity that free purposiveness conform to its own nature as a causality of concepts. Since practical reason is the necessity appropriate to freedom, Kant defines obligation as "the necessity of a free action under a categorical imperative of reason."[27] What practical reason requires is intrinsically obligatory.[28]

Kant's notion of normativeness is extraordinarily elegant. Obligation refers to what *must* be *done* (or not *done*), raising the philosophical problem of how the elements of necessity and action are com-

---

[27] Kant, *Metaphysics of Morals,* 48 [222].

[28] It must be emphasized that normative necessity is not one of efficient causes; if it were, free will—and with it wrongdoing—would be impossible. Of course, because purposive activity always strives to accomplish something, practical reason presupposes a world of efficient causes; see Kant, *Critique of Practical Reason,* 43 [42]. But it is not itself intelligible in terms of that world. From the standpoint of efficient causation, determination by practical reason is only a possibility. Accordingly, a person may be ignorant of the requirements of practical reason or may be caused by sensuous impulses to rebel against them. The capacity of practical reason to determine the will—along with the conceptual necessity that it do so—does not, therefore, abolish wrong. Rather, it shows how wrong is intelligible against the background of what freedom requires.

bined. If they were separate, how could action be subject to obligation except by an impermissible inference of what ought to be done from what is done?[29] Kant realized that no norm external to purposive activity could be relevant to it. His achievement was to elucidate purposive activity as a causality of concepts and therefore as implicitly rational, so that we are spared the Sisyphean task of separately locating the normative bearing of the practical idea of reason. Normativeness consists in the governance of purposive activity according to a standard arising from the nature of such activity. The integration of free choice and practical reason contains all the normativeness there is.

I can now sum up the significance of the practical reality of an idea of reason. A practical reality is grounded in the self-determining freedom of human action. An idea of reason is intelligible as an articulated unity of its parts. Freedom of the will, the integration of free choice and practical reason, is the principle that unites the various aspects of the practical idea of reason into a network of conceptual interdependencies. Practical reason is the determining ground that can conform free choice to its own nature as a spontaneous causality of concepts. This meshing of freedom and necessity imparts normative force—and thus practical reality[30]—to the entire idea of reason.

4.2.4. Legality as a Practical Idea

Given the significance of an idea of reason that has practical reality, how can legality be such an idea? In view of his definition of the practical as everything tied up with the free will, Kant evidently posits a connection between his conception of legality and his conception of purposive activity. Here I focus on the nature of this connection.

Kant equates the sphere of legality with a person's external relationships, thus distinguishing it from ethics, which he considers action from a standpoint internal to the actor. The focus of his legal philosophy is not on an action's goodness but on its consistency with the freedom of all persons. His exposition of the concept of right contains

---

[29] David Hume, A Treatise of Human Nature, 475–476 (Lewis Selby-Bigge, ed., 2nd ed., 1978); Critique of Pure Reason, A319/B375.

[30] Kant, Critique of Pure Reason, A808/B836. (The moral world "is a mere idea, though at the same time a practical idea, which really can have, as it also ought to have, an influence upon the sensible world, to bring that world, so far as may be possible, into conformity with the idea. The idea of a moral world has, therefore, objective reality.")

the most general formulation of this consistency. Right *(das Recht)* is "the sum of conditions under which the choice of one can be united with the choice of another in accordance with a universal law of freedom."[31] Right thus combines the notions of external relationship and free will in the most abstract way. Accordingly, the union of externality and freedom in the concept of right permits law to be understood as an idea of reason with practical reality. I must therefore turn to Kant's elucidation of the concept of right.

Kant outlines the conditions within which the concept of right applies as follows:

The concept of Right...has to do *first,* only with the external and indeed the practical relation of one person to another, insofar as their actions, as facts, can have (direct or indirect) influence on each other. But, *second,* it does not signify the relation of one's choice to the mere *wish* (hence also to the mere need) of the other, as in actions of beneficence or callousness, but only a relation to the other's *choice. Third,* in this reciprocal relation of choice no account at all is taken of the *matter* of choice, that is, of the end that each has in mind with the object he wants; it is not asked, for example, whether someone who buys goods from me for his own commercial use will gain by the transaction or not. All that is in question is the *form* of the relationship of choice on the part of both, insofar as choice is regarded merely as *free,* and whether the action of one of the two parties can be united with the freedom of the other in accordance with a universal law.[32]

As always in Kant, the three conditions mentioned in this passage are not a seriatim list of separate factors. Rather, the passage makes salient the role of free will through a three-stage movement toward an unadulterated notion of external action: by gradually removing whatever has no place in this context, it brings the concept of right into high relief.

The first condition asserts the application of the concept of right to external and practical relations. Since the practical is that which is related to the free will as ground or consequence, the field of applicability of the concept of right is located at the juncture of the volition and its external effects. This sentence, although introductory, never-

[31] Kant, *Metaphysics of Morals,* 56 [230].
[32] Id. at 56 [230]. In the last sentence I have added to Gregor's translation the phrase "of the two parties" to reflect the words *von beiden* in Kant's text.

theless has important implications. For one thing, the concept of right, because it applies to the external, does not imply the possibility of virtuous self-perfection. For another, because the concept of right is restricted to the practical, it excludes activity that is determinable only by sensuous impulse. Although animal will creates effects in the external world, it is not practical.

The second condition in the passage eliminates wishing, and with it need, as a relevant consideration under the concept of right. Wishing is purposive activity, in that a person doing so seeks to actualize the object of a mental representation. Since the representation does not directly determine the person's action but can be replaced or discarded, wishing, unlike animal will, is an aspect of the free will. The peculiarity of wishing is that it is not accompanied by the consciousness of a capacity actually to produce the object of the mental representation. The representation thus remains merely internal to the wishing person and does not assume an externalized shape in relation to anyone else. Wishing is therefore practical but has no external effect.[33]

In eliminating wishing, Kant affirms that the duties arising under the concept of right cannot be justified solely by the purported obligor's need, which, as something internal to the needy person, has no standing in the world of external relationships. Of course in satisfying someone else's need, I am acting externally to myself and in relation to someone else, and Kant holds that I am under an ethical duty to do so.[34] But since another's need, as such, does not have an external existence, it cannot create in me any legal obligation with respect to it. Therefore the practical relationship to which the concept of right refers cannot be between one person's choice and another person's wish, but must be between choice and choice.

This brings me to the third condition for the application of the concept of right. The relationship here between free wills does not deal with the specific purpose that either actor has in mind, because this purpose is only internally significant. Therefore, as Kant notes with an example drawn from commercial dealings, the failure of the act to achieve what motivated it is not relevant to the act's juridical quality. Inasmuch as it affects another, the act itself has an external status that is indifferent to the purpose that called it into being.

What matters for the concept of right is not the specific object that

---

[33] On wish *(Wunsch)*, see id. at 42 [213], 163 [356]; Kant, *Critique of Judgement*, 16 [178].
[34] Kant, *Metaphysics of Morals*, 196 [393].

free choice is attempting to achieve, but only that it is a free choice that attempts to achieve it. Only the form of the choice as free, not its content, comes into consideration. The concept of right, therefore, does not require any particular affirmative actions. It postulates an area of permissibility where the actor can strive to accomplish any purpose whatever, provided that the act is consistent with the form of the relationship between the wills insofar as they are free.

The second and third conditions for the applicability of the concept of right are the converse sides of the same notion. In the language of the common law, the concept of right deals with misfeasance and not nonfeasance. Under the second condition, one person's need does not serve as the basis for obligating another to satisfy that need; accordingly, there is no liability for nonfeasance, that is, for not providing another with a needed benefit. The third condition restricts the law's interventions to misfeasances, since it treats only acts as violations of right. The two conditions state not two independent principles, but the reciprocal entailment of no positive duties to help another and only negative duties to avoid acting inconsistently with the form of freedom between wills.

At the heart of the concept of right, then, is the form of the relationship between wills that are free. This relationship is the locus of the practical in its external orientation; the third condition for the concept of right simply articulates more precisely the first condition's joining of the external and the practical. This precision consists in leading us back to the form of free choice that is the foundational presupposition of self-determining action. The abstraction from the content of the will, which Kant notes as intrinsic to the concept of right, is also the defining characteristic of the negative aspect of freedom: free choice is the possibility of substituting one object of desire for another, so that whatever content the will has for the moment does not necessarily determine what a person does. The concept of right refers to the relationship between two beings whose activity is subject to this possibility.

By emphasizing the form of free choice, Kant makes the concept of right congruent with Aristotle's description of corrective justice. What Aristotle formulates as an abstraction from considerations of virtue ("whether a person has deprived an unworthy person or vice versa makes no difference") Kant formulates as an abstraction from the content of choice. One's worthiness reflects one's tendency to act for morally desirable ends. Corrective justice abstracts from considerations of virtue because it abstracts from all particular ends. Moreover,

Aristotle's continuation, that "the law looks to the difference in harm alone," points to a sheer relationship of act and effect that can be assessed from the standpoint of justice; that is, it points to the union of the external and the practical in Kantian right. And what Aristotle characterizes as the law's equal treatment of the doer and sufferer of harm surfaces in Kantian right as the moral compossibility of one person's action with another's freedom.

At the end of the quoted passage, the concept of right leads to what Kant terms the universal principle of right. Under the concept of right, "all that is in question is ... whether the action of one of the two parties can be united with the freedom of the other in accordance with a universal law." In thus governing bilateral relationships, the concept of right comprehends the sequence from one person's performance of an action to another's suffering of its effects. Because the parties to this relationship are free wills, the action must be consistent with the freedom of the potential sufferer. Accordingly, the concept of right constrains free and purposive action in the name of freedom itself. And because such freedom is an expression of the parties' capacity for self-determining agency, it falls under a universal law applicable to both parties as free, purposive beings. This universal law of freedom refers to what practical reason requires.

We can now appreciate the sense in which the conformity of juridical relations to the principle of right is an actualization of practical reason. Reason is practical when it is "applied to the capacity for choice irrespective of its objects."[35] Just as practical reason, or *Wille*, is the determination of free choice by its form and not its content, so the principle of right, that one person's action must be capable of coexisting with another's freedom, is the form of free choice determining the interaction of one free will with another. Practical reason is the determination of purposive activity by the causality of concepts; similarly, the principle of right is the determination by the concept of right of the relationships governed by that concept. Both practical reason and the principle of right abstract the form of free choice from whatever content it happens to have, and make this form determine the operation of the free will. The principle of right is therefore the external aspect of practical reason, or practical reason as it pertains to interaction among free wills. Under its external aspect, practical reason *(Wille)* becomes the general or universal will *(der allgemeine Wille)*.

---

[35] Id. at 42 [214].

Thus the quoted passage starts with the observation that the concept of right applies only to the external and practical relationship of one person to another, and then explains how both aspects of the combination of the external and the practical are satisfied. The wishes of the parties and the particular ends that are the content of their volitions are irrelevant to externality. What remains is the form in the relationship between formally free wills. The external and the practical have been reduced to their single abstract point. This contentless abstraction of the externally practical determines the relationships that fall under the concept of right. Just as practical reason holds free choice to the requirements of the rational nature of free choice, so the general will, as it functions in accordance with the principle of right, holds the external and practical relationship among those with free choice to the conceptual requirements of that relationship.

The connection between practical reason and free choice is conceptual and not physical. The distinction is crucial to the difference between Kantian legality and Kantian ethics. The spontaneity of free choice would be illusory unless it could be determined by the causality of concepts, which is the essence of this spontaneity. The determination is ethical when the freely choosing being adopts practical reason as the principle of an action. Here both practical reason and free choice are internal to a single actor.

However, since practical reason is conceptually and not physically connected to free choice, the locus of one can be different from the locus of the other, so that practical reason can be brought to bear on free choice from outside the being with free choice. This occurs in the realm of right.[36] Because acting out of virtue is irrelevant to the externality of the relationships governed by law, an external authority must be present to enforce upon the actor the external requirements of practical reason. The necessity of such an authority is a conceptual one, flowing from the nature of the conjunction of the practical and the external.[37] Thus the externality of right does not reflect merely the relationship between the parties to a legal transaction. In right, exter-

---

[36] Id. at 193 [389] (under right, the categorical imperative is a principle not of one's own will but of "will in general, which could also be the will of others").

[37] As Kant writes, the principle of right "lays an obligation on me, but it does not at all expect, far less demand, that I *myself should* limit my freedom to those conditions just for the sake of this obligation; instead, reason says only that freedom *is* limited to those conditions in conformity with the idea of it, and that it may also be actively limited by others." Kant, *Metaphysics of Morals,* 56 [231].

nality is a characteristic of volition itself, in that the conceptually connected aspects of free choice and practical reason are each located in mutually external entities. A rightful law is the voice of practical reason addressing from without a being with free choice.

4.3. From Free Will to the Publicness of Law

4.3.1. Ulpian's Precepts

Now it is clear how the coherence of law as a Kantian idea of reason is grounded in the will's integration of free choice and practical reason. Subjection to law can thus be the public confirmation, rather than the denial, of one's status as a free being. The concept of right is the most abstract binding of the practical and external; it is the prism that diffuses the requirements of practical reason into the external relationships of law. Here I focus on this process of diffusion by exhibiting the intricate conceptual progression through which law arises inexorably from the structure of willing. The parts of this process form the articulated unity that characterizes legality as a practical idea of reason.

Kant outlines the movement from free will to public law when he sets out a threefold division of the duties of right.[38] This division takes the form of a commentary on Ulpian's famous three precepts of right: *honeste vive* (live honorably), *neminem laede* (injure no one), *suum cuique tribue* (give each his due).[39] Kant playfully proposes to ascribe to them a sense that Ulpian himself "may not have thought distinctly in them, but which can be explicated from them or put into them."[40] That a serious purpose lurks here is evident from Kant's reference to this threefold division at other strategic junctures in his exposition.[41] The three precepts, in Kant's interpretation, are stages in the maturation of public law from its beginnings in the will.

What gives opportunity and point to Kant's use of the three precepts of Ulpian is that they feature a steady increase in the number of persons involved. The first precept, which Kant ambiguously translates

---

[38]   Id. at 62 [236–237].

[39]   *Digest*, 1.1.10.1 (Ulpian, *Regularum* 1). Kant transforms the infinitives of the *Digest* text into imperatives, presumably because he is proposing a general classification of the duties of justice. Duty is the content of obligation, and the imperative is the voice germane to obligation; Kant, *Metaphysics of Morals*, 48 [222].

[40]   Id. at 62 [236].

[41]   Id. at 87 [267], 120 [306].

as *Sei ein rechtlicher Mensch*[42]—"Be an honorable man" (but also, as we shall see, "Be, that is, assert yourself as, a juridical person")—does not explicitly require the existence of anyone but the addressee. The second precept, translated by Kant as "Do not wrong anyone,"[43] envisages a more populous world in which a second person exists who might be the victim of the injustice from which the addressee is enjoined. The final precept, "Give to each what is his,"[44] is, Kant notes, an absurdity on its face, because one cannot be given what one already has; Kant accordingly interprets it as mandating a regime of public law in which what each person owns is secured against everyone else.[45] This precept thus envisages not merely the two immediate parties to an interaction, as does the second, but also a publicly authoritative figure who confirms them in what they have and thus gives each his or her due. The successive precepts correspond to three stages that, through their increasingly dense population of the public world, represent the externality of right with progressively greater explicitness.

This emerging explicitness can be summarized as follows. In the first stage, the focus is on the lone actor, with the public aspect of action still only implicit. At the second stage, a second actor appears, so that the externally oriented action of the first stage has become an interaction, which can be ordered by the principle of right. But even this stage does not make the external aspect of free willing completely explicit because adhering to the principle of right and applying it in specific situations depend entirely upon (and are thus internal to) the subjective inclination of the interacting parties. The third stage adds a third party, the judge who impartially interprets the interaction and sets in motion the coercive apparatus of enforcement. Since the externality of the parties is regulated by the external authority of public law, the external relationship of all to all, ordered according to the principle of right, is now fully explicit.

In the same three phases practical reason also becomes more explicit. Indeed, Kant produces the precepts of Ulpian as relevant to a general classification of the *duties* of right; and because duties apply only to free acts, this classification charts a progression in the external recognition of the freedom of the will. The first stage, so Kant tells us, marks a possibility that becomes actual at the second stage and nec-

---

[42] Id. at 62 [236].
[43] Id.
[44] Id. at 62 [237].
[45] See id.

essary in the final stage.[46] When this trichotomy is applied to the volition, the actor is initially conceived as an entity for whom determination by practical reason is only possible. In the second stage, the external operation of practical reason can be actual; there can be a second free will on whom the first can impinge. These two interacting persons are bound by the principle of right to a harmony of the action of one with the free will of the other. The first stage's capacity for action in accordance with practical reason is now, at the second stage, put to the test of actual interaction. Although the second stage advances beyond the bare implicitness of practical reason to the existence of correlative rights and duties, this existence is itself not yet explicit until the third stage, when public law announces and enforces such rights and duties.

This progression from free will to public law can be further broken down. The cursory articulation that follows is partly a summary of what Kant says, partly a skeletal commentary, partly illustration, and partly a supplementary fleshing out of Kant's suggestive outline. The purpose of briefly exhibiting the components of this progression is to indicate the scope of legality as an idea of reason.

4.3.2. The First Stage

The possibility of a public world. Among the related set of possibilities in the first stage is the possibility of a truly public world. The actor, although alone at this point, is nonetheless a free will and so can abstract from the content that inclination proposes for action. Inclination as such is intrinsically private. Practical reason, in contrast, operates "through concepts which alone can be universally communicated, and not by mere sensation which is limited to the individual subjects and their susceptibility."[47] Any freely willing being can, by virtue of its independence from determination by sensuous impulse, participate in a shared world of reason. Without this possibility, the resultant polity would be nothing but a congeries of private interests randomly affecting one another in response to the impetus of inclination, rather than a civil association that can institutionalize through its public system of law the external aspect of practical reason.

---

[46] Id. at 120 [306]. This progression conforms to Kant's categories of modality; see Kant, *Critique of Pure Reason,* A80/B106.

[47] Kant, *Critique of Practical Reason,* at 60 [58]; Kant, *Foundations of the Metaphysics of Morals,* 30 [413] (subjective causes "hold only for the senses of this or that person").

The possibility of interaction. The possibility of practical reason also implies the possibility of interaction. The actor, *qua* free will and even without encountering any other actor, has the capacity to reflect upon the particular purpose he or she wants to accomplish. The actor can recognize that the possibility of choosing a purpose other than the one actually chosen means that action is not defined by any particular purpose. One is free to determine any purpose for oneself, that is, one is self-determining. In recognizing oneself as self-determining, one can recognize oneself both as the object of one's attention and as the subject that provides that attention. Implicated in this recognition is the possibility that other selves might exist who can be the object of recognition and can also recognize the actor as the object of attention. Since the participants in this possible series of reciprocal recognitions are themselves freely willing actors, the possibility of recognition is immediately conjoined to the possibility of interaction. Although actual interaction begins when at least two actors come within the range of each other's effects, its seeds are already present in the actor's essential self-consciousness.[48]

The duty of rightful honor. These possibilities can be summed up in terms of the first precept of Ulpian, *honeste vive*, that one should assert oneself as a juridical person.[49] Because the outward projection of one's action is an assertion of the actor's worth in relation to others, Kant termed the duty corresponding to this imperative "rightful honor."[50] He derived its obligatory nature from the necessity of an active being to avoid passivity, and thus reduction to a means, in the face of the external world. The duty of rightful honor is incumbent on the free will as a law of its own being, and it is expressed in the imperative "Do not make yourself a mere means for others but be at the same time an end for them."[51] Kant conceived of rightful honor as a kind of defensive imperialism,[52] whereby the actor, to realize his or her nature as a bundle of self-determining energy, presses out into the world and thus resists the pressures that other actors exert. The resulting network of reciprocal pressures actualizes the possibilities inherent in the first stage, thereby bringing us to the second stage.

---

[48] Cf. Giorgio del Vecchio, *Justice,* 77–81 (L. Guthrie, trans., 1952) (the possibility of a relationship with another is a necessary aspect of self-consciousness).

[49] Kant, *Metaphysics of Morals,* 62 [236].

[50] Id. at 62 [236].

[51] Id.

[52] Id. at 120 [306] (mentioning the "protective" aspect of justice, or *justitia tutatrix*).

4.3.3. The Second Stage

Corrective justice.[53] Here the actors encounter each other as the embodiments, in their persons and in their possessions, of free will. Their interaction as practical beings brings them under the principle of right: the free choice of the one must be capable of coexisting with the freedom of the other in accordance with a universal law. This principle abstracts from the internal factors of motivation and need, so that the formality of the relationship of will to will now becomes a framework of correlative and externally compossible rights and duties that constitute the juridical categories of property, contract, and domestic status. Interaction between free wills engages the external aspect of practical reason, which requires that each actor treat the other's personal and proprietary embodiments in a manner that does not violate their formal equality as free wills.

Externally recognizable acts. On stepping into a world of interaction, the freely willing actor establishes a presence there through acts that have an externally recognizable nature. Purely mental imaginings and reservations, however real they are to the actor or however serious the consequences to which they might in due course lead, have no status in this world of interaction. Thus criminal wrongdoing requires an *actus reus;* contract cannot be held hostage to the vagaries of a private intention; and the claim to property must involve some act in the world of appearances, such as livery of seizin or a solemn declaration *"ex iure Quiritium."*[54]

Social meanings. The external nature of action implies a world of shared social meanings. Only within such a world can juridical acts by each of the parties be interpreted from a perspective common to both and thus have significance as *external* acts. Juridically meaningful acts are, therefore, historically variable and relative to societal contexts and understandings. For example, in order to appropriate, a person will perform the act that signifies appropriation in that person's society: in one society the act may be the shoe's stepping,[55] in another the hand's seizure or the laying on of a spear.[56]

---

[53] Id. Following the terminology of the scholastic tradition—see, e.g., Thomas Aquinas, *Summa Theologiae,* II–II, Q. 57–62 (Thomas Gilby, trans., 1975)—Kant calls this "commutative justice."

[54] See, e.g., Gaius, *Institutes,* 1.119 (Francis de Zulueta, trans., 1946).

[55] See, e.g., Ruth 4:7–8; see also Thomas Thompson and Dorothy Thompson, "Some Legal Problems in the Book of Ruth," 18 *Vetus Testamentum* 79, 90–93 (1968) (explicating the passage).

[56] See, e.g., Gaius, *Institutes,* at 4.16.

4.3.4. The Third Stage

Public law. So long as it encompasses only the interactors, the interaction depends on characteristics internal to the parties: their ability to discern the significance of right and their willingness to conform to right's requirements. To make their relationship fully and explicitly external, a third person is needed who can recognize and bring home to the parties their rights and duties. The function of law as public is to supply this external standpoint. With this we enter the third and final stage of the conceptual evolution from the capacity for purposiveness to the explicitness of juridical relations—the stage that Kant called public law.[57]

The court. The first function of public law is to provide an authoritative external interpretation of the relationship between the two parties. Recourse is therefore had to a third person, the judge, who is external to them both and who can impartially and disinterestedly interpret their dealings. Impartial and disinterested adjudication between the parties means that the judge does not supervene upon the interaction with distinct interests of the collectivity or of other nonparticipants in the interaction. Hence, the judge cannot use the opportunity presented by the lawsuit to maximize the community's wealth or promote the greatest good for the greatest number. As the external actualization of the practical reason implicit in the interaction of self-determining agents, the court has only one role: to give public expression to the meaning of right in a particular interaction.[58]

The structure of legal reasoning. In elucidating the significance of the interaction, the judge must treat the parties as the free wills that his role presupposes them to be. Because the parties are affected but not determined by inclination, their needs or wants do not determine

---

[57] See Kant, *Metaphysics of Morals*, at 121 [306]. Kant also calls this stage "distributive justice," taking over the Aristotelian term but not its Aristotelian significance as a structure of justice that relates persons and benefits according to a proportion.

[58] For Kant, the common interest of all is "in being in a rightful condition"; see *Metaphysics of Morals*, at 123 [311]; the commonwealth has no concern for what Bentham later called "the sum of the interests of the several members who compose it." Jeremy Bentham, *An Introduction to the Principles of Morals and Legislation*, chap. 1, sect. IV, at 12 (reprint 1970). Kant is concerned neither with the *summing* of interests, nor with Bentham's conception of the community's *interest* in terms of the pain and pleasure of its members, nor with the interests of members of society other than the parties. "By the well-being of the state must not be understood the *welfare* of its citizens and their *happiness*. . . . By the well-being of a state is understood instead, that condition in which its constitution conforms most fully to principles of Right." *Metaphysics of Morals*, at 129 [318].

the juridical meaning of the transaction between them. The free will acts under the causality of concepts, and so the intelligibility of the relationship of one free will to another requires an abstraction from the private motivations and the particular interests of the parties to a coherent conceptual structure that can express the juridical nature of their relationship and can be the framework for the public justification of the judge's decision. From this standpoint too, elaborate calculations of collective advantage are excluded, because they are beyond the limits of judicial competence. The activity of the judge consists in making explicit the categories of property, contract, and wrong that are implied by the concept of right, in articulating the subcategories that constitute these more inclusive categories, and in exercising a judgment that relates the particular situation at hand to the general concepts that render it intelligible as an interaction of free wills.

Public justification. In functioning as the institutionalized embodiment of practical reason, the court makes explicit in its judgment the rationality that is implicit in the interaction. However, though the parties need only avoid violating right, the court must make and be seen to make its judgments on the basis of the demands of right. These judgments fully externalize practical reason only when the principles that animate them are openly declared and publicly acknowledged.[59] Adjudication involves not the achievement of a collective goal through subterfuge or manipulation, but a declaration of principles and standards that could be accepted by all as expressing their nature as free wills. The externality of right entails the public announcement of its articulations and applications.

The public aspect of adjudication. The court not only interprets the relationship between the litigants, but also makes explicit the public standpoint of such interpretation. Thus although the court has no particular collective interest that it adds to the interaction of the parties, its necessary presence as the external interpreter of the relationship's juridical quality carries with it the demand that the judgment correspond to what is publicly manifest and ascertainable rather than to the inner logic of the dispute.[60] For example, according to the inner logic of the law of sales, one cannot sell what one does not own.[61] If, however, the transaction conforms to a publicly recognized mode of acquisition, a good-faith purchaser acquires property in the thing and

---

[59] Cf. Rawls, *A Theory of Justice,* 133 (publicity as a formal condition of the concept of right).

[60] Kant, *Metaphysics of Morals,* 113–120 [297–305].

[61] Id. at 116 [301].

not merely a personal cause of action against the vendor.[62] Similarly, the inner logic of gratuitous bailment suggests that the bailor gave the bailee only the use of property and did not thereby intend to assume the risk of its destruction. What is publicly ascertainable, however, is that the gratuitous bailor, who could without prejudice have expressly allocated the risk to the bailee, omitted to do so. From the standpoint of public judgment, therefore, the bailor must bear the cost of damage to the bailed object.[63]

Publicly authorized coercion. The authority of public law is coercive as well as interpretive. Since the vindication of right includes the prevention or reversal of violations of right, the freedom of all is immediately joined with a reciprocal universal coercion.[64] But the task of coercion, like that of interpretation, cannot be placed in the hands of the interacting parties themselves. Although the parties may spontaneously observe the requirements of right either by forbearing from wrong or, once a wrong has occurred, by making or extracting proper amends, these possibilities have no juridical standing since they presuppose in the parties an internal virtue foreign to the externality of legal relations. Therefore, the public significance of wrong can be signaled only by the availability of a coercion that represents the external operation upon the parties of the concept of right.[65]

The prospectivity of law. The public functions of interpretation and coercion operate not only retrospectively to correct past wrongs, but also prospectively in anticipation of wrongful behavior. Since right does nothing more than hold a given act to the external aspect of practical reason, the specification of wrongfulness does not depend on the wrong's already having occurred. Thus although Kant's conception of law, unlike that of utilitarianism, cannot ignore or discount completed wrongs for the sake of future collective benefits, its gaze is

---

[62] Id. at 116–118 [301–303].

[63] Id. at 114–116 [248–300].

[64] Id. at 57 [232].

[65] In subjecting wrongful action to an equal reaction that undoes the wrong, law's coerciveness can be sharply distinguished from revenge. Unlike the law's impartial and external reassertion of the equality of wrongdoer and victim, revenge allows victims to mingle the satisfaction of their hurt with the exaction of the penalty due and thereby presents them with the choice between subjectively determined excess and virtuous self-abnegation. Moreover, even if avengers observe the proper measure of violence, nothing about their acts bears the external markings of a vindication of right rather than the commission of a subsequent counterbalancing wrong. Revenge is therefore not adequate to the public form required by the full explicitness of action toward another. For further discussion, see Susan M. Shell, *The Rights of Reason: A Study of Kant's Philosophy and Politics,* 122 (1980).

not exclusively fixed on the past. Indeed, the necessity for public law itself testifies to the law's prospectivity. Public law is born in the apprehension of injury: since it is inconsistent with the equality of free wills that one should refrain from wronging someone who might not exercise an equal restraint, everyone is to be coerced into a public regime of law as a way of guaranteeing in advance the equal security of everyone's freedom.[66]

Public knowability. In its prospective functioning, public law sets a standard against which actors can measure their future conduct by making public the duties incumbent upon them. If what the actor is to do or to abstain from doing is to bear on contemplated behavior, it must be publicly knowable. Hence the need for the greatest possible certainty and predictability. However, the aspect of public knowability includes but goes beyond the requirement that law be clearly formulated. Law must reflect the coherence of an idea of reason with practical reality. Public law is, accordingly, to be knowable in the deepest sense of rendering explicit the inherent rationality of purposive activity.[67]

Deterrence. Just as the law's knowability has prospective significance, so does the law's coerciveness. The requirement of right that every act of wrongdoing be answered by an equal and opposite reaction has a deterrent as well as a retributive aspect. Coercion, taken on its own, is a hindrance to freedom, but its use is consistent with freedom when it is deployed to prevent a hindrance to freedom.[68] Although the prospective knowability of right indicates the web of duties that should constrain the actor, the law does not presuppose in the actor a subjective recognition of duty as the incentive to act in accordance with it. Acting out of duty is an internal quality of a good will and therefore is not part of the external ordering contained in the concept of right. Since the point of right is to hold the external aspect of action to the external demands of practical reason, law must posit an external force capable of determining the actor's will, that is, capable of acting as a deterrent. The prospect of external coercion complements the prospectivity of legal duty, by giving potential violators notice of the consequences attending any violation.

---

[66] Kant, *Metaphysics of Morals,* 121 [307].

[67] This is not to say that positive law cannot legitimately operate unless it actually has been known to the person who falls under its strictures, for actual knowledge is an internal quality that is irrelevant to the right's externality. But public law must have a public presence that renders it capable of being known. Ignorance of knowable law is accordingly no defense.

[68] Kant, *Metaphysics of Morals,* 57 [231].

Excuse. The apprehension of coercion is not only a conceptual ingredient of law but a marker of the limits of the law's application. A wrongful act with respect to which coercion cannot exercise its function as a possible determinant of the will lies in the realm of excuse. The excused act is, to be sure, a violation of the principle of right, as when one shipwrecked sailor pushes another off a plank.[69] But since the prospect of the law's punishment cannot outweigh the evil to which the wrongdoer is currently exposed, the external operation of the law cannot function as a deterrent, and the viola-tor of right is immune to the reach of the legal process. For the law to require that one person respect the equality of another in circumstances where the anticipation of punishment cannot deter is to require virtue; to inflict afterward a penalty that previously could not determine the will is to exact revenge for a failure of virtue. From the standpoint of right, the impugned act is a wrongful one, but it is excused because any punishment would itself be inconsistent with the concept of right.[70]

4.4. The Priority of the Right

In Kant's legal philosophy, the concept of right pervades the legal sys-tem, giving it its normative character and making it the occasion for philosophic insight. Right is comprehensive, unifying, and systematic, encompassing everything from the operation of the will to substantive legal doctrines and institutions. Without the concept of right, law would be a merely empirical phenomenon: like a wooden head, beau-tiful but brainless, it would lack inner intelligibility.[71]

Kant treats private law as normatively self-sufficient. Private law draws its moral character from the notion of free will that it presup-poses. Out of the agent's capacity to abstract from particular ends

[69] Id. at 60 [235]. I am grateful to Peter Benson for his elucidation of Kant's discussion of the excuse of necessity.

[70] Kant's treatment of excuse is radically different from that proposed by George P. Fletcher, "Fairness and Utility in Tort Theory," 85 *Harvard Law Review* 537 (1972), discussed above in sec-tion 2.9.4. For Fletcher, excusing conditions give rise to humanitarian considerations that apply to one of the parties, thereby splitting the relationship between the plaintiff and the defendant. For Kant, in contrast, the excuse maintains the integrity of the relationship, but places that rela-tionship beyond the reach of the law's coercion. Whereas Fletcher's argument goes to the defendant's culpability, Kant's goes to the inherent limitations of legality. Thus while Fletcher presents excuse as an ad hoc moderation of the rigor of right, Kant derives excuse from the need to maintain the coherence of the concepts within the unifying structure of right.

[71] Kant, *Metaphysics of Morals,* 55 [230].

comes the possibility of ordering the interactions among free purposive beings without passing judgment on the virtuousness of their chosen purposes. Because of the conceptual implications of free will, the interactions of purposive beings are inevitably subject to the requirements of corrective justice. Private law becomes a normative reality when those requirements assume the form of a publicly authoritative system.

The self-sufficiency of private law denies justificatory relevance to considerations that do not express right's union of the external and the practical. Excluded, of course, are instrumentalist considerations, which, by treating individuals as means, fail to reflect their status as free purposive beings and, therefore, as bearers of rights. Also excluded, however, are ethical considerations, which depend not on the external authority of law but on the agent's internal recognition of the obligatoriness of a particular act. Understood as the manifestation of right, private law is normative without being ethical.

Both law and ethics are for Kant branches of morality, in that both require the volition to live up to the demands of practical reason. They differ in the incentive that each holds out: in law the actor responds to the prospect of external coercion, whereas in ethics the idea of duty itself motivates the action. When Kant deals systematically with both law and ethics, he treats law first,[72] thus indicating that juridical relations are somehow prior to ethical duties—that is, in contemporary parlance,[73] that the right is somehow prior to the good. This priority gives law its conceptually self-contained nature and invalidates the importation into legal analysis of considerations drawn from ethics.

In the Kantian understanding, the priority of the right over the good refers to a conceptual sequencing within the operations of practical reason. The right is prior to the good because practical reason must first traverse the domain of law before it can reach the domain of ethics. At the point in this conceptual sequence where practical reason formulates ethical duties, juridical ones have already taken hold. The juridical relationship of one party to another can therefore be understood independently of the ethical duties incumbent upon them.

This priority follows from Kant's distinction between law and ethics. The governance of free choice by practical reason, which is implicit in the capacity for self-determination, can become explicit in two ways. Either practical reason—the very thought of doing one's

---

[72] In *Metaphysics of Morals*, the *Rechtslehre* ("the doctrine of right") precedes the *Tugendlehre* ("the doctrine of virtue").

[73] See Rawls, *Political Liberalism*, 173.

duty—can be the incentive for the act, or some external party can enforce upon the actor external conformity to the requirements of practical reason. The internal avenue leads to Kantian ethics, the external one to Kantian legality.

What is crucial is that the external avenue is narrower than the internal one. Whereas legality "deals only with the *formal* condition of outer freedom...ethics goes beyond this and provides a *matter* (an object of free choice), an *end* of pure reason which it presents also as an objectively necessary end, *i.e.,* an end which, so far as men are concerned, it is a duty to have."[74] Legality abstracts from particular ends to the form of choice, whereas ethics specifies obligatory ends. In effect, ethical actors recognize their own status as self-determining beings and make practical reason, and the duties arising out of it, decisive for their actions. By contrast, legal actors do not make practical reason the determining ground of their actions. Because practical reason acts on them from without, its jurisdiction is limited to the governance of their external relations.

The priority of law over ethics is evident from the different structures of legal and ethical norms. Whereas law permits all acts except those that are inconsistent with the freedom of others and therefore comprises prohibitions that limit an area of permissibility, ethics begins with the concept of duty and seeks out obligatory ends.[75] These ends would, however, not be obligatory unless they were permissible, and they would not be permissible if they violated the juridical rights of others. Legal duties are therefore essentially negative prohibitions whose validity is presupposed in ethics' more particular structure of positive injunctions.

The right is prior to the good because relationships of right actualize the capacity for purposiveness that underlies the specification by ethics of the obligatory objects of free choice. Whereas ethics contains ends that are duties, law is concerned with the purposive capacity alone. So long as the exercise of that capacity is consistent with the purposiveness of others, law is indifferent to particular purposes. The concept of right abstracts from the content of the free choice to its form as purposive activity. Since obligatory purposes presuppose the common purposiveness that they instantiate, the harmonization through right of this common purposiveness is conceptually prior to the insistence in ethics on any of these particular purposes.[76]

---

[74] Kant, *Metaphysics of Morals*, 186 [380].

[75] Id. at 187 [382].

[76] *Zwecken überhaupt* ("purposes as such" or "ends in general") is Kant's phrase

The priority of the right over the good does not mean that for any ethical duty a parallel legal duty must be presupposed. In Kant's view, the distinctiveness of certain ethical duties (such as the duty of self-perfection or of beneficence) lies precisely in their lacking any juridical counterpart. The point, rather, is that although certain ethical duties can be conceived without anterior juridical ones, ethical duty as such cannot be conceived without the principle of right. In ethics, practical reason specifies the purposes incumbent on any purposive being. Such specification would be impossible unless the exercise of the purposive capacity, considered apart from any particular purpose, could be ordered into accordance with its nature as a causality of concepts. Practical reason could not become explicit in the actor's purpose unless it was already implicit in the purposive capacity.

The priority of the right also does not mean that the right is better than the good. Since the concept of right is prior to the intelligibility of the good, judgments of goodness or betterness are simply not apposite to it. Because law is conceptually prior to ethics, law does not occupy the whole field of moral action: law sets only the minimal—but also the maximally enforceable—moral conditions for the interaction of purposive beings. Precisely because of the conceptual priority of law over ethics, public lawful coercion, as an aspect of the practical idea of reason, would be conceptually necessary "however well-disposed and law-abiding men might be."[77]

The irrelevance of ethics to right illuminates a point made during the discussion of legal formalism in Chapter 2.[78] There I contended that morality—even noninstrumental morality—sheds light on private law only to the extent that it reflects the character of private law. Moral considerations directed at only one of the parties to the private law relationship, such as Fried's conception of promises or Fletcher's of excuses, do not correspond to the bipolarity of the private law relationship. They therefore do not assist in understanding private law, despite their noninstrumental quality.

I can now relate these observations about the bipolar character of private law to the Kantian grounding of private law. My examination of the character of the private law relationship has led back through corrective justice to the Kantian analysis of practical reason, with its

---

for what I here call "purposiveness." See *Metaphysics of Morals*, 199 [396] (distinguishing "ends in general" from "an end").

[77] Id. at 124 [312].

[78] See above, section 2.9.

distinction between right and ethics. One-sided noninstrumental considerations belong to the realm of Kantian ethics: their ultimate criterion is whether the act comes from a will that has made practical reason its determining ground. Fried's theory of contract as promise, for instance, requires a single will's choices to be consistent over time; and Fletcher's plea for excuses argues that action under exigent circumstances does not indicate the actor's lack of a good will. Not only do these justificatory considerations fail to correspond to the bipolarity of the private law relationship, but they lock into the wrong section of the Kantian moral universe.

5

Correlativity

5.1. Introduction

With the elucidation of Kantian right, the main theoretical components for understanding private law are in place. Starting from the premise that private law is an exercise in justificatory coherence that can be understood from its own immanent perspective, I have set out three mutually supporting ideas. The first, formalism, constitutes the methodological framework for integrating the unity, the kind, and the character of a juridical relationship. The second, corrective justice, is the form of the private law relationship. The third, Kantian right, allows one to trace corrective justice back to its normative roots in self-determining agency and forward to the values and institutions of a coherent legal order.

I now want to illuminate the inner workings of the private law relationship by following the implications of Kantian right into the interior of corrective justice. In Aristotle's presentation of corrective justice, the correlativity of gain and loss is the organizing feature of liability. But what exactly is the meaning of this correlativity? How do we identify the gains and losses and see them as expressions of Kantian right? And how do the main grounds of liability—tort, contract, and unjust enrichment—reflect the correlativity of gain and loss that Aristotle mentions?

In dealing with these questions, I first distinguish between two aspects of gain and loss, the factual and the normative. In their factual aspect, gains and losses refer to changes in the condition of the litigants' holdings; in their normative aspect, gains and losses refer to discrepancies between what the parties have and what they should have according to the norm governing the parties' interaction. My argument is that the gains and losses must be understood as normative, not factual, and that we can therefore identify the correlativity of this normative gain and loss as a correlativity of Kantian rights and duties. I then consider the objection that in postulating a normative rather than a factual correlativity, Kantian right ignores the particularity and concreteness of human welfare. My answer is that Kantian right does not ignore human welfare but sees it from the moral perspective appropriate to the bipolar interaction of free and purposive beings. Finally, I turn to an examination of how the structure of liability in tort, contract, and unjust enrichment reflects the correlativity of right and duty.

5.2. The Two Aspects of Gain and Loss

To clarify the meaning of gain and loss under corrective justice, I propose a distinction between what we might call the "factual" and the "normative" aspects of gains and losses. Suppose, for example, that you negligently injure me. A comparison of my present and my previous condition reveals that I am materially worse off than I was before. This is the factual aspect of the loss. In addition, however, I am also worse off than I should be, given the norm against negligent injuring. The loss considered from the standpoint of the relevant norm is the normative aspect of the loss.

Analytically, the normative and the factual aspects are distinguishable, although both may be present in a particular case. Thus, in the example of negligent injury, the injury that makes me materially worse off than I was before is also the injury that I should not have suffered, given the norm against negligence. If, however, you innocently injure me, the loss I suffer has a factual but no normative aspect.

The factual aspect of gain and loss refers to the effect of the interaction on the amount or condition of one's holdings (broadly construed to include both one's body and the external objects at one's disposal). In its factual aspect, a gain is a change for the better from the standpoint of the person whose holdings are increased; a loss is a change for the worse.

The normative aspect of gain and loss derives from the justificatory function of corrective justice. As a justificatory structure, corrective justice embodies norms that set the terms of fair interaction. In their normative aspect, gains and losses involve a comparison between what one has and what one should have through the operation of those norms. A normative gain occurs when one's holdings are greater than they ought to be under those norms; a normative loss occurs when one's holdings are smaller than they ought to be. Taking our cue from Aristotle's treatment of gains and losses as the just grounds for a court's taking from one party and giving to another, we may say that a person enjoys a normative gain when there is justification for the law's diminishing his or her holdings, and that a person endures a normative loss when there is justification for the law's augmenting his or her holdings.[1]

The two aspects reflect different conceptions of the baseline for the characterization of gain and loss. The baseline for factual gains and losses is the preexisting condition of one's holdings: a transacting party whose holdings have increased or improved as a result of the transaction has realized a factual gain; a party whose holdings have decreased or deteriorated has suffered a factual loss. The baseline for normative gains and losses is one's due under the justifications that obtain within corrective justice: a gain is an excess over, and a loss a shortfall from, one's due.

The distinction between factual and normative gains and losses allows the possibility that a gain or loss of one type may be unaccompanied by a gain or loss of the other. All the possible combinations are recognized in sophisticated systems of private law. A party may realize: (1) a normative gain but no factual gain: if I negligently injure another, I have acted wrongly but no holding of mine has been improved by the wrong; (2) a factual gain but no normative gain: if another mistakenly paves my driveway without my knowledge, the condition of my holdings has been improved, but I owe the improver nothing; (3) a normative loss, but no factual loss: if someone trespasses on my property without impairing its condition, a common law court may award me nominal damages to mark the breach of a norm, despite the absence of actual damage; (4) a factual loss, but no normative loss: if someone injures me without fault, I generally cannot recover despite the impairment of my physical condition.

Given the two aspects of gain and loss, what precisely has to be correlative to what if there is to be liability under corrective justice? We can eliminate the possibility of a factual loss correlative to a normative gain or of a factual gain correlative to a normative loss. The logic of correlativity requires that what is predicated of one element in the pairing be also predicated of the other. Accordingly, the gains and losses must be of the same kind. We are then left with the question

---

[1] The nature of such justifications is the subject of sections 5.3 and 5.4.

of whether corrective justice features a correlativity of factual gain to factual loss, or of normative gain to normative loss.

That the gains and losses of corrective justice are normative is evident from the equality that constitutes their baseline. This equality is not itself factual: as discussed in Chapter 3, it does not refer to an equality in the amount or condition of the parties' holdings. Rather, equality is a formal representation of the norm that ought to obtain between doer and sufferer. Action that conforms to this norm, whatever it is, maintains the equality between the parties, so that no complaint is justified. Action that breaches this norm produces a gain to the injurer and a loss to the person injured. Then the court, "justice ensouled" in Aristotle's graphic phrase, restores the parties to the equality that would have prevailed had the norm been observed. The normative nature of the equality indicates that the variations from that equality are also normative.

This conclusion accords with corrective justice's being a *justificatory* structure. The gains and losses have the same character as the structure they define: they refer to the norm that figures in the process of justification. Accordingly, gain and loss are the excess over and the shortfall from one's due.[2]

The modern common law confirms this conclusion by having liability reflect the correlativity of normative, rather than factual, losses and gains. Tort law allows recovery where factual loss is unaccompanied by factual gain; and the law of unjust enrichment allows recovery where factual gain is unaccompanied by factual loss.

In tort law, the plaintiff typically complains of the factual loss of injury, but only exceptionally has the defendant realized a corresponding factual gain from the wrong. If tort law insisted on factual correlativity, liability would be clear only for takings of property, where the taker's holdings are increased and the victim's diminished to the same extent.[3] Negligence would be excluded from liability, because the plaintiff's suffering of an unintended injury in no way improves the situation of the defendant. Normative correlativity, however, is present even in negligence liability, because the wrongful injury represents both a normative surplus for the defendant (who has too

---

[2] Aquinas expressly observes that "loss is so called from one having less than he should have." Thomas Aquinas, *Summa Theologiae*, II-II, Q. 62, Art. 5 (T. Gilby, trans., 1975).

[3] Other intentional wrongs would be more problematic: one would have to consider the psychic satisfaction of the tortfeasor to be a factual gain that was somehow equal to the factual loss.

much in view of the wrong) and a normative shortfall for the plaintiff (who has too little).[4]

The converse case of factual gain without a corresponding factual loss arises under the law of unjust enrichment. Suppose the defendant profits through the unauthorized use of the plaintiff's asset, and the plaintiff claims a part of the profit or, at least, the defendant's saving in not having to rent such an asset. If the plaintiff did not intend to use the thing during the period of the defendant's use and if the property was returned unimpaired at the end of that period, we have a situation where the defendant has gained but the plaintiff has realized no correlative factual loss. The modern treatment of unjust enrichment in the common law grants restitution in such a case.[5] Because of the absence of factual loss, such results accord with corrective justice only if the correlativity of loss and gain is normative. Then the restitutionary requirement that the defendant's gain be "at the plaintiff's expense" can be understood normatively, as referring to what has been called the defendant's "subtraction from the plaintiff's right to the exclusive enjoyment of the property."[6]

The conclusion that gains and losses of corrective justice are normative rather than factual ought to dispel a common error in contemporary thinking about corrective justice. The requirement of correlativity is sometimes thought to limit or undermine the Aristotelian conception of corrective justice, on the ground that if gain and loss are to be correlative, they must necessarily be equal, which is obviously not the case for the factual gains and losses resulting from neg-

---

[4] Aristotle himself points out that personal injury causes a terminological difficulty for his formulation of correlative gain and loss. After considering the infliction of death or the causing of physical harm as occasions for corrective justice, he remarks that "in such cases the word 'gain' is used generally, even though in particular cases it is not the appropriate term, as when one strikes another—and 'loss' for the one who suffers—but whenever the loss has been measured, it is called the loss on the one hand and the gain on the other." *Nicomachean Ethics*, 1132a10–1132a14. The word "gain" is inappropriate because personal injury does not in and of itself factually enrich the injurer. Yet Aristotle does not for that reason think that personal injury is beyond the scope of corrective justice. These remarks indicate that Aristotle himself did not think that corrective justice required factual correlativity.

[5] Strand Electric Ltd. v. Brisford Entertainment Ltd., [1952] 1 All Eng. Rep. 796 (C.A.); Olwell v. Nye & Nissen Co., 173 P. 652 (Wash. S.C., 1946). See Daniel Friedmann, "Restitution of Benefits Obtained through the Appropriation of Property or Commission of a Wrong," 80 *Columbia Law Review* 504 (1980); Allen E. Farnsworth, "Your Loss or My Gain? The Dilemma of the Disgorgement Principle in Breach of Contract," 94 *Yale Law Journal* 1389 (1985); J. Beatson, *The Use and Abuse of Unjust Enrichment: Essays on the Law of Restitution*, 230–234 (1991).

[6] Beatson, *The Use and Abuse of Unjust Enrichment*, 232.

ligence.[7] However, that factual gain does not necessarily equal factual loss is true but irrelevant. What matters to the justificatory structure of corrective justice is the correlativity of normative, not factual, gain and loss.[8]

Indeed, once one draws the distinction between the normative and the factual aspects of gain and loss, the conclusion that corrective justice involves a correlativity of the normative aspect can scarcely be in doubt. In the Aristotelian account, gain and loss are a way of representing the occurrence of an injustice that needs to be rectified through liability. Injustice and liability reflect the violation of certain norms, not the existence of certain facts. Even in the case of a taking, where the appropriator's gain is factually equivalent to the victim's loss, liability follows not from the fact of this equivalence, but from the breach of a property norm. Where gains and losses are solely factual (as in the case of a new enterprise that takes customers away from a competitor), there is no liability under corrective justice.

To sum up: The correlative gain and loss of corrective justice does not point to a factual loss and a corresponding factual gain. What matters is whether the transaction can be regarded as yielding a normative surplus for the defendant and a normative deficit for the plaintiff. Therefore, liability for a deterioration in the condition of the plaintiff's holdings is predicated not on some parallel improvement in

---

[7] For a recent example of this thinking, see George P. Fletcher, "Corrective Justice for Moderns," 106 *Harvard Law Review* 1658, 1668 (1993).

[8] Readers of Aristotle might suppose that his contrast of the quantitative equality of corrective justice with the proportional equality of distributive justice indicates that Aristotle himself thinks the correlativity is factual. For does not the very idea of quantitative equality point to something tangible like the quantity or quality of one's holdings? However, the quantitative equality is a mathematical representation of corrective justice's justificatory structure, and we should not confuse the image with the reality. The point of Aristotle's adducing of quantitative equality is to bring out the categorical distinction between the two forms of justice, not to tell us anything about the subject matter of the equality. Aristotle thinks the correlativity is normative, as is shown by his regarding the working of injustice as itself the gain. For example, in explaining the violation of equality under corrective justice, he says, in *Nicomachean Ethics*, 1130a5, that the law looks to whether "the one commits and the other suffers injustice." Aristotle's continuation ("and if one has inflicted harm and the other has suffered harm") also, I believe, includes the normative aspect. By "harm" Aristotle means not a physical injury simpliciter but an injury that is actionable; see his listing of the "three kinds of harm" in *Nicomachean Ethics*, 1135b10. The meaning of this last passage is itself controversial: see Richard Sorabji, *Necessity, Cause, and Blame*, 278–281 (1980), and David Daube, *Roman Law: Linguistic, Social, and Philosophical Aspects*, 142–150 (1969). My own belief, for reasons independent of the present discussion, is that Daube is closer to the truth than Sorabji.

the condition of the defendant's but on the defendant's having unjustly inflicted that loss. Similarly, the plaintiff recovers the defendant's
gain not when the plaintiff has suffered merely a factual loss but when
the defendant's enrichment represents an injustice to the plaintiff.

5.3. The Correlativity of Normative Gain and Loss

Let me next consider what it means for normative gains and losses
to be correlative. As the dynamic idea that links gain and loss, correlativity structures the normative content of corrective justice. To this
point I have described normative gain and loss in general terms
as excess and deficiency from the standpoint of a justificatory
consideration, but I have not specified any particular justificatory consideration. Correlativity enables us to discern what justificatory
considerations are possible because the only considerations that play a
role in corrective justice are those that can be applied correlatively.

Here I move toward a particular set of justificatory considerations by
following through on the structural implications of correlativity. My
procedure is formalist: instead of positing substantive norms, I look to
the conditions that any norm must fulfill if it is to conform to the
dimension of correlativity. By progressively refining the considerations
that might satisfy these conditions, I hope first to eliminate justificatory
considerations that do not fit, and then to provide an increasingly definite account of the operation of Kantian right within corrective justice.

5.3.1. The Conditions of Correlativity

To satisfy the dimension of correlativity, the justificatory considerations at work in corrective justice must be unifying, bipolar, and
expressive of transactional equality. They must be unifying in that for
normative gain and normative loss to be relative to each other, the
same norm must be the baseline for both. They must be bipolar in
that because one party's normative gain is the other's normative loss,
the justificatory considerations must link two, and only two, parties.
And they must be expressive of transactional equality in that by being
equally applicable to the party realizing the gain and to the party suffering the loss, they accord a preferential position to neither.

Consequently, a justificatory consideration that fits into the normative structure of corrective justice cannot have a justificatory force
that reaches only one of the parties. Such a one-party consideration

could account for the normative effect—be it gain or loss—on that party alone. But because the correlative normative effect on the other party lies beyond its scope, that consideration does not supply the single baseline for both gain and loss; nor does it establish a bipolar link between the gainer and the loser; nor does it express their equal normative standing in the transaction.

For instance, the idea that compensation is a goal of tort liability[9] cannot fit within corrective justice. Because compensation reposes its justificatory force solely on the plaintiff's exigence in the aftermath of injury, it applies to the plaintiff independently of the defendant. It therefore cannot serve the unifying function of supplying the baseline for both the defendant's gain and the plaintiff's loss. Moreover, the need for compensation does not forge a bilateral link between the injured party and any particular injurer. Instead, it relates the injured party to others (however many there are) who are similarly exigent and thus have similar claims as a matter of *distributive* justice. Finally, the plaintiff and the defendant do not have equal standing under this justificatory consideration—indeed, the defendant has no standing at all. In looking to the injured person's exigence, the justification is intrinsically preferential to plaintiffs. Basing liability on it would violate, not vindicate, the parties' equality.

Accordingly, the compensation rationale does not yield a correlative gain and loss. It is true that being injured might be thought of as a normative loss consisting in the shortfall from the plaintiff's entitlement under the goal of compensation. But the defendant, whose position is unaffected by that justificatory consideration, could not be said to realize a gain with respect to it. From the standpoint of the compensation rationale, the plaintiff's loss lacks bipolar significance. At most, the loss justifies improving the plaintiff's situation; it does not state a ground for taking something from the defendant. Accordingly, the compensation rationale does not support the *defendant's* liability to the plaintiff.

The same applies, *mutatis mutandis*, if the parties' positions are reversed. Suppose a justificatory consideration applies to the defendant independently of the plaintiff (as when deterrence is taken to be a goal of tort law). Then the defendant's holdings might be excessive in the light of that consideration, so that unless penalized by the law the defendant would realize a normative gain. However, because plaintiffs do not come within the reach of that justificatory consider-

---

[9] See above, section 2.6.2.

ation, they cannot be said to have less than they are entitled to under it. There is a normative gain with no correlative normative loss. Consequently, the justificatory consideration would provide no reason for the defendant's liability to the *plaintiff*.

Nor can correlativity be satisfied by an accumulation of considerations that apply separately to the two parties but embrace them both only when taken together. (An example is the explanation of tort liability by reference to the need both to deter actors and to compensate sufferers.) To be sure, such an explanation produces a normative gain for the defendant and a normative loss for the plaintiff. But because the reason for thinking the defendant to have gained is not the same as the reason for thinking the plaintiff to have lost, the gain and the loss are not normatively correlative. The considerations may justify eliminating the gain and the loss through separate operations that decrease the holdings of the defendant and increase those of the plaintiff. But they do not justify the direct legal link of liability in corrective justice.

5.3.2. Right and Duty

In contrast to the inadequacy of such one-sided goals, Kantian right fleshes out corrective justice in a way that satisfies the requirement of correlativity. The fundamental principle of Kantian right, that one person's action be united with the other's freedom in accordance with practical reason, treats the relationship between the parties as unified, bipolar, and transactionally equal. Unity is present because the concept of right integrates into an idea of reason the juridical constituents of the parties' relationship. Bipolarity obtains because of the focus on the relationship between the one person's action and the other's freedom. And the transactional equality is manifest in the equal moral status of the interacting parties as free and purposive beings.

The specific form of correlativity within Kantian right is that of right and duty. The requirement that one's action be consistent with the other's freedom means that every actor is obligated not to violate the rights of others. In Kantian theory, rights are the juridical manifestations of the freedom inherent in self-determining agency. An act is consistent with another's freedom when it is compatible with that person's rights. Thus having a right implies that other actors are under the moral necessity to refrain from infringing it. In Kant's words, rights are "(moral) capacities to put others under obligations."[10]

---

[10] Kant, *Metaphysics of Morals*, 63 [237].

The Kantian approach, then, links the interacting parties through a right, on the one hand, and a corresponding duty, on the other. The right represents the moral position of the plaintiff; the duty represents the moral position of the defendant. Right and duty—and therefore plaintiff and defendant—are connected because the content of the right is the object of the duty. The Kantian principle that the action of one party be united with the freedom of another in accordance with practical reason can be explicated in terms of right and duty as follows: that principle is satisfied when the action of one party does not violate a duty, when the freedom of the other manifests itself in a right, and when the reason inherent in free and purposive agency grounds both the right and the duty and connects one to the other.

In making Kantian right more determinate, this conjunction of right and duty maintains the shape appropriate to the correlativity of corrective justice. The relationship of the parties is unified because both right and duty are expressions of the same notion of practical reason. Moreover, the direct connection between the obligee of the duty and the holder of the right makes the relationship a bipolar one: although a single right can generate a duty in many persons, each such duty is separately correlative to the right that generates it. Finally, transactional equality is assured because the holder of the right and the obligee of the duty have equal standing as free and purposive beings.

5.3.3. *Correlativity as Articulated Unity*

Given that the conjunction of right and duty satisfies the conditions of unity, bipolarity, and equality, I must now consider a further question: how do right and duty *operate* as correlatives? To put the question more accurately: how do these conditions manifest themselves in the internal workings of a juridical relationship marked by the correlativity of right and duty?

When right and duty operate as correlatives, they constitute an *articulated* unity. By this I mean that, as the constituents of a unified but bipolar relationship, right and duty maintain their distinct moral characters while nonetheless functioning together as a unity. Correlativity does not consist in a single undifferentiated norm that takes its justificatory force from either right or duty. Just as in a transaction two separate parties form a coherent juridical relationship without losing their individuality, so in corrective justice the concepts of right and duty coalesce in a single normative structure without abandoning their own internal requirements.

The alternative to thinking of right and duty as forming an articulated unity is to regard them as analytic reflexes of each other. When right is considered an analytic reflex of duty, the entire justificatory weight of the relationship rests on the reason for considering the defendant to be under a duty; right is then immediately attributed to anyone who would benefit from the performance of that duty. The relationship is composed of right and duty, but right is merely the analytic shadow of the duty and occupies no space of its own. Conversely, when duty is considered an analytic reflex of right, the entire weight of the relationship rests on the reason for thinking the plaintiff has a right; by its very existence the right is thought to demarcate a space that the defendant is duty-bound not to enter.

This alternative view is inconsistent with the parties' transactional equality. Inasmuch as right and duty represent, respectively, the plaintiff- and the defendant-oriented aspect of the relationship, to make duty a merely analytic reflex of right, or vice versa, is to tip the equilibrium in favor of one of the parties. If right were the reflex of duty, justificatory considerations pertaining to the defendant alone would be decisive for the relationship as a whole. Similarly, if duty were the reflex of right, the judgment that the defendant breached a duty would immediately follow from an act damaging an embodiment of the plaintiff's right, thus making the normative position of the plaintiff decisive for both parties. Although couched in terms of right and duty, the justificatory considerations would be as one-sided as those of compensation and deterrence.

In contrast, the Kantian approach recognizes that right and duty have distinct normative functions that derive from their being the expressions of external practical reason. A right is not merely a benefit mandated by a moral duty; it is a juridical manifestation of a person's freedom with respect to the actions of another. Nor is there a breach of a legal duty whenever one damages another's rightful holdings; rather, duty consists in a moral necessity to act in a certain way. Because under the Kantian approach a right is the manifestation of self-determining agency and a duty governs the act that must comply with it, neither right nor duty can be regarded as the analytic reflex of the other. A right that is the analytic reflex of another's duty is not necessarily the manifestation of the right-holder's self-determining agency. And a duty that is the analytic reflex of another's right is not centered on the act of the duty-bound person.[11]

---

[11] Charles Fried's theory of contract as promise, discussed in section 2.9.3., in effect treats

So far I have been stressing the importance of respecting the articulation into right and duty of the relationship's unity. I now turn to the unity itself. This unity is achieved through the mutual moral reference of right and duty. Of course, liability under corrective justice requires that the plaintiff have a right and that the defendant act in breach of a duty. In addition, however, the plaintiff's right must be the ground of the defendant's duty, and the scope of the duty must include the kind of right-infringement that the plaintiff suffered. When these conditions are fulfilled, the breach of the duty and the infringement of the right constitute a single normative sequence in which each assumes its character from its relationship with the other. It is not sufficient, for instance, that the defendant breaches a duty to the plaintiff with respect to one of the plaintiff's rights but injures the embodiment of a different right. In such cases, the damage to the embodiment of a right is merely a historical consequence, not a normative correlate, of the breach of duty.[12]

Understood as an articulated unity, the correlativity of right and duty normatively spans the sequence from act to injury, thereby establishing the moral nexus between a specific plaintiff and a specific defendant. The correlative gains and losses of corrective justice compare what the parties have with what they ought to have under a Kantian regime of rights and corresponding duties. The defendant realizes a normative gain through action that violates a duty correlative to the plaintiff's right; liability causes the disgorgement of this gain. The plaintiff realizes a normative loss when the infringed right is within the scope of the duty violated; liability causes the reparation of this infringement. Since the normative gain is morally correlative to the normative loss, disgorgement of the gain takes the form of rep-

contractual right as an analytic reflex of contractual duty. Fried bases the contractual duty to adhere to one's promises on the need to respect the consistency of the self as a choosing entity extended over time, and gives the promisee a private law right to the enforcement of the promisor's duty. Even if Fried's argument about the self's consistency over time produces a duty in the promisor, it cannot produce a right in the promisee, because it does not engage the moral status of the promisee as a freely willing being. The fact that the promisor is duty-bound to bestow a promised benefit is not in itself a manifestation of the promisee's freedom. In bestowing the benefit, the promisor is not honoring the promisee's right to it but is merely fulfilling a self-regarding duty of consistency over time.

On the distinct normative functions of right and duty in tort law, see the critique of strict liability and the subjective standard below, section 7.3.1.

[12] The implications of this structural point for negligence liability are developed below, section 6.4.

aration of the loss. And because of the mutual moral reference of the infringement of the right and the breach of the duty, the amount of the gain is necessarily identical to the amount of the loss.[13] Hence the transfer of a single sum annuls both the defendant's normative gain and the plaintiff's normative loss.

5.4. The Relevance of the Factual Aspect

I have reached the correlativity of right and duty by elucidating the intimate connection between corrective justice and Kantian right. Following through on Aristotle's indication that correlative gain and loss operate from a baseline of equality that abstracts from the particularities of social rank and virtue, I identified that equality with the abstracting notion of agency that undergirds Kantian right. On this view, the equality of corrective justice expresses the Kantian conception of normativeness in external relationships. Being variants from a normative baseline, the gains and losses are correlative in their normative and not in their factual aspects. The nexus of right and duty under Kantian right captures this normative correlativity.

In this and the following section, I would like to make the normative content of corrective justice still more specific by exploring the relation of the normative and the factual. In doing so, I also aim to consider the objection that, by focusing on the normativeness of Kantian right, my account ignores the significance of the factual aspect of gain and loss.

The objection contends that distinguishing between the factual and the normative subverts rather than illuminates the idea of private law. Private law characteristically deals with changes in the condition of one's holdings. The plaintiff in tort, for instance, seeks reparation for factual injury suffered at the defendant's hands, not merely a declaration that the defendant's action has violated a norm. At issue in such a claim is not wrongfulness in the abstract but the concreteness of a particular loss. The transmutation of Aristotle's gains and losses into correlative rights and duties renders unexplainable the concrete factuality of the plaintiff's suffering and the role of private law in giving redress for that suffering.[14]

[13] As Aristotle says regarding personal injury, in *Nicomachean Ethics*, 1132a13 (see above, note 4), "whenever the loss has been measured, it is called the loss on the one hand and the gain on the other."

[14] Stephen R. Perry, "The Moral Foundations of Tort Law," 77 *Iowa Law Review* 449, 478–488 (1992).

Behind this objection lies an objection about the abstractive nature of agency. At the heart of the Kantian conception of the agent is the capacity for purposiveness that abstracts from particular purposes. One might think that, strictly speaking, agents so conceived cannot interact. The purposiveness characteristic of agency appears to be a mere potentiality that does not issue into the world and therefore does not act upon or interact with anything or anyone. In abstracting from particularity, agents, it might be said, withdraw from the world and cannot leave their mark upon it.

The objections assume that in the Kantian account willing is made up of the capacity for purposive action, abstracted from particular purposes and persons, and nothing else. Hence the interactional dimension of harming and the particularity of the harm suffered lie beyond the reach of Kantian right. This conclusion misconstrues the Kantian integration of purposiveness and activity. The capacity to abstract is a necessary, not a sufficient, condition of free purposive agency. This capacity is essential to the will's self-determination, in that without it the agent would be passive to circumstance and inclination. But the capacity for purposiveness must also—if it is to function as an aspect of *willing*—actualize itself in the execution of some particular purpose. To be a will, the will must will something. Accordingly, far from disavowing particularity, Kantian right requires it. Kantian right only insists that, from the normative point of view, a particular purpose be understood as the expression of the freedom inherent in the agent's capacity to reject that purpose and substitute another one for it. The capacity for purposiveness neither detaches the agent from action nor precludes the act's having a particular content; its role is rather to imbue that act with the significance of freedom.

In executing a particular purpose, agency is the free and purposive modification of the agent's given world—"reality...asserted under the category of change."[15] Therefore, although as the occasion for practical reason, agency involves abstraction from particularity, as an activity agency takes place under certain empirical conditions. For human beings, those conditions include the working of one's will through the physical organism of the body, the sentience of that organism, the presence of various satisfactions that motivate action, the possibility of acting in contravention of the requirements of practical reason, the existence of an external world populated (apparently) both by other agents and by objects that lack free will, and the absence

---

[15] Michael Oakeshott, *Experience and Its Modes*, 273 (1933).

of omniscience concerning the future effects of one's act. Agency does not form an ontological realm that is inconsistent with this empirical world or that, as it were, competes with it for the same space. Rather, the empirical world that human beings inhabit supplies the circumstances within which practical reason is and ought to be operative for them.

The abstractive aspect of willing provides the normative basis for elaborating the rights of beings so circumstanced. Although the rights do not derive their normative force from the empirical conditions of human agency, they apply to those conditions.[16] The rights are normatively immanent to agency in the circumstances in which human agents act, given their physical constitutions and the world in which they live.

Under Kantian right two kinds of rights—both applicable to the conditions of human interaction—are relevant to private law. The first is the right to one's bodily integrity. The body houses the free will and is the organ of its purposes. Thus every human being has an immediate—or, as Kant puts it, an "innate"[17]—right to the security of his or her physical constitution against injury and constraint by another, except, as in the case of legal punishment, where such constraint is itself a vindication of right. Correspondingly, everyone is under a duty to abstain from coercing or doing violence to another. A breach of this duty is incompatible with the equality of the interacting parties as free purposive beings. For by such a breach one actor treats another not as a self-determining being but as the instrument of an extrinsic purpose.

The second kind of right is to external objects of the will. Rights to external objects, including rights to property and to contractual performance, are not innate to the actor but are acquired through the execution of a juridically effective act. The will's need to express itself in particular purposes entails the moral possibility of the will's realizing itself in an external sphere. For if no such external sphere were morally available, the capacity for purposiveness would be incapable

---

[16] In *Metaphysics of Morals*, 44 [217], Kant distinguishes between the basis and the applicability of a metaphysics of morals: "[W]e shall often have to take as our object the particular nature of man, which is known only by experience, in order to show in it what can be inferred from universal moral principles. But this will in no way detract from the purity of these principles or cast doubt on their a priori source. That is to say, in effect, that a metaphysics of morals cannot be based upon anthropology but can still be applied to it."

[17] Id. at 63 [237].

of actualization—a consequence that would involve free will in the contradiction of having as its defining feature an unrealizable capacity.[18] The external sphere into which the will may realize itself is comprised of everything that is devoid of, and thus categorically different from, free will. Because external objects are categorically different from free will, they can be owned without contravening the freedom of others under the principle of right. And their being owned entails an obligation in nonowners to refrain from their use.[19]

Accordingly, particularity is essential to the conceptualization of the parties and their holdings. The principle of right allows the free will to realize itself in anything that is not already the locus of another free will. Conversely, agents are barred from interfering with things—the bodies and property of other agents—that are the embodiments of someone else's free will.

Kantian right sees the factual in the light of the normative. The normative aspect of gain and loss, that is, the correlativity of right and duty, is the vehicle for assessing the legitimacy of transactional gains or losses in their factual aspect. When the plaintiff claims compensation for a factual loss, the issue is whether by causing a deterioration in the condition of the plaintiff's holdings the defendant has breached a duty correlative to the plaintiff's right. If so, the defendant is required to undo the consequences of his or her wrongful act by making good the factual loss. Similarly, when the legitimacy of a gain is in question, the issue is whether the improvement in the condition of the defendant's holdings is compatible with the plaintiff's rights. If it is not, corrective justice requires the defendant to disgorge the gain to the plaintiff.

Thus abstract agency is the normative grounding for private law's governance of particular harms. Kantian right abstracts from particular purposes in order to construe rights as emanating from a free will. Similarly, Kantian right abstracts from the particular features of parties and their holdings in order to construe them as the embodiments of free will. In abstracting from particularity, Kantian right does not ignore it. Rather, it pays particularity the compliment of seeing it as the expression of self-determining activity.

---

[18] Id. at 68 [246] ("the postulate of practical reason with regard to rights"); Georg W. F. Hegel, *Philosophy of Right*, sect. 44–45 (T. M. Knox, trans., 1952).

[19] Kant, *Metaphysics of Morals*, 68–74 [245–252]. For illuminating analyses of Kant's discussion of acquired rights, see Mary J. Gregor, *The Laws of Freedom*, 50–63 (1963), and Leslie Mulholland, *Kant's System of Rights*, 232–265 (1990).

5.5. Rights and Welfare

The objection that Kantian right cannot account for particular losses goes hand in hand with a specific view of the normative basis of private law. Kantian right funnels the normative significance of factual gains and losses through the conceptual categories arising from the abstracting will. The objection I have been examining reacts by claiming that the concreteness of gain and loss eludes the Kantian analysis. If my remarks in the previous section are sound, this objection is overstated, but what it overstates is the perception that Kantian right does not give the concreteness of injury its due. In that perception lies a major point of difference between the position I am putting forward here and much of contemporary scholarship about private law—and indeed about law generally.

At stake is the normative significance of welfare, understood as the totality of interests constitutive of well-being. For many contemporary scholars, welfare has so immediate a normative appeal that they consider the elements of welfare to be the fundamental components of normative analysis. They may disagree on how to characterize those elements (are they preferences? utilities? wealth? basic aspects of the good?) and what to do with them (maximize them? equalize them? satisfy the most urgent? allow Pareto superior moves?). They agree, however, that law, including private law, is intelligible only in terms of welfare. Rights, if they play any role at all, are labels attached to the preferred interests at the conclusion of a legal operation on the elements of welfare.

In this approach, the factual gains and losses from the interactions governed by private law are normatively primary. One's body and the external things at one's disposal represent assets in human and other capital. The physical condition of one's holdings determines, to a considerable extent, the level of welfare that one enjoys at a particular time. A factual gain improves the condition of one's holdings and thus improves that level of welfare. A factual loss diminishes it. These variations in welfare, so it is assumed, ought to be the direct focus of normative attention.

The Kantian approach is radically different. Inasmuch as it deals with constraints on action, normativeness arises from the structure of the free will. With respect to external relations between agents, that structure leads to a regime of correlative rights and duties. Freedom, not welfare, is primary.

Welfare plays only a secondary role in rights so conceived. Because, as I just noted, Kantian right deals with the external relations of agents in the empirical conditions of their interaction, the rights pertinent to interaction among humans crystallize certain welfare advantages and protect them from wrongful interference. And when such interference occurs, the law rectifies the wrong by an award of damages that quantifies the wrong by quantifying the value of the welfare of which the plaintiff has been deprived. But right is not synonymous with welfare, nor wrong with the deprivation of it. I can infringe your rights without thereby decreasing your welfare, as in the case where a court would order me to pay you nominal damages. I can decrease your welfare without thereby infringing your rights, for instance by starting a business that successfully competes with yours.

Understood as a manifestation of Kantian right, private law protects rights, not welfare. The normative focus of private law is on welfare only inasmuch as it is crystallized in the holding of a right. Under the Kantian principle of right, private law is concerned not with whether an act has increased or diminished welfare, but with whether that act can coexist with the freedom of another in accordance with practical reason.

This relationship of right to welfare arises from the underlying conception of agency. As the actualization of purposiveness in the execution of particular purposes, agency has both a particular and a universal aspect.[20] The particular aspect consists in the circumstances that pertain to the execution of the particular purpose, including, in the case of human beings, welfare components constituting the needs and desires that the agent seeks to satisfy. The universal aspect, by contrast, consists in the agent's capacity as a free and purposive being to abstract from any particular purpose. The universal aspect characterizes the agent as free; the particular aspect constitutes the material for embodying that freedom. Both aspects are necessary for agency. Without the particular aspect, agency could not be the execution of a purpose. Without the universal aspect, agency could not be an exercise of freedom. Kantian right, therefore, does not disregard human welfare and other elements of particularity. Rather, because the universal carries the normative dimension of agency, Kantian right treats the particular in the light of the universal.

Even the idea of property takes its normative character from the abstractness of right rather than from the promotion of welfare. Of

---

[20] This paragraph follows Hegel, *Philosophy of Right*, sect. 35, and Georg W. F. Hegel, *Philosophy of Mind*, sect. 483 (William Wallace, trans., 1971).

course the activity of acquiring, preserving, and using one's property is fueled by the owner's particular needs and interests. From the normative standpoint, however, property is intelligible not through those needs and interests, but through its being an incident in the relationship between free beings. Just as a particular choice is intelligible as an operation of a free will—and is therefore subject to the requirements of practical reason—through the actor's capacity to abstract from that choice, so property is normatively intelligible by abstracting from the particular needs that impel its acquisition and use to the compatibility of property with the principle of right. Just as human agents are not beings without needs, but are freely willing actors intelligible as such whatever their needs, so property owners are property owners whatever their needs and whether what they own satisfies those needs.[21]

The Kantian treatment of welfare has important implications for the legal and scholarly analysis of private law. As a matter of legal analysis, the fact that one person's action has made another worse off can never in itself be a basis for restoring the status quo ante. The injury must be fitted into the normative structure of right and correlative duty. And the task of the courts is to articulate that normative structure into legal categories, concepts, standards, and principles, and to apply the normative structure thus articulated in the adjudication of the transactions that come before them.[22]

As a matter of scholarly analysis, Kantian right repudiates the common notion that private law theory should seek to elaborate a proper ordering of welfare interests, however conceived. It therefore rules out the economic analysis of private law. The defect of economic analysis is not merely that its instrumental conception of law is incompatible with the noninstrumental character of Kantian right. More fundamentally, by dealing with satisfactions rather than rights, eco-

---

[21] That is why Kantian right is consistent with the utmost inequality in property holdings; see *Kant: Political Writings,* 75 (Hans Reiss, 2nd ed., 1991).

[22] Courts, however, do not always adopt the Kantian perspective in carrying out their adjudications. Perhaps the most spectacular example of a court's attending to welfare rather than rights is Spur Industries v. Del E. Webb Co., 494 P. 2d 700 (Ariz. S.C., 1970), where a developer who had built a subdivision near a cattle feedlot alleged that the smells from the feedlot constituted a nuisance. Although holding that the smells were a nuisance and that the plaintiff was entitled to an injunction, the court made that injunction conditional on the plaintiff's compensating the tortfeasor by the damage that would be done by the injunction. Having determined that the defendant wronged the plaintiff, the court nonetheless ensured that the wrongdoer's position was not worsened by the operation of the remedy to which the plaintiff was entitled.

nomic analysis makes the wrong kind of considerations the primary building blocks of its enterprise.

At the core of this treatment of welfare lies a straightforward idea: welfare cannot supply the normative underpinning for private law because private law relationships are bipolar and welfare is not. Whatever its normative appeal, welfare does not connect the doer to the sufferer of a harm. Of course a person grievously injured by another suffers a dramatic decrease in welfare. But the normative claim thereby generated on the score of welfare results from the victim's present condition, not from the role of another in causing that condition. To make sense of private law, the justificatory considerations we deploy must reflect the bipolar character of the private law relationship. Kantian right, with its correlative rights and duties, fully satisfies this requirement.

5.6. Reparation and Restitution

I want now to outline how the correlativity of right and duty applies to the main categories of liability. My purpose at this point is not to deal with private law doctrine in detail (the next two chapters contain a more extended account of tort liability), but rather to present a general picture that highlights the immanence of corrective justice in tort, contract, and restitution. I hope thereby to illustrate how corrective justice sees factual gains and losses in the light of the normative correlativity of right and duty.

The structure of private law confirms the significance of normative correlativity. Correlativity is presupposed in the directness of the defendant's liability to the plaintiff. That this correlativity is not the factual equivalence of gain and loss is shown by the difference that private law maintains between suing in tort or contract for reparation of a loss and suing for restitution of a gain. This difference depends on normative correlativity rather than factual equivalence, because if gain and loss had to be factually equivalent, it would not matter which of them was the basis of the claim.

The normative correlativity of corrective justice allows for the difference between suing to repair a loss and suing to recover a gain. Considered normatively, loss refers to the infringement of the plaintiff's right, and gain to the breach of the defendant's duty. Under corrective justice, the plaintiff's claim for compensation of a factual loss succeeds if the loss to the embodiment of a right occurs through the breach of a correlative duty. Conversely, the plaintiff's claim for restitution of a factual gain succeeds if the defendant's gain is realized through breach of a duty correlative to the plaintiff's right.

5.6.1. The Reparation of Tort Losses

Tort liability reflects corrective justice in the following respects. First, to recover in tort, the plaintiff's injury must be to something, such as personal integrity or a proprietary entitlement, that ranks as the embodiment of a right. It is therefore not sufficient that the plaintiff has suffered the merely factual loss of being made worse off or of being deprived of a prospective advantage.[23] Second, the defendant must have committed an act that violates a duty incumbent on the defendant and thus can be regarded as an act of wrongdoing. Accordingly, the modern common law emphasizes the importance of fault, since the defendant is duty-bound not to perform the intentional or negligent acts that constitute faulty conduct. Third, the duty breached by the defendant must be with respect to the embodiment of the right whose infringement is the ground of the plaintiff's cause of action. In Justice Cardozo's words, "The plaintiff sues in her own right for a wrong personal to her, and not as the vicarious beneficiary of a breach of duty to another."[24]

---

[23] For example, in Fontainebleau Hotel Corp. v. Forty-Five Twenty-Five, Inc., 114 So. 2d 357 (Fla. C.A., 1959), the plaintiff hotel sued its neighbor for building a structure that cast an afternoon shadow on its bathing area. In dismissing the action, the court remarked, at 358, that the maxim *sic utere tuo ut alienum non laedas* "does not mean that one must never use his property in such a way as to do any injury to his neighbour....It means only that one must use his property so as not to injure the lawful *rights* of another." The same issue arises when the defendant causes economic loss by negligently interfering with some facility—e.g., a tunnel, as in Cattle v. Stockton Waterworks, (1875) L.R. 10 Q.B. 453; a power line, as in Spartan Steel and Alloys Ltd. v. Martin & Co. (Contractors) Ltd., [1973] Q.B. 27 (C.A.); a pipeline, as in Caltex Oil v. The Dredger "Willemstad," 176 Comm. Law Rep. 529 (H.C. Aust., 1976); a bridge, as in Norsk Pacific Steamship Co. Ltd. et al. v. Canadian National Railway Company, [1992] 1 Sup. Ct. Rep. 1021—that is not owned by the plaintiff but is essential for the carrying on of the plaintiff's business. Historically, the common law denied recovery except to the extent that the economic loss was a quantification of the damage done to something that embodied the plaintiff's right. The economic loss standing on its own was insufficient for liability. The historic common law result is in accord with corrective justice. More recently, Commonwealth courts have experimented with allowing recovery so long as they felt that the claim could be limited through notions of proximity; see *Caltex Oil* and the opinions favoring liability in *Norsk Pacific Steamship*. The problem of limiting recovery, however, presupposes that one has located (as these judgments do not) the entitlement with respect to which the recovery is to be limited.

[24] Palsgraf v. Long Island Railroad, 162 N.Y. 99, at 100 (N.Y. C.A., 1928). Cor-

When the defendant thus breaches a duty correlative to the plaintiff's right, the plaintiff is entitled to reparation. The remedy reflects the fact that even after the commission of the tort the defendant remains subject to the duty with respect to the plaintiff's right. The defendant's breach of the duty not to interfere with the embodiment of the plaintiff's right does not, of course, bring the duty to an end, for if it did, the duty would—absurdly—be discharged by its breach. With the materialization of wrongful injury, the only way the defendant can discharge his or her obligation respecting the plaintiff's right is to undo the effects of the breach of duty. Just as the plaintiff's right constitutes the subject matter of the defendant's duty, so the wrongful interference with the right entails the duty to repair. Thus tort law places the defendant under the obligation to restore the plaintiff, so far as possible, to the position the plaintiff would have been in had the wrong not been committed.[25]

rective justice allows one to understand why the doctrine of transferred intent, under which the defendant is held liable for harm done to one person as a result of an act performed with the intent to harm another, is indeed "something of a freak," as it is termed in William L. Prosser, John W. Wade, and Victor E. Schwartz, *Torts: Cases and Materials* (7th ed., 1982). This doctrine, exemplified in Talmage v. Smith, 59 N.W. 656 (Mich. S.C., 1894), in effect holds that there is liability even where the defendant's breach of duty is not correlative to the plaintiff's infringed right. The doctrine is discussed in William L. Prosser, "Transferred Intent," 45 *Texas Law Review* 650 (1967). Prosser treats the doctrine as a curious survival of the criminal law aspect of the old writ of trespass. Aside from the dictum by Chief Justice Latham in Bunyan v. Jordan, 57 Comm. Law Rep. 1, at 12, (H.C. Aust., 1937), there is, to my knowledge, no trace of this doctrine in Commonwealth tort law.

[25] It is worth drawing attention to two implications of this statement. First, under corrective justice damages are compensatory, not punitive. Therefore, the common law jurisdiction whose attitude regarding punitive damages comes closest to conformity to corrective justice is England, which since Rookes v. Barnard, [1964] App. Cas. 1129 (H.L.), has restricted punitive damages to cases of oppressive, arbitrary, and unconstitutional governmental action and to cases where the defendant has calculated that the gain from misconduct will exceed the compensation payable to the plaintiff. In Cassell & Co. v. Broome, [1972] App. Cas. 1027 (H.L.), Lord Diplock explained this second category in terms of unjust enrichment. This explanation would make this category, at least, consistent with corrective justice's treatment of illegitimate gains; see below, section 5.6.3. For a survey and discussion of different approaches to punitive damages, see Bruce Chapman and Michael Trebilcock, "Punitive Damages: Divergence in Search of a Rationale," 40 *Alabama Law Review* 741 (1989).

Second, corrective justice is applicable in the modern world despite the fact that the prevalence of liability insurance means that the defendant personally does not compensate the plaintiff for the loss. Corrective justice goes to the nature of the obligation; it does not prescribe the mechanism by which the obligation is discharged. Liability insurance presupposes liability, and it is that liability which is intelligible in the light

On the commission of a tort, the plaintiff suffers a normative loss, and the defendant realizes a correlative normative gain. The plaintiff's normative loss consists in the shortfall from what the plaintiff is entitled to under the norm that the defendant's action violated. Conversely, the defendant's normative gain consists in the excess in the defendant's holdings, given the defendant's violation of the norm that the duty signifies. Since the norm underlying both the gain and the loss consists in the defendant's being under a duty not to infringe the plaintiff's right, the normative gain and the normative loss are correlative to each other. Consequently, the defendant's liability to the plaintiff rectifies both the normative gain and the normative loss in a single bipolar operation.

5.6.2. The Reparation of Contract Losses

Like tort law, contract law is a regime of correlative right and duty. The unity of the contractual relationship consists in the fact that contractual performance is the content of both the defendant's duty and the plaintiff's right. Because a breach of the defendant's duty is an infringement of the plaintiff's right, the law requires the defendant, through expectation damages or specific performance, to place the plaintiff in the same position he or she would have been in if the contract had been performed.

Both tort law and contract law rectify losses through corrective justice. In both branches of law, the plaintiff alleges the violation of a right that the defendant is duty-bound to observe. In both, damages compensate for the defendant's infringement of the plaintiff's right.[26]

The difference between tort law and contract law lies in the origin of the right. In tort law, the plaintiff's right exists independently of the defendant's action; the damage award therefore aims at eliminating the effects on the plaintiff of the defendant's wrong. In contract law, the parties themselves create the plaintiff's right to the defendant's performance of the promised act; the damage award therefore gives the plaintiff the value of that performance.

---

of corrective justice. Nothing about corrective justice precludes the defendant from anticipating the possibility of liability by investing in liability insurance.

[26] Because expectation damages are in lieu of the contractual performance to which the plaintiff is entitled, it is wrong to assume, as do Lon L. Fuller and William R. Perdue, Jr., in "The Reliance Interest in Contract Damages," 46 *Yale Law Journal* 52, 56 (1936), that contract law passes "from the realm of corrective justice to that of distributive justice" because its damage award "no longer seeks merely to heal a disturbed status quo, but to bring into being a new situation."

Accordingly, the correlativity of contractual right and duty emerges from the interlocking role of the two parties in creating the contract. Because the contract works a voluntarily assumed correlative change in their moral position, both parties contribute as moral equals in the formation of a unified but bipolar relationship. The common law governs the contract-creating acts through the doctrines of offer and acceptance, consideration, and unconscionability. As I shall now indicate, all these doctrines construe the contract-creating acts as a single normative sequence marked by unity, bipolarity, and equality.[27]

Under the doctrine of offer and acceptance, formation of the contract is complete when the offer of one party is accepted by the other. This doctrine serves the unifying function of setting out the circumstances under which two temporally disconnected acts—offer and acceptance—are construed as the components of a single continuous sequence. On the one hand, the two acts must be temporally disconnected, because simultaneous offers are mutually independent acts that do not bind the parties to each other.[28] On the other hand, the gap between the two acts is bridged by the idea that the offer, unless revoked, is continuously available for acceptance by the offeree. In serving this unifying function, the doctrine of offer and acceptance also manifests bipolarity and equality. The bipolarity consists in the fact that neither offer nor acceptance has juridical significance standing on its own. The former only creates the possibility of the latter; the latter only completes the process initiated by the former. The equality consists in the fact that offer and acceptance are equally necessary, since the presence of one without the other does not create a valid contract.

Under the doctrine of consideration, a promise is contractually binding only if the promisee has promised or done something in

---

[27] A detailed discussion, which I largely follow, of the connection between corrective justice and the doctrines of offer and acceptance, consideration, unconscionability appears in the work of Peter Benson. See Peter Benson, "Toward a Pure Theory of Contract" (LL.M. diss., Harvard Law School, 1983); Peter Benson, "Grotius' Contribution to the Natural Law of Contract," 6 *Canadian Journal of Netherlandic Studies* 1 (1985); Peter Benson, "External Freedom according to Kant," 87 *Columbia Law Review,* 559, especially 563–568; Peter Benson, "Abstract Right and the Possibility of a Nondistributive Conception of Contract: Hegel and Contemporary Contract Theory," 10 *Cardozo Law Review* 1077 (1989); Peter Benson, "The Basis of Corrective Justice and Its Relation to Distributive Justice," 77 *Iowa Law Review* 515 (1992), especially 591–601; Peter Benson, "Contract Law and Corrective Justice" (paper prepared for the 22nd Annual Workshop on Commercial and Consumer Law, McGill University Faculty of Law, October 1992).

[28] Tinn v. Hoffman, (1873) 29 Law Times 271 (Exch. Ch.).

return. The principal function of this doctrine is to capture the bipolarity of the contractual relationship by affirming the promisee's participation in creating the right to the promisor's performance. The doctrine also reflects the unity of the parties' relationship: promise and consideration are not bounties unilaterally volunteered to each other; rather, the consideration is something that the parties understand to be given in return for the promise.[29] Furthermore, the doctrine attests to the equality of the contracting parties, since it requires that both parties give tokens of their will and thus participate as equal agents in the creation of the contract.[30]

Under the doctrine of unconscionability, courts do not enforce contractual exchanges where, owing to urgent need or inexperience, the value of one party's performance substantially exceeds the value of the other's. From the standpoint of corrective justice, the basic idea behind this doctrine is that, unless one party intends to bestow an unrequited benefit on the other, the value of what they exchange should be approximately equal.[31] Agreeing out of urgent need or inexperience signifies not an intention to confer an unrequited benefit, but merely a failure to exchange on equal terms. Once beneficence is ruled out, the parties must be understood as being present to each other solely through the value of what they exchange. Therefore, equal value is necessary if they are to count for each other as equals within the transaction. Moreover, in thus underlining the equality of the parties, the doctrine also reflects the transaction's bipolarity, because the doctrine treats the transaction not as a combination of independent yet

---

[29] American Law Institute, *Restatement (Second) of Contracts,* sect. 71 (1981).

[30] The phrase "tokens of the will" is taken from Hobbes's description of the law of nature concerning contracts. See Thomas Hobbes, *Man and Citizen,* 124–127 (Bernard Gert; ed., 1972). Since I am looking at contract law as the juridical embodiment of corrective justice, the validity of unilateral promises under seal is not relevant. As Benson points out in "Contract Law and Corrective Justice," promises under seal do not reflect the normative contours of transactions as such; rather, they are creations of positive law, which for instrumental purposes makes available a means of juridically binding oneself. Hobbes's discussion of contract implicitly illustrates Benson's point. Hobbes assumes that the natural law of contract, which is used to emerge from the state of nature, incorporates the doctrine of consideration, not the doctrine of seals, presumably because seals, being creations of positive law, have no validity in the state of nature.

[31] The equality is approximate because only substantially unequal transfers are justiciable on a case by case basis. Some legal systems specify the range of allowable deviation from equality; see the discussion of *laesio enormis* in Alan Watson, *Roman Law and Comparative Law,* 201–206 (1991). Jewish law specifies that the deviation can be no more than one-sixth; see *Babylonian Talmud, Baba Mezia,* 49b (I. Epstein, ed., 1935).

coincident transfers, but as an exchange in which what is transferred by one party is worth what is received from the other. Finally, by abstracting from what is particular about the transfers and relating them to each other through the approximately identical value that both represent, the doctrine also affirms the unity of the transaction.[32]

A contract transforms the promisor's choice to perform the promised act into an external object that juridically belongs to the promisee.[33] Before the contract, the choice to act in a specific way is a function of the actor's self-determining agency. This choice is normatively restricted only by the principle that the act not wrongfully infringe the right of anyone else. After the contract is formed, the promisor's choice to perform the promised act—what Kant calls "the causality of another's choice with respect to a performance he has promised me"[34]—becomes part of the promisee's belongings. Correlativity is achieved because the promisor's duty is the content of the promisee's right. Consequently, a breach of the duty is also an interference with the right.

The promisee's acquisition of the entitlement to determine the promisor's action requires that both parties contribute on an equal basis to the formation of a unified and bipolar relationship. As my

---

[32] On the place of equality of exchange in corrective justice, see Hegel, *Philosophy of Right*, sect. 77. For a detailed exposition of this passage, see Benson, "Abstract Right and the Possibility of a Nondistributive Conception of Contract," 1187–1196. Alan Brudner, "Hegel and the Crisis of Private Law," 10 *Cardozo Law Review* 949, at 996 (1989), claims that Hegel is referring only to "the narrow grounds for contractual relief based on duress of the person or on the exploitation of life-threatening situations." Brudner's interpretation is certainly wrong, as is evident from sect. 77 itself (which deals with whatever is the subject matter of the contract, not merely with Brudner's concern with duress and threats to life), from Hegel's reference to *laesio enormis* (which did not deal at all with duress and threats to life; see above, note 31), and from Hegel's cross-reference to sect. 63 (which deals with value in connection with any thing in use).

As Benson's exposition makes clear, value becomes determinate through a competitive market. One should not think that this reference to the market implies that corrective justice has the goal of promoting efficiency. Corrective justice does not serve the market; rather, the market makes corrective justice more determinate. In other words, the relationship of law to economics should be understood not as the instrumentalism of the contemporary economic analysis of law, but as the congruence of juridical and economic form that figures prominently in Marxist legal theory. See especially Evgeny Pashukanis, "The General Theory of Law and Marxism," in *Pashukanis: Selected Writings on Marxism and Law*, 36–131 (Piers Beirne and Robert Sharlet, eds., 1979).

[33] This paragraph is drawn from Kant's treatment of contract in *Metaphysics of Morals*, 68–70 [245–248], 90–95 [271–276].

[34] Id. at 98 [273].

brief survey of the doctrines of contract formation indicates, the juridical meaning of each party's contract-forming acts—whether under the doctrine of offer and acceptance, or consideration, or unconscionability—depends on the acts of the other. In this way the two parties interact as equal agents in effecting their common purpose to modify their mutual rights and obligations. By then breaching the contract, the promisor infringes an existing right. The award of expectation damages rectifies the promisor's breach of duty by restoring to the promisee the value of the right infringed.

5.6.3. The Restitution of Gains

Restitution is the law's response to one person's unjust enrichment at the expense of another. The requirement that the enrichment be "at the expense of" the plaintiff reflects the bipolarity of corrective justice by encapsulating the plaintiff's entitlement to what the defendant must disgorge. Because the defendant's enrichment was at the plaintiff's expense, the plaintiff can be said to be suffering a deprivation through the defendant's enrichment. Restitution rectifies this deprivation by forcing the defendant to surrender the enrichment (or its value) to the plaintiff.

One can broadly classify the situations that give rise to a restitutionary response according to the absence or presence of a wrongful act by the defendant.[35] Exemplifying the first situation are benefits conferred through mistake, where the defendant has to disgorge despite having been innocently passive in the receipt of a benefit from the plaintiff. Exemplifying the second situation are gains realized through breaches of fiduciary duty or through the wrongful appropriation and subsequent sale of someone else's property.

Each of these situations features the correlativity of right and duty, though they construe the right and duty differently. In the first situation, the plaintiff recovers the gain even in the absence of wrongdoing by the defendant. The ultimate basis of this recovery is that corrective justice, being in Aristotle's words "towards another," assumes the mutual externality of the parties and the consequent separateness of their interests. Accordingly, corrective justice recognizes no obligation to enrich another. The conferral of a benefit is literally within the free gift of the donor as a self-determining agent. Consequently, only if the

---

[35] Peter Birks, *An Introduction to the Law of Restitution*, 23–24 (1989); Peter Birks, "The Independence of Restitutionary Causes of Action," 16 *University of Queensland Law Journal* 1 (1990).

donor acts in execution of a donative intent is the transfer of the benefit an expression of right. Unilateral transfers, such as mistaken payments, that are not the product of a donative intent are juridically ineffective, regardless of the absence of wrongdoing by the donee.[36] Their restitution can therefore be demanded as a matter of corrective justice.

In such circumstances, the enrichment itself represents something that is rightfully the plaintiff's. Because its retention by the defendant is an infringement of the plaintiff's right, the defendant has a duty to restore it to the plaintiff. Liability is the juridical confirmation that, by holding on to the factual gain, the defendant breaches a duty that is correlative to the plaintiff's right.

In the second situation, where the enrichment is the consequence of a wrongful act, the right and the duty that define the wrongfulness are the basis of the plaintiff's claim to the defendant's enrichment. For instance, where a tortfeasor appropriates and sells the property of another, the plaintiff's entitlement to the tortfeasor's gain reflects the plaintiff's right in the appropriated property and the defendant's breach of the corresponding duty to abstain from that property. The money produced by the sale is the factual gain that embodies the plaintiff's right to the object; indeed, that money can be thought of "as a replacement or substitute for the property."[37] Similarly, the disgorging of profits by a fiduciary responds to the breach of the duty of unqualified loyalty owed to the principal. Existence of the fiduciary obligation means that the loyalty demanded by that obligation is included within the plaintiff's possessions.[38] Because the fiduciary has wrongly replaced duty with interest, the resulting profits can be thought of as the factual embodiment of the plaintiff's right to the fiduciary's loyalty.

Restitution in the aftermath of wrongdoing amply illustrates the

---

[36] In the words of the comprehensive formula that the Canadian courts use in restitution cases, there is an "absence of any juristic reason—such as a contract or disposition of law—for the enrichment." Pettkus v. Becker, [1980] 2 Sup. Ct. Rep. 834, at 848.

[37] Dan B. Dobbs, *Law of Remedies*, 368 (Hornbook Series, 2nd ed., 1993).

[38] Courts sometimes express this idea by describing the opportunity to profit as the principal's "property." See Boardman v. Phipps, [1967] 2 App. Cas. 46, at 107, 115 (H.L.). Such property is odd in that it entails the right to exclude only the fiduciary, not the whole world. As Lord Cohen remarked, id. at 102, the opportunity "is not property in the strict sense." Nonetheless, the term "property" is an acceptable way of representing the idea that the loyalty of a particular person—what we might call, paraphrasing Kant (see above, text at note 34), "the causality of another's choice with respect to performance as a fiduciary"—is a right belonging to the principal.

point that the correlativity of gain and loss is normative, not merely factual. The plaintiff is entitled to recover the gain even without having suffered a corresponding factual loss. For example, if the defendant commercially exploits a cave that opens only onto his property but runs beneath his neighbor's as well, the neighbor can recover a portion of the profits.[39] In such a case the plaintiff suffers no factual loss, since he has no way of using a cave to which he has no access. Nonetheless, by exploiting the plaintiff's part of the cave, the defendant infringes the plaintiff's right, and the plaintiff has a claim to profits attributable to that wrong. Similarly, the fiduciary can be required to surrender unauthorized profits even if those profits could not practically or legally be acquired for the principal.[40]

This kind of restitutionary claim is the mirror image of negligence claims in tort. Liability for negligence requires the plaintiff to suffer a factual loss without the defendant's needing to realize a corresponding factual gain. Liability to restitution requires the defendant to have realized a factual gain without the plaintiff's needing to realize a corresponding factual loss. In both categories of liability, the bipolar link between the parties is established through the correlativity of duty breached and right infringed.

5.7. Liability as Corrective Justice

I can now summarize the conception of liability that reflects the correlativity of right and duty. Because of this correlativity, the private law relationship forms a normative unit that integrates the doing and suffering of harm and that dovetails with the bipolar litigation between plaintiff and defendant.

First, the correlativity of right and duty indicates the kind of justificatory argument that counts in determining liability. Correlativity locks the plaintiff and defendant into a reciprocal normative embrace, in which factors such as deterrence and compensation, whose justificatory force applies solely to one of the parties, play no role. The only pertinent justificatory considerations are those that articulate the correlational nature of right and duty.

---

[39] Edwards v. Lee's Administrators, 96 S.W. 3d 1028 (Kentucky C.A., 1936). For a recent discussion of this and similar cases, see John Glover, "Restitutionary Principles in Tort: Wrongful User of Property and the Exemplary Measure of Damages," 18 *Monash University Law Review* 169 (1992).

[40] Keech v. Sandford, 25 Eng. Rep. 223 (1726).

Moreover, correlativity highlights the moral reason for singling out the defendant for liability. Because the actor's breach of duty infringes the sufferer's right, liability reflects the defendant's commission of an injustice. Liability is therefore not the retrospective pricing or licensing or taxing of a permissible act. Nor is the defendant singled out as a convenient conduit to an accessible insurance pool that might spread the overall cost of harm. Conversely, correlativity also indicates why the plaintiff in particular is entitled to recover. The defendant violates a normative bond not with the world at large but specifically with the person to whom the defendant owed the duty. In bringing an action, the plaintiff does not step forward as the representative of the public interest in economic efficiency or in any other condition of general welfare. The plaintiff sues literally in his or her own right as the victim of the defendant's unjust act.

Consequently, by linking a particular plaintiff and a particular defendant, the remedy maintains the correlativity of right and duty. Liability transforms the victim's right to be free from wrongful suffering at the actor's hand into an entitlement to reparation that is correlative to the defendant's obligation to provide it. The remedy consists not in two independent operations—one penalizing the defendant and the other benefiting the plaintiff—but in a single operation that joins the parties as obligee and obligor.

When the remedy takes the form of an award of damages, a single amount undoes the injustice both of what the defendant has done and of what the plaintiff has suffered. The award's simultaneous performance of this dual role also reflects the correlativity of right and duty. Only because the plaintiff's right is the subject matter of the defendant's duty can the same sum represent the injury to the plaintiff's right and the violation of the defendant's duty.

Thus the various aspects of the damage remedy—that the defendant is obligated to pay, that the plaintiff is entitled to be paid, and that the same amount undoes the injustice perpetrated by the defendant and suffered by the plaintiff—constitute a single whole. The origin, destination, and quantum of the damages can be understood together: a particular quantum is taken from a particular defendant because it is paid to a particular plaintiff. The taking of money from the defendant and the giving of money to the plaintiff cannot be ascribed to independent justifications (the deterrence of defendants and the compensation of plaintiffs, for instance) that make their conjunction in private law a merely conventional arrangement. Rather, the justifica-

tion for obligating the defendant to pay is correlative to the justification for entitling the plaintiff to be paid. Neither justification
is intelligible without the other, and together they form an intrinsic unity.

This conception of liability assigns the court a properly adjudicative
function. The court's task is to specify what the relationship of doer
and sufferer requires in the context of a particular dispute. Because
private law adjudication involves justifications that pertain only to the
relationship between the parties as doer and sufferer of the same harm,
a court cannot impose on the relationship an independent policy of
its own choosing. Rather, a court intervenes at the instance of the
wronged party to undo the unjust harm.[41] Adjudication thus conceived gives public and authoritative expression to what is implicit in
the correlativity of right and duty. So understood, private law adjudication works justice between the parties without legislating to promote the general welfare.

Accordingly, the intrinsic unity of the private law relationship can
be seen in private law's embodying in its structure, procedure, and remedy the correlativity of right and duty. The plaintiff's right to be free of
wrongful interferences with his or her entitlements is correlative to the
defendant's duty to abstain from such interferences. The plaintiff's suffering of a unjust loss is the foundation of his or her claim against the
person who has inflicted that loss. The transference from the defendant
to the plaintiff of a single sum undoes the injustice done by the former
to the latter. Whether the issue is the ground of the claim or the
mechanics of processing it, each litigant's position is the mirror image
of the other's. Conceived in this way, private law makes a coherent
juridical reality out of the relationship of doer and sufferer.

---

[41] I do not mean to imply that only an award of damages or other ex post relief conforms
to corrective justice. Corrective justice refers to a structure of wrongfulness that directly links
doer to sufferer. Any remedy responding to liability that reflects that structure is consonant
with corrective justice. Corrective justice thus allows for injunctions that prevent unjust
harm as well as for awards of damages and other specific reliefs that undo unjust harm. See,
for example, the discussion of nuisance in section 7.4.3 below. On the role of prospectivity
in Kantian right, see section 4.3.4.

6

Negligence Liability

6.1. Introduction

In this chapter I elucidate the immanence of corrective justice in negligence liability. My discussion so far has focused on the theoretical notions of form, corrective justice, and Kantian right, with only sporadic and general treatment of legal doctrine. In this chapter, in contrast, I present a sustained account of a specific area of common law liability.

The reason for dealing with negligence law in particular is that it poses an especially strong challenge to the unity of doing and suffering that corrective justice postulates. Negligence law holds the defendant liable for the harm that materializes from the creation of an unreasonable risk. Because the harm is an unintended consequence of the defendant's action, one might suppose that its occurrence is a fortuity that is morally irrelevant to the defendant's culpability. On this view, negligent harming is comprised of two separate episodes, the defendant's risk-creating act and the plaintiff's consequent injury. Postulating the unity of doing and suffering appears particularly unpromising.

To show how negligence law unifies doing and suffering, I shall pay particular attention to its ensemble of concepts: duty of care, proximate and factual cause, misfeasance, and the standard of the reasonable person. Each of these concepts, I contend, can be understood as expressing the normative correlativity of doing and suffering harm. Together, they treat the progression from the defendant's action to the plaintiff's injury as a single moral sequence. The negligence concepts allow the negligence relationship to be constructed, in two related senses: each concept can be *construed* as linking doer and sufferer and, taken as a group, they *construct* the liability that coherently connects the defendant's risk creation and the plaintiff's injury.

The assumption behind my account of negligence liability is that legal concepts are the provisional signposts of the law's coherence. Because a sophisticated legal system, such as the common law, values and tends toward its own coherence, one can adopt as a working hypothesis the idea that the concepts of the common law are constitutive of the unity of the plaintiff-defendant relationship. Over the centuries, the common law has engaged in the reasoned elaboration of its doctrine through cases in which plaintiffs vindicated their entitlements against defendants. It would be remarkable if the bipolarity of such litigation did not structure the legal doctrine that it spawned. If, as I claim, corrective justice and Kantian right truly are the unifying structure and normative ground of the private law relationships, the legal concepts that make up that relationship should be expressive of that structure and ground. Of course it may turn out, on examination of those concepts, that the hypothesis of the law's coherence cannot be sustained. Then the law will have failed to live up to its own aspirations to be a truly justificatory phenomenon.

In affirming the coherence of the common law's treatment of negligence, my account of negligence liability illustrates the formalist idea that corrective justice is immanent in a sophisticated system of private law. Given the juridical necessity for such a system to have its concepts and discourse express coherent bipolar relationships, corrective justice and Kantian right are theoretical notions that must be seen as implicit in the system's functioning. Private law does not refer to these theoretical notions explicitly, because private law is not a theory but a normative practice. Nonetheless, corrective justice and Kantian right are as immanent in its discourse as principles of syntax and logic are in discourse generally.

In this chapter I also illustrate formalism's acceptance of the concepts of private law on their own terms. Such acceptance is an aspect of the immanence of corrective justice and Kantian right in private law as a normative practice. Because formalism assumes that private law strives to be an expression of justificatory coherence, formalism treats the law's concepts as pathways into an internal intelligibility. The formalist therefore tries to understand these concepts as they are understood by the jurists who funnel their thinking and their discourse through them. Instead of looking upon legal concepts as proxies for extrinsic goals or as an alien vocabulary that requires translation into the discourse of another discipline, formalism sees them as having the meaning that juristic thought supposes that they have. For instance, whereas the practitioner of economic analysis might construe the plaintiff's cause of action as a mechanism for bribing someone to vindicate the collective interest in deterring the defendant's economically inefficient behavior, the formalist interprets that cause of action simply as what it purports to be: the assertion of right by the plaintiff in response to a wrong suffered at the hands of the defendant.

My argument in this chapter is that, understood in their own terms, the concepts of the common law of negligence constitute a single normative sequence that begins in the defendant's action and ends in the plaintiff's suffering. I will first consider the concepts that mark the two termini of this sequence: the standard of reasonable care, whose violation by the defendant creates the wrongful risk, and the concepts of factual cause and misfeasance, which represent the effects of that wrongfulness on the plaintiff. I will then consider the concepts of duty of care and proximate cause, which, I shall argue, span the moral space between these two termini. Together these concepts form an integrated ensemble that is the expression in common law of the unity of negligent doing and suffering.

6.2. Reasonable Care

Under negligence law, wrongdoing consists of the failure to live up to the standard of reasonable care. The standard is breached by action that creates a risk that no reasonable person would impose upon others. Presupposed is the existence of a certain level of risk to which the defendant can expose the plaintiff without committing a wrong, even if injury should result. The defendant is liable only for injuries that materialize from risks above that level.

The focus on risk is significant for corrective justice because risk is a relational concept that connects doing and suffering. As used in negligence law, risk refers to the potential for harm that is present in an act. Through the notion of risk, what one person does can be regarded from the standpoint of what another person might suffer. Risk thus links the active and passive aspects of injurious conduct.

Although the common law determines the acceptability of the risk on a case by case basis, there have been two attempts to schematize the significance of risk more explicitly. The American approach compares the risk and the cost of precautions. The English and Commonwealth approach disregards the cost of precautions. As I shall now argue, the second of these approaches rather than the first conforms to corrective justice.

The classic formulation of the American approach is in the famous case of United States v. Carroll Towing.[1] There Judge Learned Hand proposed that the defendant's duty is a function of three variables: the probability of an accident's occurring, the gravity of loss if it should occur, and the burden of adequate precautions. He then continued: "Possibly it serves to bring this notion into relief to state it in algebraic terms: if the probability be called P; the injury, L; and the burden, B; liability depends upon whether B is less than L multiplied by P: i.e., whether B [is less than] PL." In this formula P and L constitute the ingredients of risk. Risk creation is tortious when PL exceeds B.

The role of B in controlling the legitimacy of PL renders the test problematic from the standpoint of corrective justice. The test centers on whether the defendant who does not take precautions gains more ex ante than those exposed to the risk lose. It thus pivots not on the equality of the parties to the transaction but on the surplus that one party realizes at the expense of others. As its role in economic analysis shows, the Learned Hand test aims not at achieving corrective justice between the plaintiff and the defendant, but at maximizing the aggregate wealth of those affected by the risk-creating act.

In contrast, the English and Commonwealth approach to reasonable care ignores B almost completely and focuses narrowly on the risk, consisting in the combination of P and L. From a corrective justice standpoint, disregard of B makes sense, because it is the risk, not the cost of eliminating it, that connects the parties to an accident as doer and sufferer.

In determining whether the defendant has lived up to the standard of care owed to the plaintiff, Commonwealth courts proceed in several stages.[2] They first ask whether the risk was "reasonably foreseeable." In this inquiry, reasonableness refers to the degree of risk itself, rather than to the relationship of risk to prevention cost. The question reflects

---

[1] United States v. Carroll Towing Co., 159 F. 2d 169, at 173 (2d Cir., 1947).

[2] The following description of the English and Commonwealth approach is drawn from the three leading cases: Bolton v. Stone, [1941] App. Cas. 850 (H.L.), Overseas Tankship (U.K.) Ltd. v. The Miller Steamship Co. Pty. (Wagon Mound No. 2), [1967] 1 App. Cas. 617 (P.C., on appeal from Australia), and Wyong Shire Council v. Shirt, 29 Aust. Law Rep. 217 (H.C., 1979). Of course the practice is not as explicit as this description makes it. The three cases are remarkable precisely because they show the courts reflecting on a process normally treated merely as a casuistic determination by the trier of fact.

the sense that there is a threshold degree of risk that a reasonable person ought not to ignore. The assumption is that in any particular case one can distinguish risk that is "real" and ought not to be brushed aside even if it is quite unlikely to occur from risk that is "so fantastic or far-fetched that no reasonable man would have paid any attention to it."[3] Once a plaintiff gets over this undemanding[4] threshold, "it is then for the tribunal of fact to determine what a reasonable man would do by way of response to the risk."[5]

The reasonable response in turn depends on the risk's magnitude. For a real risk that is not small (the adjective used is "substantial," but, as we shall see at once, this does not mean that it must be large), the cost of precautions is irrelevant. In the leading case of Bolton v. Stone,[6] for example, the House of Lords decided that the defendant cricket club was not negligent when a ball hit over the fence of the cricket pitch struck the plaintiff. Lord Reid formulated the conception of reasonable care as follows: "[I]t would be right to take into account not only how remote is the chance that a person might be struck, but also how serious the consequences are likely to be if a person is struck, but I do not think it would be right to take into account the difficulty of remedial measures. If cricket cannot be played on a ground without creating a substantial risk, then it should not be played there at all."[7] Unlike the Learned Hand test, the consideration that the cost to the defendant of precautions would exceed the ex ante quantification of the plaintiff's injury does not exonerate the defendant from liability. The defendant can therefore be liable even for a cost-justified action.

Only if the risk, although real, is fairly small does one consider the cost of precautions. The idea here is that it might be reasonable not to go to considerable expenditure to eliminate a risk that, while not "fantastic and far-fetched," was nevertheless very unlikely to occasion harm. Lord Reid subsequently explained the holding in Bolton v. Stone on this basis.[8] Hitting a cricket ball onto the street was not "fantastic and far-fetched"; indeed, it had happened six times in twenty-eight years. And if the ball was so hit, it was not "fantastic and far-fetched" that it would strike someone. But since the street was a relatively unfrequented side road, "the chance of its happening in

[3] *Wagon Mound No. 2*, at 641.
[4] Wyong Shire Council v. Shirt, at 218.
[5] Id. at 221.
[6] Bolton v. Stone, [1951] App. Cas. 850 (H.L.).
[7] Id. at 867.
[8] *Wagon Mound No. 2*, at 641.

the foreseeable future was infinitesimal. A mathematician given the data could have worked out that it was only likely to happen once in so many thousand years." Therefore, explained Lord Reid, "[t]he House of Lords felt the risk was so small that in the circumstances a reasonable man would have been justified in disregarding it and taking no steps to eliminate it." Referring to the significance of high precaution costs, Lord Reid continued:

It does not follow that, no matter what the circumstances, it is justifiable to neglect a risk of such a small magnitude. A reasonable man would neglect such a risk if he had some valid reason for doing so, e.g., that it would involve a considerable expense to eliminate the risk. He would weigh the risk against the difficulty of eliminating it...Bolton v. Stone did not alter the general principle that a person must be regarded as negligent if he does not take steps to eliminate a risk which he knows or ought to know is a real risk and not a mere possibility which would never influence the mind of a reasonable man. What that decision did was to recognise and give effect to the qualification that it is justifiable not to take steps to eliminate a real risk if it is small and if the circumstances are such that a reasonable man careful of the safety of his neighbour would think it right to neglect it.

In Bolton v. Stone, then, the risk, though real, was so small that the defendant might reasonably forgo the large expenditure required to eliminate it. Even here, however, we are still far from the Learned Hand test. On Lord Reid's explanation, precaution costs are relevant to a very small risk only if they are "considerable" and only as a "qualification" to the general principle.[9]

In the English and Commonwealth approach, the conclusion that a

---

[9] Bolton v. Stone was a controversial decision. Commentators criticized it as explicable only on the ground that it involved "an accident arising out of...a highly meritorious national pastime"; see Dennis Lloyd, Note, 14 *Modern Law Review* 499 (1951). (Compare the comment of Justice Murphy that "[p]olicy considerations concerning English cricket seem to have been paramount in that case which, in my opinion, is not a guideline for negligence law in Australia." Wyong Shire Council v. Shirt, at 223.) In response to a public outcry, the defendant made an ex gratia payment to compensate the injured plaintiff. Note, 68 *Law Quarterly Review* 3 (1952). No doubt Lord Reid's subsequent gloss, which requires distinguishing between a risk so small that it is not real ("fantastic and far-fetched") and a risk that is real but very small ("infinitesimal"), is artificial. Moreover, the gloss creates the oddity that, despite the language in the text at note 7 above, Bolton v. Stone does not turn on the presence or absence of substantial risk. What the controversy indicates is that even the modest role the English approach assigns to Learned Hand's B may be excessive.

particular risk is unacceptable generally reflects not a comparison with the cost of taking precautions but a casuistic judgment concerning the magnitude of the risk. Negligence consists in exposure to "real" risk, that is, to risk that, even if unlikely, cannot reasonably be regarded as "fantastic and far-fetched." The greater the risk, the greater the precautions incumbent on the risk-creator, regardless of cost, to lower the risk to the level of the "fantastic and far-fetched." As Lord Reid says, the question that arises is "whether the risk of damage was so small that a reasonable person in the position of the [defendants], considering the matter from the point of view of safety, would have thought it right to take steps to prevent the danger."[10] Because this "is a question, not of law, but of fact and degree,"[11] it is reserved to triers of fact who apply the judge's general instructions about reasonableness on a case by case basis.[12]

This conception of reasonable care gives expression to the idea of agency that underlies corrective justice. Two aspects of the relationship of risk to human action are pertinent here, the first dealing with the legitimacy of action and the second with the illegitimacy of indifference to the suffering that action can cause.

First, risk is an unavoidable concomitant of human action. Although action is the attempt to realize some purpose that the actor sets, it takes place in a world that is not completely within the actor's control. As Lord Reid observes, "[i]n the crowded conditions of modern life, even the most careful person cannot avoid creating some risks and accepting others."[13] The actor therefore cannot be under a

---

[10] *Wagon Mound No. 2*, at 641.

[11] Id.

[12] Textbooks include the utility of the defendant's conduct as a consideration going to negligence. One should not conclude from this that the determination of negligence is a utilitarian judgment. The utility of conduct is usually relevant only where public authorities or public champions cause injury while attending to emergencies. See, e.g., the leading cases in Canada and England: Priestman v. Colangelo and Smythson, [1959] Sup. Ct. Rep. 615 (Can.) (police officers under statutory duty to apprehend criminals); Watt v. Hertfordshire County Council, [1954] 2 All Eng. Rep. 368 (C.A.) (fire brigade engaged in emergency rescue). In such cases the social role of the defendant moves the litigation closer to the judicial review of administrative action, where a court might be properly deferential about substituting its assessment for that of officers with specialized expertise who are charged with the responsibility of acting for the public good. The leading Australian case refers to this factor as "consideration of…any other conflicting responsibilities which the defendant may have." Wyong Shire Council v. Shirt (1980), at 221.

[13] Cf. Lord Radcliffe's comment that "a social being is not immune from social risk." Bolton v. Stone, at 869.

duty not to impose risk. Such a duty would deny the moral possibility of action and, since duty presupposes the exercise of agency, would therefore be self-contradictory.

Second, although risk is a concomitant of action, it can nonetheless be affected by the actor. Through action, actors attempt to work their purposes in the world. Nothing prevents actors from including among their purposes the reduction of the risks that accompany their own actions. Actors who implicitly claim that they can change the world through action (and therefore through the creation of risk), and yet that they cannot affect the risks that attend such action, assert a convenient but incoherent powerlessness in the exercise of power. Because action by its very nature involves the possibility of unintended consequences, the harm into which risk materializes is not alien to the risk-creating actor. To refuse to mitigate the risk of one's activity is to treat the world as a dumping ground for one's harmful effects, as if it were uninhabited by other agents.

From the standpoint of Kantian right, which conceives of doing and suffering as a relationship of free wills, these two considerations are mirror images of each other. Under the Kantian principle of right, the position of each party must be consistent with the other's being a self-determining agent. Accordingly, the plaintiff cannot demand that the law regard as wrongful the creation of all risk; such a judgment of wrongfulness would render action by the defendant impermissible, thus denying to the defendant the status of agent. Similarly, the defendant cannot claim immunity regarding risks that could have been modulated; that claim would ignore the effect of one's action on other agents and would treat them as nonexistent. When combined, these two considerations constitute a standard of care in which doer and sufferer rank equally as self-determining agents in judgments about the level of permissible risk creation.

The Commonwealth conception of reasonable care reflects the role within Kantian right of these two considerations. On the one hand, the actor is not held liable for the "fantastic and far-fetched" possibilities of injury that inevitably accompany human action. On the other hand, the creation of risks from which injury is reasonably foreseeable is grounds for liability, because of the failure to modulate one's action in view of its potential to cause others to suffer. Thus the requirement not to create what Lord Reid terms "real risk" translates these two considerations about human action into a standard governing the relationship of doer and sufferer.

6.3. Misfeasance and Factual Cause

6.3.1. The Bounds of the Parties' Relationship

Just as the defendant's negligent action initiates the tortious sequence from doing to suffering, so the resulting harm to the plaintiff completes it. Lack of reasonable care and the consequent occurrence of injury are the termini of the progression from doing to suffering.

For liability under corrective justice, the defendant's negligent conduct must have materialized in injury to the plaintiff. Without injury at the actor's hands, there is no sufferer to whom the actor is liable. And without the causal connection of suffering to the wrongful creation of risk, there is no actor responsible for the suffering and thus no one from whom, as a matter of corrective justice, the sufferer can recover.

Two doctrines of the common law deal with the effects of the defendant's wrongdoing on the plaintiff. The first is the distinction between nonfeasance and misfeasance:[14] for the plaintiff's injury to be actionable, it must be the consequence not of mere failure to act but of the defendant's risk creation. The second is the requirement of factual causation:[15] for the defendant's creation of risk to be actionable, it must result in injury to the plaintiff. These doctrines mirror each other in relating doing to suffering. The first prevents liability for the plaintiff's suffering apart from the defendant's action. The second prevents liability for the defendant's action apart from its consequences for the sufferer.

Through the first of these doctrines, the distinction between misfeasance and nonfeasance, the common law recognizes that for the injured person to recover, the suffering must be the consequence of what the defendant has done. Except under special circumstances, defendants are not liable unless they have participated in the creation of the risk that materialized in the plaintiff's injury.[16] Suffering by the

---

[14] William L. Prosser and W. Page Keeton, *Prosser and Keeton on the Law of Torts*, 373–385 (5th ed., 1984).

[15] Id. at 263–272.

[16] These special situations fall into certain groups. The first is comprised of situations where a public authority is under a statutory duty to act for the benefit of a class that includes the plaintiff; e.g., O'Rourke v. Schacht, 55 Dom. Law Rep. (3d) 96 (S.C. Can., 1974) (duty of the police to make highways safe for traffic); Jane Doe v. Metropolitan Toronto Commissioners of Police, 74 Ont. Rep. (2d) 225 (Div. Ct., 1990) (duty of the police to prevent sexual assault); City of Kamloops v. Neilson, 10 Dom. Law Rep. (4th) 641 (S.C. Can., 1980) (duty of a municipality to prevent the construction of houses with defective foundations). This category reflects the difference between the juridical standing of private parties,

plaintiff that does not result from the defendant's action has no significance for corrective justice. Accordingly, no liability lies for failure to prevent or alleviate an independently arising danger. The plaintiff's unilateral need for assistance, no matter how urgent, falls outside the relationship of doing and suffering.[17]

As for the second of these doctrines, some scholars have called the factual causation requirement into question. This assertion of "the decline of cause"[18] takes its cue from cases where difficulties of proving cause have led courts to lighten or reverse the plaintiff's evidentiary burden.[19] To the extent that these cases still allow defendants to exculpate themselves by disproving their causal role,[20] they merely modify

whose freedom would be infringed by the coercion of a benefit, and that of public authorities, which exist for the public good.

The second group is comprised of situations of particular intimacy or dependency. These include family situations, which are special applications of the principle of right; see Immanuel Kant, *The Metaphysics of Morals,* 95–100 [276–282] (Mary Gregor, trans., 1990).

The third group is comprised of situations where the defendant takes charge of an injured person and is obligated not to worsen that person's position. An example is Farwell v. Keaton, 240 N.W. 2d 217 (Mich. S.C., 1976), where the defendant was held liable for not securing medical attention for a friend injured during a joint activity.

The fourth group is comprised of situations where the defendant's failure to act takes place in the context of the defendant's risk-creating activity. Examples are Horsley v. MacLaren, 22 Dom. Law Rep. (3d) 545 (S.C. Can., 1972) (duty of the operator of a boat to rescue a person who has fallen overboard); Kline v. 1500 Massachusetts Avenue Apartment Corp., 439 F. 2d 477 (D.C. Cir., 1970) (duty of a landlord to provide adequate security for rented premises); Crocker v. Sundance Northwest Resorts, 51 Dom. Law Rep. (4th) 421 (S.C. Can., 1988) (duty of a resort operator to control participation in potentially dangerous resort entertainment).

The first and second groups are governed by considerations peculiar to their situations. The third and fourth are not so much exceptions to the general rule as particular applications of it.

[17] For the basis of the misfeasance/nonfeasance distinction in Kantian right, see above, section 4.2.4. In failing to recognize a general duty to rescue, the common law presses the implication of the nonfeasance/misfeasance distinction to an extreme not shared by other legal systems. See Aleksander W. Rudzinski, "The Duty to Rescue: A Comparative Analysis," in *The Good Samaritan and the Law* (James M. Ratcliffe, ed., 1966). But the distinction is implicit even in these other systems, which impose a less onerous duty on nonfeasant persons than they do on misfeasant ones. For the situation in Jewish law, see Ernest J. Weinrib, "Rescue and Restitution," 1 *S'vara: A Journal of Philosophy and Judaism* 59 (1990).

[18] Judith J. Thomson, "The Decline of Cause," 76 *Georgetown Law Review* 137 (1987).

[19] Summers v. Tice, 199 P. 2d 1 (Calif. S.C., 1948); Sindell v. Abbott Laboratories, 607 P. 2d 924 (Calif. S.C., 1980).

[20] The notable exception is Hymowitz v. Eli Lilly Co., 539 N.E. 2d 1069 (N.Y. C.A., 1989)

the evidentiary mechanisms regarding causation without negating its systemic importance for tort liability. Nonetheless, these cases have spurred the suggestion that the wrongful creation of risk may suffice for liability even in the absence of factual causation. Some have even claimed that this suggestion is consistent with corrective justice.[21] Let me here briefly indicate why it is not.

6.3.2. The Fortuity of Factual Causation

One version of the argument against factual causation goes like this.[22] Assume that both A and B negligently shoot in C's direction, but only A's shot strikes C. A and B are equally culpable, with the difference between them being a matter of chance that should not affect our moral assessment. If we hold A liable but not B, we allow the fortuity of causation to distinguish between morally equivalent wrongdoings.

By comparing the culpability of possible defendants, this argument ignores tort law's particular mode of moral assessment. Tort law is not interested in the defendant's culpability aside from the plaintiff's entitlement to redress. The bipolar nature of tort law requires our asking not only "Why can this plaintiff recover from *this* defendant?" but also "Why can *this* plaintiff recover from this defendant?" Even

---

(holding the defendant drug manufacturer liable for market share despite disproof of causation of the plaintiff's injury).

[21] See especially Glen O. Robinson, "Probabilistic Causation and Compensation for Tortious Risk," 14 *Journal of Legal Studies* 779, 789–791 (1985); Glen O. Robinson, "Risk, Causation, and Harm," in *Essays in Law and Liability* 317, 331–341 (Raymond G. Frey and Robert C. Morris, eds., 1991); Richard W. Wright, "Causation, Responsibility, Risk, Probability, Naked Statistics, and Proof: Pruning the Bramble Bush by Clarifying the Concepts," 73 *Iowa Law Review* 1001, 1072 (1988); Christopher H. Schroeder, "Corrective Justice and Liability for Increasing Risks," 37 *University of California at Los Angeles Law Review* 439 (1990); Christopher H. Schroeder, "Corrective Justice, Liability for Risks, and Tort Law," 38 *University of California at Los Angeles Law Review* 143 (1990). Robinson and others—e.g., Alan Schwartz, "Causation in Private Tort Law: A Comment on Kelman," 63 *Chicago-Kent Law Review* 639, 646 (1987)—have also made arguments in favor of liability for risk exposure within the framework of economic analysis. My concern here is only with corrective justice. It is apparent from section 2.9.1 above that, with respect to economic analysis, the question is not whether liability for risk exposure fits within the framework but whether the framework is itself an illuminating way of thinking about private law.

[22] This version has been explored by Thompson, "The Decline of Cause," and in Judith J. Thompson, *Rights, Restitution, and Risk* 192 (1986). It also plays a role in the work of Robinson, "Probabilistic Causation and Compensation for Tortious Risk," and of Schroeder, "Corrective Justice and Liability for Increasing Risks."

if culpability suffices to implicate the defendant, the plaintiff can complain only about the violation of a right. The acts of A and B may be morally equivalent, but it does not follow that C is entitled to claim indifferently against either of them.

From the standpoint of corrective justice, tort liability operates through and upon the relationship of plaintiff and defendant. Although C's injury does not distinguish A from the equally culpable B, it does distinguish C's relationship with A from C's relationship with B. A and C are linked as doer and sufferer of the same harm; no such connection exists between B and C. When A and B fired they created an unreasonable risk to C, so that at that moment C was identically related to both of them in terms of the potentiality of injury. That moment has, however, been superseded in a different way for each of the defendants. In hitting C, A's bullet joined A and C as the active and passive components of the same causal nexus. B's bullet flew by, harmlessly dissipating the possibility of injury into the environment. The relationship of doer and sufferer that B's negligence might have created between B and C can now never come into being. Although B acted culpably, the absence of injury to C precludes C from claiming reparation.[23]

The defect, then, of this version of the "decline of cause" argument is that in focusing on the culpability of the defendant, it leaves the plaintiff's injury out of account. It thereby introduces a one-sidedness inconsistent with the bipolarity of corrective justice.

6.3.3. Probabilistic Causation

The second version of this argument purports to plug this gap by including, but redefining, the causation of injury.[24] On this version,

---

[23] Kant is often invoked to support the moral arbitrariness of factual causation. See, e.g., Thompson, "The Decline of Cause," 143; John M. Fischer and Robert H. Ennis, "Causation and Liability," 13 *Philosophy and Public Affairs* 33 (1986); Robinson, "Risk, Causation, and Harm," 338; Schroeder, "Corrective Justice and Liability for Increasing Risks." These references draw on Kant's notion that the good will is the only unqualified good, regardless of what it accomplishes. Immanuel Kant, *Foundations of the Metaphysics of Morals*, 16 [400] (Lewis White Beck, trans., 1969). In the context of liability, however, this invoking of Kant is misleading. For Kant, the operation of the good will falls under ethics, not right, and is therefore irrelevant to liability. On the relation between the right and the good in Kantian moral philosophy, see above, section 4.4.

[24] See especially Robinson, "Probabilistic Causation and Compensation for Tortious Risk"; Robinson, "Risk, Causation, and Harm"; Schroeder, "Corrective Justice

liability flows from the probability that the injury will occur: this probability itself, "the present actuarial value of possible future loss-es,"[25] counts as the injury required by corrective justice. For instance, a defendant who dumped carcinogenic chemical waste would be liable for increasing the likelihood of the plaintiff's contracting cancer. Instead of regarding injury in the traditional tort way as the materiali-zation of an unreasonable risk, this argument considers causation to consist in the very creation of the unreasonable risk and injury to consist in exposure to the risk so created. Such redefinition preserves the moral equality of culpable actors and yet allows each actor and each prospective sufferer to be conceived as a participant in a bipolar relationship.

The argument construes the plaintiff's exposure to risk as the loss that corrective justice corrects. To be sure, exposure to risk, to the extent that it depreciates the value of the body considered as a capital asset, might be considered a factual loss, a change for the worse in the plaintiff's condition. But such loss is an inadequate basis for liability. Corrective justice requires not factual but normative loss consisting in wrongful infringement of the plaintiff's right.

For risk exposure to count as an actionable loss under corrective jus-tice, the prospect of bodily injury, rather than actual bodily injury, would have to constitute the violation of the plaintiff's right. Conversely, the right would have to consist not in actual bodily integrity, but in the absence of the prospect of injury. But the absence of the prospect of injury cannot count as a right under the Kantian gloss of corrective jus-tice. Rights are juridical manifestations of the will's freedom. The absence of the prospect of injury is not in itself a manifestation of the plaintiff's free will. In this respect, risk of bodily injury decisively differs from bod-ily injury itself: a human being has an immediate right in his or her body because it houses the will and is the organ of its purposes.[26] The prospect of injury is, at most, something that may affect the embodiment of the plaintiff's free will in the future. Therefore, security from this prospect does not rank as a present right.[27]

---

and Liability for Increasing Risks"; Schroeder, "Corrective Justice, Liability for Risks, and Tort Law."

[25] Robinson, "Probabilistic Causation and Compensation for Tortious Risk," 790.

[26] See above, section 5.5.

[27] Proponents of probabilistic causation (e.g., Robinson, "Probabilistic Causation and Compensation for Tortious Risk," 795) point out that the estimate of probabilities already plays a role in the calculation of damages. So far as corrective justice is con-

Accordingly, traditional tort law reflects corrective justice in refusing to treat risk as an independent kind of harm. Risk is always the risk *of something*. In corrective justice, that *something* encompasses the right that defines the plaintiff's claim. Risk refers to the possibility of a normative loss. It is not itself the normative loss.

6.4. Duty of Care and Proximate Cause

6.4.1. Two Approaches

Duty of care and proximate cause are the concepts the common law of negligence uses to connect the defendant's lack of reasonable care and the resulting injury to the plaintiff. The duty issue focuses on the link between the defendant's negligence and the person injured, proximate cause on the link between the negligence and the resulting accident or injury. The two concepts follow through on the idea of unreasonable risk creation by addressing, respectively, the questions of risk to whom and risk of what.[28] Since one cannot characterize the persons affected by the risk apart from the accident or injury they might suffer, the two issues are frequently interchangeable.

Much discussed under both duty and proximate cause is the problem of negligence resulting in unforeseeable injury. In such cases wrongdoing and the causation of injury are both present, but the injury is not the materialization of the potential for harm that renders the defendant's action wrongful. Can the plaintiff recover?

The two opposing responses essayed by the common law[29] represent different ways of connecting wrongdoing and causation. One response holds that although wrongdoing and a resulting injury are both necessary to liability, the injury need not be within the wrongful risk for the plaintiff to recover. Negligence determines who is liable; it does not determine the consequences for which that person is liable. In Lord Sumner's famous formulation, the reasonable foreseeability of harm is relevant to whether the defendant was negligent, and this "goes to

---

cerned, this is true but irrelevant. There is a difference between using probabilities to quantify the value of a violated right and using them to identify the violated right.

[28] Cecil A. Wright, *Cases on the Law of Torts*, 172 (4th ed., 1967).

[29] The history of these two responses has often been told. See especially John G. Fleming, "The Passing of Polemis," 39 *Canadian Bar Review* 489 (1961); Patrick J. Kelley, "Proximate Cause in Negligence Law: History, Theory, and the Present Darkness," 69 *Washington University Law Quarterly* 49 (1991).

culpability, not to compensation."[30] Of course, even on this approach the defendant cannot be held liable for the possibly endless consequences of negligence. The limitation on liability, however, arises through a division of the causal chain (into direct and indirect consequences, for example) without reference to what underlies the decision about culpability. Negligence and the causation of injury do not participate in a single integrating idea, but are separate conditions that must be satisfied if the defendant is to be held liable. In the language of Chapter 2, negligence and injury form a merely accidental unity.[31]

The second response treats the parties' relationship as an intrinsic unity. On this view, unreasonable risk is the idea that integrates the defendant's wrongdoing and the plaintiff's injury. The defendant's wrongdoing consists in creating the potentiality of a certain set of harmful consequences; the plaintiff recovers only if the injury is within that set. The consequences for which the defendant is liable are restricted to those within the risks that render the act wrongful in the first place. In Warren Seavey's words, "[p]rima facie at least, the reasons for creating liability should limit it."[32]

Only the second of these approaches conforms to corrective justice. The first approach—as I shall now show—fails to maintain the correlativity of right and duty and thereby leaves us without a reason for holding this particular doer liable to this particular sufferer.

6.4.2. The Palsgraf Case

To illustrate, let us examine the *Palsgraf* case.[33] In addition to being the leading United States decision on duty of care, the *Palsgraf* opinion is the most considered judicial exposition of the competing approaches just adumbrated. Justice Cardozo's majority judgment treats wrongdoing and the resulting injury as intrinsically unified; Justice Andrews' dissenting opinion treats them as disconnected requirements that can be independently satisfied.

In *Palsgraf*, an employee of the defendant railroad negligently pushed a passenger, causing him to drop a package he was carrying. The package turned out to contain fireworks. The resulting explosion overturned scales at the other end of the platform. The scales struck

---

[30] Weld-Blundell v. Stephens, [1920] App. Cas. 956, 984.

[31] See section 2.6.1 above.

[32] Warren S. Seavey, "Mr. Justice Cardozo and the Law of Torts," 39 *Columbia Law Review* 20, 34 (1939).

[33] Palsgraf v. Long Island Railroad, 162 N.E. 99 (N.Y. C.A., 1928).

the plaintiff. By endangering the property of the pushed passenger, the act of the defendant's employee fell below the standard of care. But since the package gave no notice of its contents; the effect of this negligence on the plaintiff could not reasonably have been anticipated.

In a four to three decision, the New York Court of Appeals denied liability. Speaking for the majority, Cardozo held that because the defendant's negligence was not a wrong relative to her, the plaintiff could not recover. Andrews, dissenting, held that the duty to avoid creating unreasonable risks is owed to the world at large, not merely to the person who might be expected to be harmed. Since harm is the natural consequence of the negligent act, anyone in fact harmed can complain. The only limitation on liability is that the negligent act must be the proximate cause of the injury. This means that the injury must be within the series of events past which the law, as a matter of practical politics, arbitrarily declines to trace consequences.

Cardozo's majority opinion emphasizes the relational quality of negligence. The wrongfulness of negligence consists not in unsocial conduct at large, but in the potential violation of another's right. The tort plaintiff must therefore sue "in her own right for a wrong personal to her, and not as the vicarious beneficiary of a breach of duty to another."[34] Since the defendant's negligence was to the package's owner, the harm done to the plaintiff was the result of a wrong to someone else. For such harm the plaintiff is not entitled to recover.

As Cardozo points out, the relational quality of risk corresponds to the relational quality of negligence. "The risk reasonably to be perceived defines the duty to be obeyed and risk imports relation; it is risk to another or to others within the range of apprehension."[35] Risk is not intelligible in abstraction from a set of perils and a set of persons imperiled. As a way of referring to the harmful potentialities inherent in a given act, risk extends from the defendant's creation of these potentialities to their actualization in the plaintiff's injury. In Cardozo's view, the same wrongful risk must qualify both the defendant's action and the plaintiff's injury.

Cardozo's opinion integrates wrongfulness and the resulting injury. Only when the plaintiff's injury is within the risk that renders the defendant's act wrongful is the plaintiff entitled to recover in tort. Then, because the plaintiff's right is the ground of the duty that the defendant breached, the parties are intrinsically united in a single juridical relationship.

[34] Id. at 100.
[35] Id.

In contrast, Andrews' dissent juxtaposes but does not integrate the defendant's negligence and the plaintiff's injury. Causation links the litigants as doer and sufferer, but the wrongfulness of the defendant's action is independent of whether the plaintiff is within the range of its foreseeable effects. The plaintiff's injury therefore need not be the materialization of the unreasonable risk created by the defendant.

Andrews' approach to the duty of care makes manifest his failure to integrate negligence and injury. In Andrews' view the duty of care involves "not merely a relationship between man and those whom he might reasonably expect his act to injure" but also a relationship "between him and those whom he does in fact injure."[36] Once the defendant commits an act that unreasonably endangers someone, any resulting injury to anyone falls within the scope of the breached duty. This approach incorporates two different conceptions of the defendant's wrong. One is that the wrong is "to the public at large" because "due care is a duty imposed on each of us to protect society from unnecessary danger."[37] Injury is irrelevant to this conception; society is endangered as soon as the negligent act is performed.[38] A second is that the wrong consists in an injury to the plaintiff's rights.[39] Negligence is irrelevant to this conception; the plaintiff's rights would be as injured by nonnegligent acts as they are by negligent ones. Each conception makes paramount what is immaterial to the other. Although injury and negligence are thus conceptually unconnected, Andrews has the injury determine the recipient and the extent of the compensation for the negligence.

Moreover, even when taken on its own terms, Andrews' comprehensive view of the duty of care is at odds with his narrow conception of proximate cause. As long as the focus is on culpability, the duty is expansively owed to the world at large, so that "all those in fact injured may complain."[40] When Andrews turns specifically to the injury, the limitation of proximity is suddenly introduced—and expressly justified by its arbitrariness.[41] The breach of the obligation at large wrongs everyone who has been injured as a result, but only an arbitrarily specified subset made up of those whose injuries are proximate can receive compensation in tort.

---

[36] Id. at 102.

[37] Id.

[38] "Where there is an unreasonable act and some right that may be affected, there is negligence whether damage does or does not result. That is immaterial." Id.

[39] "The plaintiff's rights must be injured ..." Id. at 103.

[40] Id.

[41] Id. at 103.

This failure to integrate injury and wrongdoing brings into question the appropriateness of entitling this plaintiff to damages from this defendant. Andrews treats injury as singling out the plaintiff, and wrongdoing as singling out the defendant. The difficulty lies in finding a basis for joining these two parties, out of all those who suffer injury or commit negligence, in one lawsuit that makes this particular defendant liable for this particular plaintiff's injuries. If the wrong consisted in endangering one person's package, why must the defendant compensate a different person for physical injuries?

Several answers, none of them satisfactory, are available. One might first argue that the defendant's wrongdoing is the key to the link with the plaintiff. But since Andrews regards due care as an obligation owed to the world at large, its breach does not in itself give the plaintiff any special status to complain. Once the negligence has been committed, the function of the plaintiff in Andrews' conception should be to vindicate wrong done to the public at large. This function has no necessary connection with the injury suffered by any particular individual. On Andrews' conception of the duty of care, its breach is not correlative to the infringement of any right specific to Mrs. Palsgraf.

Second, one might suppose that the causal connection between the defendant's negligence and the plaintiff's injury links the parties. However, because on Andrews' argument the negligence violates a duty to the whole world without establishing a particular normative bond with the plaintiff, the defendant's negligence is merely a historically causal antecedent of the plaintiff's injury. But then the question presents itself again: what entitles the plaintiff to single out the defendant's negligence from among the numerous historically causal antecedents, whether innocent or culpable, of that injury?

Third, although neither wrongdoing nor the causation of injury, taken each without the other, justifies holding this particular wrongdoer liable to this particular victim, perhaps in combination these concepts have a potency that they lack separately. This answer presupposes that wrongdoing and causation together form a whole greater than the sum of its individual parts. But without an integration of wrongdoing and causation there is no such whole. Since the plaintiff's injury is outside the range of the consequences that makes the defendant's action wrongful, wrongdoing and the causation of injury are mutually independent. Accordingly, their joint power cannot exceed the aggregate of their individual powers.

Fourth, the defendant's liability to the plaintiff has been supported on the ground that it is fairer for the negligent perpetrator than for the innocent victim to bear the costs of the injury.[42] This defense, however, merely reproduces the problem in a different form. It invites us to allocate the costs of this injury according to a comparison of the parties' guilt or innocence. But unless the defendant's negligence is correlative to the plaintiff's right, this moral ledger involves factors that apply not only to the particular accident at issue but also to the entire extent of a person's life and activity.[43] Why, then, should our interest in the parties' comparative innocence play itself out within the restrictive framework of this incident? The scope appropriate to the enterprise of comparison is at odds with the occasion and the form of the litigation.[44]

The root of Andrews' problem is that he joins wrongdoing and injury without preserving the normative correlativity of the parties' relationship. Inasmuch as the plaintiff was beyond the ambit of the unreasonable risk, her right in her bodily security was not the ground for the employee's duty to abstain from pushing the passenger. Hence the duty breached was not relative to the plaintiff's right. The defendant committed a wrong and the wrong caused the plaintiff's injury, but since the prospect of the injury was not what made the defendant's

---

[42] Herbert L. A. Hart and Tony Honoré, *Causation in the Law*, 267 (2nd ed., 1985); William L. Prosser, "Palsgraf Revisited," 52 *Michigan Law Review* 1, 17 (1953).

[43] Robert E. Keeton, *Legal Cause in the Law of Torts*, 21 (1963).

[44] The argument illustrates the incoherence of combining distributive and corrective considerations within a single relationship. On the one hand, the claim that "as between the innocent victim and the culpable actor the latter should bear the cost of the accident" sets up a ratio that distributes the cost of injury according to the parties' respective innocence and culpability. This ratio mediates the parties' relationship through a comparison of their culpability. On the other hand, causation of injury connects the particular parties immediately in accordance with corrective justice. But if culpability is decisive, why not distribute the costs among all who share this quality regardless of causation? There is no reason either to single out this particular defendant from the pool of negligent actors or to compensate this particular plaintiff because of an innocence equally found in other sick or injured persons. The distributive and corrective features of the relationship point to justifications that pull in different directions.

Closely related is the argument that the fact that the defendant may often have been negligent without having had to pay compensation justifies liability on the odd occasion when harm turns out to be unforeseeable. Hart and Honoré, *Causation in the Law*, 268. Here, too, the consideration invoked goes beyond the incident in question. Whereas the consideration in the text implicitly invites a global comparison of innocence and guilt, this one assumes both that the unknown negligence of other occasions is relevant and that it is always to be debited to the defendant rather than to the plaintiff.

act wrongful, no wrong was done to the plaintiff. The plaintiff's injury was historically consequent on, but not normatively correlative to, the defendant's wrongdoing.

In *Palsgraf*, then, only the defendant's act, not the plaintiff's resulting injury, was wrongful. Given my account of the reasonable care standard, this is not as paradoxical as it might seem. The negligence standard entails dividing the possible consequences of the defendant's acts into those that are the materialization of what Lord Reid called a real risk and those that are not. A negligent actor creates both real and far-fetched risks, but the negligence consists only in the former. In *Palsgraf* the defendant's employee created a real risk of damaging the property of the shoved passenger but a far-fetched risk of injuring Mrs. Palsgraf. As it happened, the far-fetched risk materialized. Since this risk was not wrongful, its materialization did not make the plaintiff the victim of a wrong.

To sum up: In the absence of normative correlation, the concepts that mark the juridical relationship do not form an integrated whole. The result is that Andrews' treatment of wrongdoing does not cohere with his treatment of injury. And because wrongdoing in this case defines the moral character only of the doing and not of the suffering, there is no normative link between the parties, and therefore no justification for requiring this particular defendant to compensate this particular plaintiff.

6.4.3. Describing the Risk

The lesson of *Palsgraf* is that for the defendant to be liable, the wrongfulness of the defendant's risk creation must be correlative to the wrongfulness of the plaintiff's injury. The concepts of proximate cause and duty of care connect wrongful doing to wrongful suffering by requiring the plaintiff's injury to be the fruition of the unreasonable risk that renders the defendant's action wrongful. The function of these concepts is to span the normative space between the parties by treating the injury that occurred in terms of the wrongful risk out of which it materialized.

This function involves the interplay of general and particular characterizations of the risk. When the wrongful act is committed, the risk is, as Cardozo observes, relational, but in a general way. Because it refers to the *possibility* of harm, the risk does not include all the specific attributes of circumstance and person that qualify any actual harm. Risk at this point refers generally to a class of persons that it might affect, a kind of injury that might result, and a type of mechanism by which the injury might come to pass. In the *Palsgraf* case, for instance, it does not matter whether the defendant foresaw the danger to the plaintiff, Mrs. Palsgraf, as a specific and identified person; the reasonable foresight on which Cardozo insists is relative to a class of persons to whom Mrs. Palsgraf may or may not belong. Indeed, even if the defendant had every reason to suppose that Mrs. Palsgraf would not be at the station at that time, he would nonetheless be liable if she turned up as part of the class relative to which the defendant's action was negligent.

Only when the harm materializes does this generality narrow to a particular victim and a particular injury. Duty of care and proximate cause, in Cardozo's approach, are the headings we use to subsume the particularity of the actual injury under the generality of risk. Duty addresses the question of whether the plaintiff, as the person in fact affected, is to be regarded as within the class foreseeably affected by the defendant's negligence. Proximate cause performs a parallel function with respect to the injury and the process through which the harm comes into being.[45]

To understand how duty and proximate cause perform their function, we must keep in mind two features of risk. First, as I have just noted, risk is a process of maturation from general to particular. Second, risk is always the risk of something: because risk is unintelligible without reference to what is at risk or how the danger might come to pass, risk must be conceived under a description of its potential effects. When we put these two features together, we see that evaluating risk creation involves a description of potential effects in terms of some point on the spectrum from general to particular. In the common law of negligence, duty of care and proximate cause are the rubrics under which one describes the risk at an appropriate degree of generality.[46]

Formulating a risk description of appropriate generality implicates the same considerations encountered in the determination of reasonable care. This is not surprising, since duty of care and proximate

---

[45] Hughes v. Lord Advocate, [1963] App. Cas. 837 (H.L.); Doughty v. Turner Manufacturing, [1964] 1 Q.B. 518 (C.A.).

[46] See McCarthy v. Wellington City, [1966] N.Z.L.R. 481, 521 (C.A.) (holding that "the injury which happened to the respondent was of the *general* character which a reasonable person would have foreseen as being likely to happen to the *class* of which the respondent was one, and that *class* was so closely and directly affected by the appellant's acts that the appellant owed a duty of care to those in it") (emphasis added).

cause trace the wrongfulness of the defendant's risk creation through to the maturation of the risk. The description of the risk should therefore reflect the wrongful quality of the act. As with the reasonable care standard, the rubrics of proximate cause and duty must neither delegitimize action nor legitimize indifference to the effect of action on other agents.

On the one hand, too particular a description would legitimize indifference to the effects of action and thus fail to reflect the wrongfulness of the act. What makes risk creation wrongful is not that it might produce a particular wound in a particular person through a particular sequence, but that it might produce a type of wound in a class of persons through a certain kind of accident. At the time of the defendant's action, there could never be, in Lord Reid's formulation, a real risk that the injury would in all its details turn out precisely as it did. To require that the risk be described in terms of its particular impact would immunize any act from liability.

On the other hand, an excessively general risk description would also fail to capture the wrongfulness, but with the opposite effect of implicitly delegitimizing action. Take the most general description of the risk, that the risk is simply "of injury." Since all action produces such a risk, allowing liability on the materialization of this risk would be equivalent to judging action itself to be illegitimate. The wrongful quality of the defendant's act evaporates in so general a description. What we need is a characterization of the risk that allows us to distinguish the potential for harm in the defendant's act from the background harms that are part and parcel of all action. The very characterization of the risk as unreasonable means that the qualification takes place with respect to a more limited category of injury than injury simpliciter.

Obviously, these considerations about generality and particularity do not yield a formula for solving problems of duty and proximate cause. They only indicate the normative framework within which such problems arise. As every lawyer knows, determining the appropriate degree of generality does not involve recourse to an apodeictic decision procedure. Indeed, given that we are dealing with a qualitative spectrum, any proposed apodeictic procedure would be unintelligible, and is thus impossible even in principle.[47] The duty and proximate cause issues demand a judgment, which different people might plausibly

---

[47] What would it mean, for instance, to lay down a rule that the proximate cause requires that the description be at 63 percent generality?

make differently, about what, on the facts of a specific case, is the sort of consequence that a reasonable person ought to have anticipated and guarded against.[48]

Thus proximate cause and duty do not themselves set the level of generality. They are the legal vehicles for the expression of such generality as seems appropriate for individual cases or for groups of cases.[49] Since these categories connect specific accidents to the risks out of which they materialize, the application of the categories is peculiar to the circumstances of the injury. The most that the courts can accomplish through abstract prescription is to point out that foreseeability of "the precise concatenation of events" is irrelevant,[50] while also cautioning against setting up excessively broad tests of liability. The description of the risk can be formulated only case by case in terms of what is plausible in any given fact situation as compared with analogous fact situations.[51]

---

[48] Keeton, *Legal Cause*, 49–60; Clarence Morris, "Duty, Negligence, and Causation," 101 *University of Pennsylvania Law Review* 189, 196–198 (1952). Morris puts the point in terms of the rhetoric of litigation, but this rhetoric reflects the conceptual requirements of negligence law as an intrinsic ordering. On the nonpolitical nature of the indeterminacy of proximate cause, see below, sections 8.3 and 8.4.

[49] For an example of the approach to proximate cause outlined here, see the judgment of Chief Justice Magruder in Marshall v. Nugent, 222 F.2d 604, 610, (1st Cir., 1955): "[T]he effort of the courts has been, in the development of this doctrine of proximate causation, to confine the liability of a negligent actor to those harmful consequences which result from the operation of the risk, or a risk, the foreseeability of which rendered the defendant's conduct negligent. Of course, putting the inquiry in these terms does not furnish a formula which automatically decides each of an infinite variety of cases. Flexibility is further preserved by the further need of defining the risk, or risks, either narrowly or more broadly, as seems appropriate or just in the special type of case." Compare also the remarks of Justice Windeyer in Mt. Ida Mines Ltd. v. Pusey, 125 Comm. Law Rep. 383, at 402 (H.C.Aust., 1971): "Foreseeability does not mean foreseeability of the particular course of events causing the harm. Nor does it suppose foresight of the particular harm which occurred, but only of some harm of a like kind....This comfortable latitudinarian doctrine has, however, the obvious difficulty that it leaves the criterion for classification of kinds or types of harm undefined and at large ...Lord Wright in Bourhill v. Young, [1943] A.C., at p. 110, said: 'The lawyer likes to draw fixed and definite lines and is apt to ask where the thing is to stop. I should reply it should stop where in the particular case the good sense of the jury or of the judge decides.' That perhaps does not reckon with courts of appeal, and varying judicial opinions of where in good sense the proper stopping place is."

[50] See, for example, Hughes v. Lord Advocate, [1963] App. Cas. 837, 855 (H.L.), The Queen v. Cote, 51 Dom. Law Rep. (3d) 244, 252 (S.C. Can., 1974).

[51] The recoil from excessive generality in the duty formulations of recent English cases is instructive. In Home Office v. Dorset Yacht, [1970] App. Cas. 1004 (H.L.), the House of Lords was confronted with the novel question of whether borstal officers

6.5. Conclusion

From this survey one can see how corrective justice is immanent in the most fundamental concepts of negligence law. By tracing different aspects of the progression from the doing to the suffering of harm, these concepts coalesce into a single normative sequence and thus instantiate corrective justice. Throughout, negligence law treats the plaintiff and the defendant as correlative to each other: the significance of doing lies in the possibility of causing someone to suffer, and the significance of suffering lies in its being the consequence of someone else's doing. Central to the linkage of plaintiff and defendant is the idea of risk, for "risk imports relation."[52] The sequence starts with the

---

were responsible for damage done by borstal boys in the course of their escape from supervision. Members of the Court who favored liability adopted two different approaches. Lord Reid, arguing from the general to the particular, held that the reasonable foreseeability of injury should yield liability unless there was some justification for an exception. Lord Diplock, in contrast, proposed that one must start with "the relevant characteristics" of the present situation as compared with those at issue in previous decisions; the general conception of reasonable foreseeability is to be "[u]sed as a guide to characteristics which will be found to exist in conduct and relationships which give rise to a legal duty of care," but not "misused as a universal." Id. at 1060. Lord Diplock was explicitly concerned to distinguish the damage suffered here from "the general risk of damage from criminal acts of others which [the plaintiff] shares with all members of the public." Id. at 1070. Unique among judicial opinions, Lord Diplock's judgment sets out a methodology for arriving at an appropriate general description of the risk on a case by case basis. Lord Reid's approach triumphed, with Lord Diplock's surprising concurrence, in Anns v. London Borough of Merton, [1977] 2 All Eng. Rep. 492 (H.L.). That this leads to an excessively general description of the risk became evident in Junior Books Ltd. v. Veitchi Co. Ltd., [1982] 3 All Eng. Rep. 201 (H.L.) (liability of a contractor for the substandard quality of a floor laid by a subcontractor), a decision that lower courts have—remarkably in the English context—treated as a dead letter. See, e.g., Simaan General Contracting v. Pilkington Glass Ltd., [1988] 1 All Eng. Rep. 79 (C.A.). Moreover, *Anns* postulated a test comprising two stages (a prima facie duty based on reasonable foreseeability, and then limiting or negativing considerations) that, arguably, were not coherently connected; see, for example, the controversy about the second stage among the judges in McLoughlin v. O'Brian, [1982] 2 All Eng. Rep. 298 (H.L.). In the last few years, in a series of cases culminating in Caparo Industries plc. v. Dickman, [1990] 1 All Eng. Rep. 568 (H.L.), the English courts have retreated from *Anns* to an approach that is close to Lord Diplock's. Significantly, in rejecting excessive generalization, *Caparo* also draws attention to the intrinsically unified nature of negligence liability: "His duty of care is a thing written on the wind unless damage is caused by the breach of that duty; there is no actionable negligence unless duty, breach and consequential damage coincide...For purposes of determining liability in a given case, each element can be defined only in terms of the others." Id. at 599 (per Lord Oliver, quoting Justice Brennan in Sutherland Shire Council v. Heyman, 60 Aust. Law Rep. 1, 48 [1985]).

    [52] Palsgraf v. Long Island Railroad, 162 N.E. 99, 100 (N.Y. C.A., 1928).

potential for harm inherent in the defendant's wrongful act (hence the standard of reasonable care) and concludes with the realization of that potential in the plaintiff's injury (hence the role of misfeasance and factual causation). The concepts of duty of care and proximate cause link the defendant's action to the plaintiff's suffering through judgments about the generality of the description of the action's potential consequences. Each of the negligence concepts traces an actual or potential connection between doing and suffering, and together they translate into juridical terms the movement of effects from the doer to the sufferer. In this way the negligence concepts form an ensemble that brackets and articulates a single normative sequence.[53]

As promised at the outset of this chapter, I have been examining the construction, in two senses, of the negligence relationship. One sense is that negligence law constructs a conceptual bridge over the gap—both temporal and (one might suppose) moral—between doing

---

[53] It might be appropriate at this point briefly to indicate how the defenses based on the plaintiff's conduct fit into this picture of negligence liability.

(1) *Contributory negligence.* This defense applies when the plaintiff's failure to exercise reasonable care is a contributing cause of the damage suffered. The defense expresses an idea of transactional equality: the plaintiff cannot demand that the defendant should observe a greater care than the plaintiff with respect to the plaintiff's safety. See Francis H. Bohlen, "Contributory Negligence," 21 *Harvard Law Review* 233, at 255 (1908). This idea of equality underlies both the traditional common law rule, which denies all recovery, and the comparative negligence rule, pioneered in Ontario but now widely adopted, which apportions damages on the basis of degree of fault. The traditional common law rule arose because, on the assumption that partial damages could not be awarded under the common law of torts, denying recovery was fairer than the only perceived alternative, which was to hold the defendant liable. Because contributory negligence looks at the fault of the plaintiff relative to the fault of the defendant in their interaction, it is entirely a transactional notion. The same idea of equality also applies to the principle of mitigation of damages.

(2) *Voluntary assumption of risk.* This defense expresses the idea, congenial to the rights-orientation of corrective justice, that a plaintiff who decides to allow his or her rights to be imperiled cannot complain when the risk materializes. The defense formulates the conditions relating knowledge, appreciation, and acceptance of the risk under which the plaintiff can fairly be said to have determined to allow his or her rights to be imperiled.

(3) *Illegality.* It is sometimes said, on the basis of the maxim *ex turpi causa non oritur actio,* that a plaintiff who was negligently injured while committing an illegal act cannot recover. This defense is inconsistent with corrective justice, because illegality as such is not relevant to the direct interaction of doer and sufferer. For a critique of this defense and a discussion of the very limited circumstances in which it should apply, see Ernest J. Weinrib, "Illegality as a Tort Defence," 26 *University of Toronto Law Review* 28 (1976), the argument of which was largely adopted in Jackson v. Harrison, 138 Comm. Law Rep. 438 (H.C. Aust., per Justice Murphy, 1978), and in Hill v. Hebert, 101 Dom. Law Rep. (4th) 129 (S.C. Can., 1993).

and suffering. Negligence law sets the failure to exercise reasonable care and the causation of injury as the termini of the juridical relationship. Each of these termini makes implicit reference to the other: reasonable care by anticipating the prospect of injury, and injury by being the materialization of an unreasonable risk. Moreover, to preserve the normative correlation of doer and sufferer, the concepts of duty of care and proximate cause link the termini by characterizing the wrongfulness of both doing and suffering in terms of the same risk.

The second sense of construction is interpretive: we construe the concepts of reasonable care, misfeasance, factual causation, duty of care, and proximate cause as components of a single normative sequence. As the products of juristic thinking, the concepts are presented to us by positive law, and they invite us to make sense of them and of their normative dimension. The formalist approach treats these concepts as expressing private law's aspiration to be truly justificatory. Therefore, they must be construed from the perspective of their possible coherence and integration.

In construing them in this way, formalism claims to capture their immanent significance for the negligence relationship. One aspect of this immanence is that coherence here refers to the intrinsic unity of the juridical relationship rather than to any extrinsic goal. A second is that liability is the concrete legal reality embodying corrective justice and Kantian right; this reality thus makes explicit what is presupposed in negligence law as a justificatory enterprise. A third aspect—and perhaps the most pressing for understanding the positive law—is that the concepts, when so construed, are not, as economists and other instrumentalists would have us believe, the proxies for a different discourse. They are rather what the law holds them out to be: the apparatus through which courts consider the entitlement of this particular plaintiff to reparation from this particular defendant.

7

Strict Liability

7.1. Introduction

In this chapter I continue my treatment of the immanence of corrective justice in tort law by focusing on strict liability, often regarded as the great competitor of negligence liability. To view negligence liability as corrective justice, as I did in the preceding chapter, implies the rejection of strict liability. Here I set out the reasons for this rejection and deal with the pockets of strict liability found in the common law. Taken together, the discussions in Chapters 6 and 7 reverse the more standard picture, in which strict liability is thought to be a more plausible manifestation of corrective justice than is negligence law.

To be sure, aligning corrective justice with strict liability has a superficial attraction. Under strict liability *causa*, not *culpa*, is paramount: liability follows from the occurrence of the damage at the defendant's hands, regardless of whether the defendant's behavior was faulty. By focusing on the sheer impact of one person's behavior on another, strict liability links the parties only as doer and sufferer, and cuts off inquiry into distributive considerations that interrupt the immediacy of their relationship. Strict liability thus appears to fit easily within corrective justice. And this fit seems to be corroborated by the presence in the common law of doctrines that hold faultless defendants liable.

My argument that strict liability is nonetheless incompatible with corrective justice divides into two parts. First, I present the theoretical inadequacy of strict liability. To this end, I criticize Richard Epstein's sustained effort to vindicate strict liability as a requirement of justice between the parties.[1] My argument will be that Epstein's position is

---

[1] See Richard A. Epstein, "A Theory of Strict Liability," 2 *Journal of Legal Studies* 151 (1973); Richard A. Epstein, "Defenses and Subsequent Pleas in a System of Strict Liability," 3 *Journal of Legal Studies* 165 (1974); Richard A. Epstein, "Intentional

consistent neither with corrective justice's equality nor with its idea of agency nor with its correlativity of right and duty.

This part of the chapter contains a Kantian reformulation of Oliver Wendell Holmes's masterly survey, more than a century ago, of the competing liability regimes.[2] In seeking to discover "the common ground at the bottom of all liability in tort,"[3] Holmes set out to explain why liability for unintended harm employs the objective standard of negligence rather than either the more expansive idea of strict liability or the more restrictive standard that reflects the actor's subjective moral shortcoming. Holmes rooted his views in utilitarian considerations of the community's expedience, rather than in the immediate normative connection of doer and sufferer. As we shall see, however, his arguments against strict liability and the subjective standard fit readily within Kantian right.

In the second part of the chapter, I go on to consider particular common law doctrines that are often thought to embody strict liability: *respondeat superior*, liability for abnormally dangerous activities, liability for nuisance, and liability for the use of another's property to preserve one's own. The question here is whether corrective justice can be seen as immanent in these well-established doctrines. My argument is that if we have regard for their specific contours, we shall see that these doctrines are either extensions of fault liability or are ways in which the common law regulates the use of property in accordance with corrective justice. Their existence, therefore, poses no challenge to the ideas I have been developing so far.

7.2. Is There a Case for Strict Liability?

Epstein's case for strict liability takes two forms. The first, which can be termed the argument from the hypothetical of self-injury, contends

---

Harms," 4 *Journal of Legal Studies* 391 (1975). For Epstein's more recent thoughts on strict liability, see his article "Causation—In Context: An Afterword," 63 *Chicago-Kent Law Review* 653 (1987).

Because corrective justice refers to a structure of justification reflecting the immediate normative connection of doing and suffering, we can exclude from consideration versions of strict liability based on distributive justice ("strict liability is desirable because it spreads losses most broadly") or efficiency ("strict liability is desirable because, as compared to liability for negligence, it yields an economically superior set of incentives for actors"). Regardless of whether such arguments are correct in their own terms, they have no place in corrective justice, because they are insensitive to the justificatory coherence of the private law relationship.

[2] Oliver Wendell Holmes, *The Common Law*, lecture III (1881).

[3] Id. at 77.

that strict liability follows from the fact that the actor would bear the loss if he or she had also suffered the injury. The second, which can be termed the argument from the concept of property, contends that strict liability is the analytic concomitant of the plaintiff's ownership of what was injured. By setting up a framework within which commonsense notions of causation lead to liability even in the absence of fault, each of these arguments treats strict liability as corrective justice. Yet, as we shall see, they both fail.

7.2.1. The Argument from the Hypothetical of Self-Injury

Epstein raises the hypothetical of self-injury in his analysis of Vincent v. Lake Erie Transportation Co.[4] The issue in that case was whether the plaintiff could recover for damage to his dock after the defendant deliberately kept his boat moored there to protect it from a storm. Epstein's justification for imposing liability is as follows:

Had the Lake Erie Transportation Company owned both the dock and the ship, there could have been no lawsuit as a result of the incident. The Transportation Company, now the sole party involved, would, when faced with the storm, apply some form of cost-benefit analysis in order to decide whether to sacrifice its ship or its dock to the elements. Regardless of the choice made, it would bear the consequences and would have no recourse against anyone else. There is no reason why the company as a defendant in a lawsuit should be able to shift the loss in question because the dock belonged to someone else. The action in tort in effect enables the injured party to require the defendant to treat the loss he has inflicted on another as though it were his own. If the Transportation Company must bear all the costs in those cases in which it damages its own property, then it should bear those costs when it damages the property of another.[5]

Epstein accordingly proposes to determine the liability regime through a thought experiment that unites the interests of the plaintiff and the defendant and holds the defendant liable for whatever costs would be sustained by the amalgamated individual. The argument moves from the actual separateness of plaintiff and defendant, to the identification of the two in a superindividual who bears the costs of self-inflicted

---

[4] Vincent v. Lake Erie Transportation Company, 124 N.W. 221 (Minn. S.C., 1910).
[5] Epstein, "A Theory of Strict Liability," 158.

injuries, and then back again to the actuality of separate existences. In Epstein's view, this procedure yields a justification for holding the defendant liable for damage done to the plaintiff whether negligently or not. The argument for strict liability proceeds "on the assumption that the defendant must bear the costs of those injuries that he inflicts upon others as though they were injuries that he suffered himself."[6]

However, Epstein's argument does not in fact point unambiguously to strict liability. Two other liability rules can be elicited from the amalgamation of the litigants:

A. The defendant should be liable even for harm that results from behavior that does not manifest the defendant's volition. Epstein's premise that "the defendant must bear the costs of those injuries he inflicts upon others as though they were injuries that he suffered himself" allows the argument that just as I would myself bear the costs of whatever injuries I sustained while sleepwalking or in the course of an epileptic seizure, so I should be held liable for any such harms that I inflicted on you. Since Epstein's theory of strict liability accepts the uncontroversial common law doctrine that the defendant cannot be held liable for behavior that does not manifest volition,[7] the hypothetical of self-injury can lead to a liability rule broader even than the one he supports.

B. The losses should lie where they fall. Once the parties are amalgamated, the person suffering the loss has no cause of action, since one cannot sue oneself. On this argument, the consequence of combining the litigants is to preclude tort liability for any losses.

Thus Epstein's hypothetical of self-injury presents a large menu of possible liability regimes, from strict liability (Epstein's preference) to liability even for nonvolitional conduct (possibility A) to the absence of liability (possibility B). It does not, however, make strict liability more plausible than any alternative. Epstein's argument from the hypothetical of self-injury merely announces a conclusion that must be supported on other grounds.

Moreover, possibility B underlines the futility of reducing the two parties to one. Tort law presents the problem of whether the plaintiff or the defendant should bear the loss. Epstein's amalgamation of the two parties merely transforms this problem into one of selecting the feature of the resulting hypothetical situation that is to be regarded as decisive. Is the decisive feature, as Epstein assumes, that the super-

---

[6] Id. at 159.
[7] Id. at 166.

person suffers a *loss* that should remain the actor's loss in the two-party situation? Or is it that the superperson suffers an *irrecoverable* loss that should remain irrecoverable when transposed into the actuality of litigation? Epstein views the harm as something that the defendant would have to bear in the hypothetical situation. But one can equally view it as something for which the plaintiff would not be able to recover. Thus the distinct normative claim of each of the parties survives their fusion into the notional superperson. The thought experiment that unites the parties cannot determine which of them is to bear the loss in the real world.

The root problem with the hypothetical of self-injury is that its notional amalgamation of the litigants is at odds with the irreducibly bipolar nature of corrective justice. As the ordering of the relationship of doer and sufferer, corrective justice necessarily connects two parties, no more and no less. Epstein's transformation of the two-party problem of justice into a one-party loss is a misleading diversion. And as the need to choose between strict liability (Epstein's preference) and no liability (possibility B) indicates, the amalgamation of the litigants does not in the end obviate the necessity of dealing with the irreducible bipolarity of the parties' relationship.[8]

7.2.2. *The Argument from the Concept of Property*

Epstein's second argument is that "the idea of ownership necessarily entails a strict liability standard in all tort cases between strangers."[9] Ownership and property are, for Epstein, omnibus terms that refer to the entire range of one's entitlements to external possessions and personal integrity.[10] Viewing corrective justice noninstrumentally as a regime of rights, Epstein conceives of property as "an external manifestation of the principle of personal autonomy."[11] He contends that strict liability is conceptually implied by the very notion of private

---

[8] Kantian right grounds the irreducible bipolarity of corrective justice in the self-determining agency of the parties, each of whom is a separate bearer of rights. Dissolving the litigants into an amalgamated individual is a move more characteristic of instrumentalist theories than of the Kantian tradition of right. See John Rawls, *A Theory of Justice*, 27 (1972).

[9] Richard A. Epstein, *Takings: Private Property and the Power of Eminent Domain*, 239 (1985). See also Richard A. Epstein, "Causation and Corrective Justice: A Reply to Two Critics," 8 *Journal of Legal Studies* 477, 500 (1979).

[10] Id. at 500.

[11] Richard A. Epstein, "Nuisance Law: Corrective Justice and Its Utilitarian Constraints," 8 *Journal of Legal Studies* 49, 63 (1979).

property because the absence of liability for nonnegligent injury amounts to the taking of a limited property interest.[12] Epstein regards the boundary of what I own as circumscribing the area of my moral space, the domain within which I am entitled to be free of the intrusions of others. Your damaging my Ming vase even without fault, for example, is a penetration of this space that ought to trigger your liability. The idea of property makes the location of the action's effects, not its innocence, decisive for liability. Allowing you to harm what I own is inconsistent with its being my property.

This argument mistakenly supposes that ownership immediately entails the immunity of what is owned from change through someone else's action. That no such immediate entailment obtains is apparent as soon as you accidentally drop my Ming vase. I notice at once that the physical condition of my vase has changed drastically. What was previously a thing of beauty and value is now a worthless scattering of shards. Nothing, however, has affected my ownership as such. What had been my vase has become my shards, and the idea of property is embodied in the shards as surely as it was in the vase.

Epstein's argument from property to liability is missing an intermediate step. With respect to my Ming vase, all we have so far is the conjunction of my owning it and your damaging it. These are merely two separate facts about the vase which in themselves no more entail liability than do any other facts about the vase (its color, its shape, its hardness, and so on). The normative connection between my property and your action is yet to be established. We must still determine what it is about property that morally limits the action of others. The question is not whether you have intruded into my moral space but whether the intrusion is compatible with the idea of moral space that this particular chunk of it, the Ming vase, instantiates.

For corrective justice, Kantian right supplies the applicable idea of moral space. Grounded as it is in the normative dimension of free and purposive agency, Kantian right construes the right of property as the embodiment of the agent's freedom in the external world. To this extent Kantian right coincides with Epstein's notion of property as the external manifestation of the principle of personal autonomy. In governing the interaction of free and purposive agents, Kant's principle of right requires that the action of the defendant be capable of coexisting with the freedom of the plaintiff. As I have noted, this principle reflects the equality of the parties under corrective justice. Liability

---

[12] Epstein, *Takings*, 97–98.

therefore arises when the defendant's act is inconsistent with the very idea of free agency underlying both the defendant's act and the plaintiff's proprietary and other rights.

We thus return to the workings of corrective justice and Kantian right. In the following section I suggest that the ideas of equality under corrective justice and the concept of agency under Kantian right exclude strict liability. In other words, once we fill in the missing step in Epstein's argument, we see that the case for strict liability is not only unsupported but wrong.

7.3. Strict Liability and the Subjective Standard

7.3.1. Equality under Corrective Justice

At common law, negligence is a failure to act in accordance with an objective standard of reasonableness. As Holmes observed, in making negligence the criterion of liability the common law rejects two other possibilities. One is strict liability. The other is that actors be liable on a subjective standard for failing to act as safely as their personal capacities allow. Each of these alternatives embodies apparently plausible normative claims. Strict liability reflects the idea that one should not be allowed to encroach on another's moral space with impunity. The subjective standard reflects the idea that individuals should not be held to a standard they are incapable of meeting.

I propose to argue that neither strict liability nor the subjective standard conforms to corrective justice. My reason for considering them together is that, from the standpoint of corrective justice, the two have parallel defects. Whereas corrective justice treats the litigants as equals, strict liability and the subjective standard center themselves on only one of the parties—the former on the plaintiff, the latter on the defendant.

The inequality in strict liability emerges from the principle that the defendant is to be liable for any penetration of the plaintiff's space. What is decisive for the parties' relationship is the demarcation of the domain within which the law grants the plaintiff immunity from the effects of the actions of others; the activity of the defendant is then restricted to whatever falls outside this sphere. Thus the interests of the plaintiff unilaterally determine the contours of what is supposed to be a bilateral relationship of equals.

That the subjective standard is the mirror image of this inequality is apparent from the defendant's argument in the leading common law case on the point. In Vaughan v. Menlove[13] the defendant had placed his rick of hay close to his neighbor's barn, ignoring warnings that spontaneous combustion in the rick might set the barn afire. When the barn subsequently burned down after fire spread to it from the rick, the defendant's lawyer argued that his client should be absolved because he meant no harm: he was a stupid man, and "he ought not to be responsible for the misfortune of not possessing the highest order of intelligence."[14] The court, however, ruled that his lack of subjective blameworthiness was legally irrelevant: his failure to act as a person of reasonable and ordinary prudence was sufficient for his liability.

The court's rejection of the subjective standard accords with corrective justice. The defendant's argument, with its one-sided attentiveness to subjective moral capacity, is inconsistent with the transactional equality of the parties. The argument sets the boundary between the defendant's right to act and the plaintiff's freedom from the effects of that action at the limits of the defendant's powers of evaluation. This means that a feature personal to the defendant sets the terms upon which the plaintiff must tolerate impingements. Whereas under strict liability something about the plaintiff is decisive in restricting the defendant to the space left over, under the subjective standard the positions are reversed.

In their preoccupation with one or the other of the poles of the relationship, neither strict liability nor the subjective standard treats the parties as equals. Strict liability one-sidedly orients the relationship to the standpoint of the plaintiff; the subjective standard one-sidedly orients the relationship to the standpoint of the defendant. Both liability regimes are inconsistent with corrective justice, and for the same reason.

Corresponding to such inequality is the absence, under both of these liability regimes, of right and correlative duty. Strict liability and the subjective standard are each marked by a converse one-sidedness: strict liability has right without duty, the subjective standard has duty without right.[15]

Because it is triggered solely by the causation of injury, strict liability

---

[13] Vaughan v. Menlove, 132 Eng. Rep. 490 (Comm. Pl., 1837).

[14] Id. at 492.

[15] Another way to put this is that instead of allowing tort law to be an articulated unity of right and duty, strict liability treats duty as the analytic reflex of right, and the subjective standard treats right as the analytic reflex of duty. As noted in section 5.3.3, the notion that either right or duty is the analytic reflex of the other is inconsistent with the transactional equality of corrective justice and with the nature of right and duty under Kantian right.

has right without duty. Strict liability reflects extreme solicitude for the plaintiff's rights. Under strict liability, the plaintiff's person and property are a sacrosanct domain of autonomy, within which the plaintiff is entitled to freedom from interference by anyone else. But strict liability protects the plaintiff's rights without allowing room for an intelligible conception of the defendant's duty. A duty must be operative at the time of the act that the duty is supposed to govern. Under strict liability, however, the actor's duty not to do the harm-causing act need not appear until the moment of injury. Only retro-spectively through the fortuity of harm does it then turn out that the defendant's act was a wrong. Thus under strict liability, the sufferer has a right to be free from the harm, but that right is not correlative to a duty, operative at the moment of action, to abstain from the act that causes the harm.

Under the subjective standard, by contrast, duty is present without right. Actors are under a duty to exercise care in accordance with their personal capacities, and when they fail to do so, those harmed can sue for compensation. The victim's freedom from harm is thus derivative from the actor's capacity to be aware of the harm's likeli-hood. This freedom, however, is not the victim's as of right. A right reflects the self-determining agency of the agent whose right it is. Persons have rights by virtue of being ends in themselves, not deriva-tively from the moral situation of others.[16]

7.3.2. Agency and Liability

The absence of equality under strict liability and the subjective stand-ard reflects the incoherent conception of agency implicit in these lia-bility rules. Because the equality of corrective justice is grounded in the equality of agents under Kantian right, an inequality under correc-tive justice also represents an incoherence regarding the outward exer-cise of one's agency. This incoherence is evident in the judgment concerning the defendant's action that the proponent of the subjective standard or of strict liability is implicitly inviting the court to make.

The incoherent judgment about action implicit in the defendant's

---

[16] In Kantian legal philosophy, the right is the basis for, not the reflex of, the correlative duty; Immanuel Kant, *The Metaphysics of Morals*, 63 [237] (Mary Gregor, trans., 1991). Kant specifically denies that every duty has corresponding juridical rights; some duties may be merely ethical. Id. at 188 [383]. The duty asserted by the defendant in *Vaughan* takes the internal standpoint of one's own abilities as the standard, and is therefore ethical rather than juridical.

plea in Vaughan v. Menlove can be formulated as follows. An action is the actualization of the capacity for purposiveness in the external world. The initial stage of this actualization, in which a person's purposive capacity is directed to a specific purpose, is on the Kantian view completely within the range of the actor's self-determination: I can decide to put my rick of hay here or there. But the exercise of my freedom requires entry into a domain beyond my freedom. In extending my purposive capacity into the external world, I must step into a realm of nature, contingency, and the cross-purposes of others. In placing my rick here, I render it contiguous to my neighbor's barn, and I expose both rick and barn to natural forces through which both may be destroyed.

The defendant's argument that his purity of heart ought to constitute the standard of liability is an argument appropriate to the evaluation of action at the stage of potentiality, when the actor's self-determination has not yet issued into the world beyond him and when an internal standpoint of judgment corresponds to the internal locus of the inchoate action. However, the judgment that he is inviting the court to make about his action is inconsistent with the stage to which the maturation of his purpose had progressed. In pleading that he is too stupid to have taken account of the external effects of his action, the defendant is claiming an entitlement to realize his projects in the world while retaining the exclusively internal standpoint applicable to projects as mere possibilities. He wishes to have the actuality of his projects treated from the standpoint of a now superseded potentiality.

Strict liability similarly fails to respect agency as a normative phenomenon. Oliver Wendell Holmes pointed to this failure when he argued that liability without fault is inconsistent with the well-established doctrine that the defendant is not liable in tort for nonvolitional behavior. The point of this doctrine is to allow an opportunity of choice with reference to the consequence complained of, and "a choice which entails a concealed consequence is as to that consequence no choice."[17] Once injury is divorced from a normatively viable conception of the injurer's agency, Holmes continued, it ranks as a misfortune rather than as a justiciable wrong. "Unless my act is of a nature to threaten others, unless under the circumstances a prudent man would have foreseen the possibility of harm, it is no more justifiable to make me indemnify my neighbor against the consequences, than to make

---

[17] Id. at 94.

me do the same thing if I had fallen upon him in a fit, or to compel me to insure him against lightning."[18]

One can restate Holmes's argument against strict liability in terms of the equal status of the interacting parties as agents. The injurer can be liable only for action that flows from the capacity for purposiveness. Such action characterizes the injurer's status as an agent, and differentiates the injurer from an irresponsible force of nature. Because an agent is a locus of self-determining activity and not merely a passive recipient of effects from other sources, the injurer cannot consistently assert a right to act and yet treat other agents as the merely passive recipients of the act's effects. The injurer's right to act implies the victim's right to complain about the consequences of the act.

And vice versa. Because the standing of the plaintiff is a reflection of the agency that both litigants embody, the complaint cannot demand a judgment on action that renders action illegitimate. Liability implies that what the defendant did was inconsistent with the plaintiff's equal status as an agent. The point of an award of damages is to vindicate the moral dimension of agency by undoing those acts that cannot coexist with the agency of others. An agent, therefore, ought not to be held liable merely for being active.[19]

Strict liability, however, implies that the very production of external effects—an indispensable part of agency—can itself be a violation of the equality of agents. The difficulty with this is that, precisely because action has effects, those effects cannot in themselves constitute the plaintiff's case. Effects are merely the fruition of activity. To ascribe liability to an action, regardless of culpability, for whatever harmful effects it has had simply because they *are* its effects, is to hold the agent liable for being active.

In judging action by its effects, strict liability treats the defendant's agency as an incoherent normative phenomenon. On the one hand, strict liability regards the effect as integral to the defendant's action (otherwise, the defendant would not be held liable); on the other hand, because the effect is not the outcome of culpability, its link to the defendant's action consists solely in its being an effect. Thus the act turns out to be wrongful—and therefore impermissible—because of the effect that completes the action. The agent is conceded a capacity

---

[18] Id. at 96.

[19] In Hegelian terminology, liability can be only the negation of a negation of action, not a negation of action itself; see Georg W. F. Hegel, *Philosophy of Right*, sect. 96–101 (T. M. Knox, trans., 1952).

for purposiveness that, when harm occurs, turns out to have been morally incapable of being exercised and therefore to have been no capacity at all.

This account highlights the parallel between strict liability and the subjective standard. Both liability regimes implicitly treat the defendant's completed action as merely potential. The defendant's argument in Vaughan v. Menlove was that despite the materialization of his projects into effects harmful to the plaintiff, he should be entitled to invoke his moral innocence and thereby to limit his liability to the stage appropriate to an unrealized capacity. The argument for strict liability passes adverse judgment on the harmful effects constitutive of the act's completion and thereby exposes to liability action that has progressed beyond the stage of mere potentiality. The subjective standard confines action to potentiality by ignoring its completion and adopting a standard appropriate to a capacity; strict liability confines action to potentiality by holding the actor liable for the contingencies inherent in the act's completion and thus implying that its completion is beyond the limit of the actor's entitlement. Both standards accordingly presuppose a conception of action that fails to carry the action through from its origination in the actor to the materialization of its effects.[20]

These observations about agency can also be formulated in terms of the Kantian principle of right. That principle, it will be recalled,[21] requires that the freedom of one agent be capable of coexisting with the freedom of another. Both strict liability and the subjective standard are inconsistent with that principle. In strict liability, the protection

---

[20] It might be argued that strict liability does not make action incoherent but rather imposes a cost upon it. Accordingly, some legal commentators have analyzed strict liability as a judicially imposed "activity tax"—this revealing term is taken from James A. Henderson, "Process Constraints in Tort," 67 *Cornell Law Review* 901, at 915 (1982)—that forwards the purpose of compensation or loss-spreading or cheapest-cost avoidance. See, for example, Guido Calabresi and Jon T. Hirschoff, "Toward a Test of Strict Liability in Tort," 81 *Yale Law Journal* 1055 (1972). Since the incidence of a tax can fall on any feature of the actor or any segment or effect of conduct as specified by positive law, the connection between liability and the coherent maturation of action is broken. The language of costs and taxes, however, belongs to distributive justice, not corrective justice. An activity tax would take the interaction outside corrective justice by depriving it of its immediacy, because the relation between the parties would now be mediated by the purpose of the tax. Liability under corrective justice is not a tax but a judgment. The tort plaintiff's status in corrective justice is not that of a lobbyist approaching a taxing authority for a private bounty equal to the tax to be imposed on the defendant. The plaintiff claims, rather, to be the victim of a wrong at the defendant's hand, and therefore to be entitled to have this wrong corrected.

[21] See above, section 4.2.4.

of the plaintiff's right cuts off the defendant's moral power to actualize his or her purposive capacity, so that the vindication of the plaintiff's agency comes at the price of denying the defendant's. Under the subjective standard the converse occurs: the defendant subordinates the plaintiff to the operation of the defendant's moral abilities.[22]

---

[22] Following Vaughan v. Menlove, the common law rejects the use of a subjective standard as the normal baseline of liability. It does, however, consistently with Kantian right, allow subjective factors to exonerate when their presence precludes seeing the plaintiff's injury as a consequence of the defendant's self-determining agency. Consideration of subjective factors takes place principally in four situations:

(1) The clearest example is that the defendant is not liable for conduct that is not a manifestation of the volition—e.g., Slattery v. Haley, [1923] 3 Dom. Law Rep. 156 (Ont. S.C., App. Div.), where the defendant suffered an unanticipated blackout).

(2) Closely related to this example are the cases where an insane delusion prevents the defendant from discharging the duty to act reasonably—e.g., Breunig v. American Family Insurance Co., 173 N.W. 2d 619 (Wisc. S.C., 1970), or the parallel Canadian case, Buckley v. Smith Transport Ltd., [1946] 4 Dom. Law Rep. 721 (Ont. C.A.), which, more clearly than Breunig, brings out the connection between this situation and the cases where there is no manifestation of the volition).

(3) Another example concerns situations in which the physically disabled are liable not for failing to act like persons who have no disability, but only for acting unreasonably in the light of the knowledge they ought to have of their disabilities. The common law's differentiation of physical characteristics from the stupidity of the defendant in Vaughan accords with Kantian right. Kantian right regards agency as a causality of concepts, thereby treating the agent as a thinking will. Intellectual processes are constitutive of the exercise of agency, whereas physical characteristics are part of the context within which, under the conditions of human existence, agency occurs. Accordingly, the characteristics of the agent's physical embodiment are distinguishable from the intellectual processes through which agency operates as a causality of concepts. Moreover, ignoring physical disability would be a denial of the agency of the disabled, since it would make their interaction with others impossible.

(4) In cases involving children, the law must accommodate the development of self-determining agency through a process that starts with the almost complete absence of liability and culminates in the objective standard of the reasonable person. By holding children to the standard of children of like age, intelligence, and experience, the common law uses an incremental standard that reflects this process. See the remarks of Justice Wilson in The Queen v. Hill, [1986] 1 Sup. Ct. Rep. 313, 350 (Can.). The classic analysis of the objective nature of the children's standard is by Justice Kitto in McHale v. Watson, 115 Comm. Law Rep. 199, 213 (H.C. Aust., 1966): "The standard of care being objective, it is no answer for him, any more than it is for an adult, to say that the harm he caused was due to his being abnormally slow-witted, quick-tempered, absent-minded, or inexperienced. But it does not follow that he cannot rely in his defence upon a limitation upon the capacity for foresight or prudence, not as being personal to himself, but as being characteristic of humanity at his stage of development and in that sense normal. By doing so he appeals to a standard of ordinariness, to an objective and not a subjective standard." As Justice Windeyer remarked in his trial judgment, id. at 204, "Childhood is not an idiosyncrasy."

I am grateful to Mayo Moran for discussion of the issues in this footnote.

7.4. Some Problematic Doctrines

So far I have considered the theoretical question of whether the causation of injury is in principle sufficient for liability under corrective justice. In fact, however, the common law does not now—and probably never did[23]—pervasively embody liability based on causation alone. Fault, consisting in either intentional or negligent harm, is the organizing principle of the common law. Liability without fault is confined to a limited number of special situations.

These situations, problematic on any theory, will occupy my attention for the remainder of this chapter. I will look in turn at liability for the torts of one's employees, for abnormally dangerous activities, for private nuisance, and for damage caused while preserving one's property. In view of my account of negligence liability and my criticism of strict liability, can these pockets of what is often regarded as strict liability be understood as instantiating corrective justice? Does the immanence of corrective justice in private law extend even to these special liability rules?

My contention is that these rules conform to corrective justice and do not involve the conception of strict liability that I have been criticizing.[24] The first two—liability for the torts of one's employees and for abnormally dangerous activities—extend the notion of fault by imputing the injurious wrong to larger units, the former to the employer's organization as a whole, the latter to the activity as a whole. The last two—liability for nuisance and for damage caused while preserving one's property—apply corrective justice to the interaction of owners of property; they therefore deal not with the creation of unreasonable risk, but with the role of the use and the value of property in the transactional equality of owners.

---

[23] Percy Winfield, "The Myth of Absolute Liability," 22 *Law Quarterly Review* 37 (1926); S. F. C. Milsom, *The Historical Foundations of the Common Law*, 295–300 (2nd ed., 1981).

[24] I omit consideration of products liability, which in the common law world has been judicially created only in the United States. If products liability is based on instrumentalist considerations of policy, such as those mentioned by Justice Traynor in Escola v. Coca Cola Bottling Co., 150 P. 2d 436 (Calif. S.C., 1944), discussed above in section 2.6.2, it is inconsistent with corrective justice. Some commentators regard products liability as a specialized form of negligence liability. For example, see William C. Powers, Jr., "The Persistence of Fault in Products Liability," 61 *Texas Law Review* 777 (1983), William M. Landes and Richard A. Posner, *The Economic Structure of Tort Law*, 283 (1987).

7.4.1. Respondeat Superior

Under the doctrine of *respondeat superior*, "an employer, though guilty of no fault himself, is liable for the damage done by the fault or negligence of his servant acting in the course of his employment."[25] This doctrine, which makes defendants pay for wrongs they have not committed, has been the subject of much speculation for more than a century.[26] So far as the employer is concerned, the liability can be regarded as strict, because the exercise of reasonable care by the employer to prevent the accident is no defense. Is such liability, which has proven itself to be difficult for any theory, consistent with corrective justice?

Taken in its entirety, *respondeat superior* is not a pure instance of liability without fault. The liability imposed on employers is an adjunct to a tort committed by the employee. Although employers cannot plead their own reasonable care in selecting or supervising the employee, the employee's exercise of reasonable care precludes liability. Thus to the extent that the tort regime governing the employee's acts is one of fault, the employer's liability is liability for fault.[27]

The peculiarity of *respondeat superior* lies in its linking of the suf-

---

[25] Stavely Iron & Chemical Co. v. Jones Ltd., [1956] App. Cas. 627, at 643 (H.L., per Lord Reid).

[26] Recall Holmes's scathing comment in "The History of Agency," 5 *Harvard Law Review* 1, 14 (1882): "I assume common sense is opposed to making one man pay for another man's wrong, unless he has actually brought the wrong to pass according to the ordinary canons of legal responsibility....I therefore assume that common sense is opposed to the fundamental theory of agency."

[27] In the measured words of *Prosser and Keeton on Torts*, 499: "Since B himself has been free from all fault, when he is held liable to C it is in one sense a form of strict liability. In another it is not. The foundation of the action is still negligence, or other fault on the part of A; and all that the law has done is to broaden the liability for that fault by imposing it upon an additional, albeit innocent, defendant." Failure to keep in mind the fault-based nature of *respondeat superior* has led to misconceptions. For instance, it is sometimes said that the employer's liability rests on considerations of loss-spreading. As shown in Chapter 2, these considerations are not consistent with corrective justice; see Izhak Englard, *The Philosophy of Tort Law*, 51–54 (1992). Loss-spreading cannot, however, account for *respondeat superior* in its entirety: if *respondeat superior* were really based on loss-spreading, not only would it preclude the further shifting of the loss to the employee, which was sanctioned in Lister v. Romford Ice and Cold Storage Co. Ltd., [1957] App. Cas. 555 (H.L.), but it would apply even to injuries that were not the result of the employee's fault. Similarly, commentators often point to the closeness of *respondeat superior* and workers' compensation. For example, see Guido Calabresi, "Some Thoughts on Risk Distribution and the Law of Torts," 70 *Yale Law Journal* 499, 543 (1961). In fact, the two differ in this crucial respect: *respondeat superior* presupposes the existence of tortious wrong.

ferer to the employer. Since corrective justice is the normative relationship of sufferer and doer, *respondeat superior* fits into corrective justice only if the employer can, in some sense, be regarded as a doer of the harm. Corrective justice requires us to think that the employee at fault is so closely associated with the employer that responsibility for the former's acts can be imputed to the latter.

To allow this imputation, *respondeat superior* construes (indeed, constructs) the doer as a composite: the-employer-acting-through-the-employee. When the conditions that permit this construction of the doer are present, "the enterprise may be regarded as a unit...Employee's acts sufficiently connected with the enterprise are in effect considered as deeds of the enterprise itself."[28] The oft-cited maxim *qui facit per alium facit per se* ("whoever acts through another acts through himself") encapsulates this construction of the doer.

The main thrust of the doctrines constituting *respondeat superior* is to set out the conditions under which identifying the employee's act with the employer's business is plausible. In holding the employer liable for torts committed by the employee in the course of employment, *respondeat superior* needs two sets of doctrines, the first defining "employee," and the second defining an act done "in the course of employment." At common law, whether one is an employee is determined by the degree of one's integration into the employer's business,[29] and whether the tort occurs in the course of employment depends on the closeness of the connection between the assigned task and the tortious act.[30] Together, the two sets of doctrines flesh out what it means for the employer to act through the employee.

Thus *respondeat superior* is not at odds with the notion of fault that animates corrective justice. Rather, it extends that notion by imput-

---

[28]   Fruit v. Schreiner, 502 P. 2d 133, 141 (Alaska S.C., 1972). These statements occur in an opinion that sees loss distribution as the rationale of *respondeat superior*.

[29]   The traditional test of employment is whether the employer has the right to control the work done by the employee by giving instructions not only as to what, but also as to how, work is to be done. More recently, in the Commonwealth at least, in recognition of the fact that a person can be an integral part of the employer's enterprise without being under the employer's control (a doctor working in a hospital, for instance), the courts have moved to a test that asks whether the supposed employee is, in effect, a cog in the defendant's organizational machinery. For a clear statement, see Lord Denning in Stevenson Jordan and Harrison, Ltd. v. Macdonald and Evans, [1952] 1 Times Law Rep. 101, 111 (C.A.): "[U]nder a contract of service, a man is employed as part of the business, and his work is done as an integral part of the business; whereas, under a contract for services, his work, although done for the business, is not integrated into it but is only accessory to it."

[30]   *Prosser and Keeton on Torts*, 501–507.

ing the injurious wrong to the employer's organization as a whole. Where the faulty actor is sufficiently integrated into the enterprise and where the faulty act is sufficiently close to the assigned task, the law constructs a more inclusive legal persona, the-employer-acting-through-the-employee, to whom responsibility can be ascribed. In the words of a leading judgment, "*[R]espondeat superior*...rests not so much on policy grounds...as in a deeply rooted sentiment that a business enterprise cannot justly disclaim responsibility for accidents that may fairly be said to be characteristic of its activities."[31]

Of course, the-employer-acting-through-the-employee, as well as its Latinized version *qui facit per alium facit per se*, may be regarded as a fiction, because, aside from the law's construction of it, such a composite persona has no empirical existence. However, the law is full of fictions, as well as of concepts that cannot be empirically validated.[32] Although law applies to the empirical world, it is a normative enterprise that constructs its own distinctive reality.[33] The question here is not whether the employer-acting-through-the-employee is a fiction, but whether it brings out the immanent connection between the doctrinal structure of *respondeat superior* and the normative structure of doing and suffering. The maxim *qui facit per alium facit per se* is the common law's invitation to view the employee's tort in a certain light. That light illuminates *respondeat superior* as an instantiation of corrective justice.

7.4.2. Abnormally Dangerous Activities

At common law, a plaintiff injured through the operation of an abnormally dangerous activity can recover without proof of fault.[34] The

---

[31] Ira S. Bushey & Sons, Inc. v. United States, 398 F. 2d 167, 171 (2nd Cir., 1968).

[32] Lon Fuller, *Legal Fictions* (1967).

[33] This view of law is especially appropriate to Kantian right. Kantian moral theory does not depend on the empirical existence even of so basic an aspect of our moral lives as free will, for what empirically exists falls under theoretical rather than practical reason. Free will is something constructed to make sense of our moral experience. Similarly, we need not assume that Kantian right precludes positive law from constructing more capacious bearers of responsibility than the individual whose act was faulty. (If it did, corporate liability as well as vicarious liability would be excluded.) Indeed, a recent article argues (invoking Kant and using *respondeat superior* as an example) that responsibility involves constructing a self through the consequences for which responsibility is ascribed or assumed; see Meir Dan-Cohen, "Responsibility and the Boundaries of the Self," 105 *Harvard Law Review* 959, at 975, 981 (1992).

[34] American Law Institute, *Restatement (Second) of Torts*, sect. 519 (1977); I take liability for wild animals and liability under Rylands v. Fletcher, L.R. 3 H.L. 33 (1868),

liability is strict because the law does not regard the activity that pro-duces the injury as itself wrongful.[35] Yet, as I shall now indicate, this liability is an extension, not a denial, of the fault principle.

Liability for abnormally dangerous activities lies at the juncture of three considerations. First, although sometimes regarded as depending on *causa* not *culpa*,[36] the strictness of the liability consists in limiting rather than eliminating the relevance of culpability.[37] The fact that defendants can exonerate themselves by showing that the injury resulted from acts of God, *vis major*, or acts of third parties shows that culpability is still operative. The basis of these exonerating conditions is that, as in the corrective justice approach to proximate cause in neg-ligence, liability is restricted to injuries that fall within the ambit of the risk.[38] Otherwise, the harm takes place "through no default or breach of duty of the defendants."[39] Thus judgments about culpability are present as judgments about the scope of the risk and the role of the defendant in causing that risk to materialize.

Second, the restriction of the defendant's ability to invoke lack of fault echoes the commonplace of negligence law, that the more risky the defendant's activities, the more diligent the defendant must be to prevent the risk from materializing. Because each increase in the riski-ness of the defendant's conduct brings a corresponding decrease in the court's receptivity to exonerating considerations, there must be some point on this continuum where activity is sufficiently risky that lack of care can be imputed from the very materialization of the risk. Strict liability for abnormally dangerous activities represents the law's judg-ment that such activities are at that point.

Third, the law's ascription of faultlessness applies to the activity as a whole, not to the performance of any particular act within that

---

to be examples of this sort of liability; see Allen M. Linden, "Whatever Happened to Rylands v. Fletcher?" in *Studies in Canadian Tort Law*, 325 (Lewis Klar, ed., 1977).

[35] "The nuisance is not in the reservoir but in the water escaping...[T]he act was lawful, the mischievous consequence is a wrong." Baron Bramwell in Fletcher v. Rylands, 3 H. & C. 774 (Exch., 1865). See also North Western Utilities Ltd. v. London Guarantee and Accident Co. Ltd., [1936] App. Cas. 108, at 118 (P.C., per Lord Wright); Exner v. Sherman Power Con-struction Co., 54 F. 2d 510 (2nd Cir., 1931).

[36] Benning v. Wong, 122 Comm. Law Rep. 249, at 299 (H.C. Aust., 1969).

[37] Frederick Davis, "Strict Liability or Liability Based on Fault? Another Look," 1 *Dayton Law Review* 5, 22–24 (1984); Samuel J. Stoljar, "Concerning Strict Liability," in *Essays on Torts*, 267 (Paul D. Finn, ed., 1989).

[38] Nichols v. Marsland, 2 Ex. D. 1 (1876); Madsen v. East Jordan Irrigation Co., 125 P. 2d 794 (Utah S.C., 1942).

[39] Box v. Jubb, 4 Ex. D. 76, at 79 (1879).

activity. Because the abnormal danger consists in the gravity of the loss rather than in its likelihood (the L rather than the P of the Learned Hand test), the law permits the activity on the assumption that it can be carried out safely. The occurrence of injury indicates that the defendant must have done something inconsistent with that assumption. The lawfulness of the activity, therefore, does not imply that when injury does occur all the defendant's acts within the activity were faultless. The effect of liability "without fault" is only to relieve the plaintiff of the need to locate the specific faulty act.[40]

From these three considerations, the following picture emerges. The singling out of abnormally dangerous activities for a more stringent liability rule carries on the negligence idea that the requisite degree of care is proportionate to the magnitude of the risk. The implication of combining this idea with the possibility of culpability-based defenses is that the law assumes that the injury would not have occurred unless the defendant had failed to live up to the heightened standard that the riskiness of the activity imposes. The strictness of the liability indicates that when injury occurs, unless the defendant can point to a clearly external or idiosyncratic force, fault can be imputed to the activity without the plaintiff's identifying the faulty act.[41]

---

[40] The function of strict liability for abnormally dangerous activities is similar to that of *res ipsa loquitur* for negligent ones. Both doctrines reflect the sentiment that the accident in question would not have happened unless the defendant were negligent, and both doctrines relieve the plaintiff of the need to identify a specific negligent act. As befits its application to more dangerous risks, strict liability has a more drastic effect, because it does not go merely to proof.

[41] The relevance to strict liability of the distinction between engaging in an activity and performing a specific act with due care is now a commonplace of economic analysis, owing to Steven Shavell, "Strict Liability versus Negligence," 9 *Journal of Legal Studies* 1 (1980). The basic idea for economic analysis is that whereas negligence liability governs acts within the activity, strict liability induces the defendant to modulate the level of the activity. For a judicial statement of this, see Judge Posner in Indiana Harbor Belt R.R. v. American Cyanamid Co., 916 F. 2d 1174, 1177 (7th Cir., 1990): "By making the actor strictly liable ... we give him an incentive, missing in a negligence regime, to experiment with methods of preventing accidents that involve not greater exertions of care, assumed to be futile, but instead relocating, changing, or reducing (perhaps to the vanishing point) the activity giving rise to the accident....The greater the risk of an accident ... and the costs of an accident if one occurs ... the more we want the actor to consider the possibility of making accident-reducing activity changes; the stronger, therefore, is the case for strict liability." From the standpoint of corrective justice, this reasoning is unsatisfactory because its one-sided focus on the activity level of the defendant does not give any particular plaintiff a right to sue. Nonetheless, the underlying distinction between an activity and a particular act can be adapted to the needs of a corrective justice account of strict liability for abnormally dangerous activities.

Thus strict liability for abnormally dangerous activities is not at odds with the fault-based liability of corrective justice. Although the activity is not itself wrongful, its extraordinary riskiness carries with it the obligation to be extraordinarily careful. Materialization of the risk is taken as conclusively showing that the defendant did not fulfill that obligation. The occurrence of injury triggers a liability that extends, rather than denies, the fault principle.

7.4.3. Nuisance

Let me now examine whether nuisance liability also can be understood as corrective justice. Historically, nuisance has been closely associated with—and indeed was one of the sources for—strict liability for abnormally dangerous activity. Nonetheless, although in particular circumstances liability may be justified on either basis, nuisance is significantly different because its concern is not the riskiness of the defendant's conduct, but the defendant's interference with the use and enjoyment of the plaintiff's land.

The attention I have paid to negligence might lead one to suspect that because nuisance is not about unreasonable risk creation, it is especially problematic for corrective justice. Two factors, one judicial and the other academic, buttress this suspicion. The first is that because in nuisance law the reasonableness with which defendants carry on their operations is no defense, the cases have sometimes suggested that liability for nuisance is strict.[42] The second is that economic analysis has almost monopolized the great outpouring of recent literature about nuisance.[43] However, nuisance law can readily be understood as actualizing corrective justice.

---

[42] The modern Commonwealth cases make it clear that liability for nuisance is not strict. See Sedleigh-Denfield v. O'Callaghan, [1940] 2 All Eng. Rep. 349, 365 (H.L.); Overseas Tankship (U.K.) Ltd. v. Miller Steamship Co. (Wagon Mound No. 2), [1967] 1 App. Cas. 617, 639 (P.C.). The leading United States textbook also treats nuisance liability as not strict; see *Prosser and Keeton on Torts*, 629–630.

[43] The main contributions to this literature are summarized in Jeff L. Lewin, "*Boomer* and the American Law of Nuisance: Past, Present, and Future," 54 *Albany Law Review* 191, 236–265 (1992). The proliferation of economic analysis is all the more surprising in view of the fact that nuisance law does not regard as a nuisance the causing of the one kind of harm most relevant to an economic approach: a decline in the value of the plaintiff's property. The principal exception to the ignoring of corrective justice is Richard Epstein's article "Nuisance Law: Corrective Justice and Its Utilitarian Constraints," 8 *Journal of Legal Studies* 49 (1979). Although Epstein's article deserves the most serious attention, it is vitiated by two defects characteristic of his understanding of corrective justice. First, because he thinks that, in principle,

In making the use and enjoyment of property a protected interest, nuisance law conforms to Kantian right. Under the Kantian approach, the right to property is the moral concomitant of the operation of self-determining agency under human conditions, because the right to property makes it morally possible for the free will to realize itself in an external sphere.[44] Agency manifests itself in property through the use that the property owner makes of what he or she owns. Thus a property right carries with it an entitlement to the use and enjoyment of what is owned.

Nuisance law regulates conflicts between the owners of real property in accordance with the Kantian principle of right. That principle affirms the equality of doer and sufferer by treating as wrongful an action that cannot coexist with the freedom of other agents. In a nuisance situation, where the interacting agents are owners of real property, the principle of Kantian right vindicates their equal status by insisting that the defendant's use be capable of coexisting with the uses that plaintiffs make of their properties.[45] For were the law to legitimize the defendant's incompatible use, it would preclude the plaintiff from making use of his or her property, and would thereby negate the plaintiff's status as owner. The maxim that encapsulates nuisance law, *sic utere tuo ut alienum non laedas* ("use your own in a way that does not harm another's") reflects the requirement of Kantian right that uses must be compatible.[46]

---

corrective justice is entirely a matter of causal impingement (see above, section 7.2), he identifies the tortiousness of nuisance with physical invasion. This approach leaves unexplained the categorical difference in law between nuisance, which deals with interferences with use and requires damage, and trespass, which deals expressly with physical invasions and does not require damage. Second, because Epstein thinks that corrective justice involves the interaction between two individuals divorced from society, he regards the social indicia of ordinary use as utilitarian in nature. On the social nature of corrective justice, see below, Chapter 8.

[44] See above, section 5.4.

[45] I am indebted to Peter Benson for the suggestion that nuisance law is the expression of Kantian equality for the interaction of property owners.

In what follows, "property" and "ownership" refer not necessarily to the fee simple estate, but to whatever proprietary interest is sufficient to support the plaintiff's action in nuisance. See Cooper v. Crabtree, 20 Ch. D. 589 (1882); Malone v. Laskey, [1907] K.B. 140 (C.A.).

[46] In Bonomi v. Backhouse, 120 Eng. Rep. 643, at 651 (Exch. Ch. 1858), Justice Erle criticizes the maxim as "mere verbiage" because "[a] party may damage the property of another where the law permits; and he may not where the law prohibits: so that the maxim can never be applied until the law is ascertained; and, when it is, the maxim is superfluous." To be sure, the maxim is too indeterminate to function as a rule and needs to be fleshed out by more specific doctrine. But the maxim does usefully

To achieve compatibility of uses, Kantian right follows its usual strategy of seeking legal categories that abstract from the particularity of the interaction. The owner's use is fueled by, and is indeed the external realization of, the owner's particular needs. However, Kantian right requires that that use be viewed not from the standpoint of the particular need it satisfies but from a more general standpoint that brings the parties' different uses under a common standard. Nuisance law is the contextualized articulation of this common standard.

Nuisance law assesses the parties' particular uses in the light of the most general use applicable to their situation. Hence where uses conflict, nuisance law favors the ordinary use over the extraordinary one. An extraordinary use can be regarded as an assertion of particularity that attempts unilaterally to set the terms of the relationship between equals. An ordinary use, in contrast, represents the most general use applicable to the situation. Parties whose uses conform to what is ordinary treat each other equally as owners, because each use allows the other what it takes for itself. Of course the general use itself satisfies a particular need. Nonetheless, it is the generality of the use, not the particularity of the need, that is juridically relevant.

A conspicuous example of the relevance of the ordinary is the plaintiff's right to be free from "inconvenience materially interfering with the ordinary comfort physically of human existence."[47] This formulation, applied on a case by case basis, protects so basic an aspect of use that its denial would amount to a deprivation of the possibility of treating what one owns as property. The idea is that property, as a juridical expression of the agent's freedom, entails the possibility of uses that serve "the ordinary purposes of life."[48] Uses incompatible with the ordinary purposes of life are comparatively particular, and cannot, therefore, represent a generally shared standard. For instance, the pungent smells emanating from a tobacco factory constitute an interference with the neighbors' use of their properties,[49] because it

---

indicate the need for the compatibility of uses. As I shall argue in the following chapter, indeterminacy is not a vice from the standpoint of corrective justice.

[47] This phrase is taken from the oft-quoted statement of Vice-Chancellor Knight Bruce, in Walter v. Selfe, 64 Eng. Rep. 849, 852 (1851): "Ought this inconvenience to be considered in fact as more than fanciful, more than one of mere delicacy and fastidiousness, as an inconvenience materially interfering with the ordinary comfort physically of human existence, not merely according to the elegant or dainty modes and habits of living but according to plain and sober and simple notions among English people?"

[48] Fleming v. Hislop, 11 App. Cas. 686, 691 (H.L., 1886).

[49] Appleby v. Erie Tobacco Co., 22 Ont. Law Rep. 533 (Div. Ct., 1910).

would be inconsistent with property, as something that all property owners had an equal right to use and enjoy, to have a property regime in which everyone always had to tolerate another's unpleasant smells.[50]

However, the plaintiff's right to use property free from material discomforts is subject to several qualifications that themselves reflect the equal status of the parties as owners of property. First, because the defendant's use of property is, despite the plaintiff's discomfort, a manifestation of the defendant's freedom, circumstances must exist in which that use can be carried on without being subject to interruption at the suit of the plaintiff.[51] The law of nuisance permits such uses where they are ordinary in the locality, for then the locality renders the plaintiff's use the more particular one. When the defendant's use conforms to that of the locality, the law regards a claim based on the plaintiff's material discomfort not as a demand for equality with the defendant but as the unilateral assertion of a particular interest.

Similarly, nuisance law disallows claims based on the plaintiff's hypersensitivity because they reflect the less ordinary of the parties' competing uses. Such claims have the same defect that the invocation of a subjective standard has for negligence liability: the particular condition of one party is asserted to be decisive for the bipolar relationship of equals. Moreover, allowing the claims of the hypersensitive would

---

[50] This account draws on the influential paragraph from Hay v. Cohoes Co., 2 N.Y. 159, 160–161 (1849), a case in which the defendant was held liable for damage caused by blasting while excavating a canal: "It is an elementary principle with reference to private rights, that every individual is entitled to the undisturbed possession and lawful enjoyment of his own property. The mode of enjoyment is necessarily limited by the rights of others—otherwise it might be made destructive of their rights altogether. Hence the maxim sic utere tuo, & c. The defendants had the right to dig the canal. The plaintiff had the right to the undisturbed possession of his property. If these rights conflict, the former must yield to the latter, as the more important of the two, since, upon grounds of public policy, it is better that one man should surrender a particular use of his land than that another should be deprived of the beneficial use of his property altogether, which might be the consequence if the privilege of the former should be wholly unrestricted. The case before us illustrates this principle. For if the defendants in excavating their canal, in itself a lawful use of their land, could, in the manner mentioned by the witnesses, demolish the stoop of the plaintiff with impunity, they might, for the same purpose, on the exercise of reasonable care, demolish his house, and thus deprive him of all use of his property."

[51] Sturges v. Bridgman, 11 Ch. D. 852, 865 (C.A., 1879), dealing with the hypothetical that "a man might go—say into the midst of the tanneries of Bermondsey, or into any other locality devoted to a particular trade or manufacture of a noisy or unsavoury character, and, by building a private residence upon a vacant piece of land, put a stop to such trade or manufacture altogether."

be incompatible with the nature of property. Because use would depend on the individual conditions of everyone affected, it would be a contingency rather than an entitlement implicit in property.[52]

Furthermore, the plaintiff cannot complain of the minor discomforts that inevitably accompany ordinary use. Under the conditions of human existence, the use of property cannot be carried on without these. Therefore, the legitimacy of property use implies the legitimacy of the mutually imposed discomforts that are necessary for property use. In such cases, the reciprocity of mutual imposition and tolerance—the idea that one should "give and take, live and let live"[53]—preserves the equality of the interacting property owners.

As with other instances of corrective justice, nuisance liability requires the occurrence of a normative, and not merely a factual, loss. The insufficiency of factual loss is evident in the following two nuisance doctrines.

First, the defendant cannot be held liable for building something up or taking something down, even if the plaintiff is detrimentally affected by the shadow of the new structure or by the exposure resulting from removing the old one.[54] Compared with the situation previous to the defendant's action, the plaintiff has suffered a loss. The defendant, however, has violated no norm. The defendant's action consists merely in the occupation of, or the withdrawal from, the space comprising the property. If the sheer occupation of or withdrawal from space was unlawful, the use of property would be impossible. Liability would entail the contradiction of protecting property uses by making the use of property impermissible.

Second, the temporal precedence of one party's use to another's is irrelevant. It may well be the case that if the second use is allowed to continue, or if its arrival renders the first use comparatively particular and thus exposes it to liability, the owner whose use came first will suffer a factual loss. That, however, does not matter. Nuisance law is concerned with the relative generality, not the sequence, of the two uses. Until there are incompatible uses, no issue of nuisance law arises; and once there are incompatible uses, the issue is which use is the more

---

[52] Rogers v. Elliot, 15 N.E. 768 (Mass. S.J.C., 1888), in disallowing a claim based on a hypersensitive condition, mentions both the parallel with the subjective standard and the uncertainty of property rights.

[53] Bamford v. Turnley, 122 Eng. Rep. 27, 33 (Exch., 1862).

[54] Aldred's Case, 77 Eng. Rep. 816, 821 (K.B., 1610); Fontainebleau Hotel Corp. v. Forty-Five Twenty-Five, Inc., 114 So. 2d 357 (Fla. C.A., 1959); Phipps v. Pears, [1965] 1 Q.B. 76 (C.A.).

general. Being first in time has no bearing on this issue. From the standpoint of corrective justice, preference for the first use would violate the equality between the parties, for it would make the particularity of the first use decisive for what could be done with adjacent properties.[55] Coming second, therefore, cannot in itself be the violation of a transactional norm.

Finally, Kantian right accounts for the injunction that remedies the nuisance.[56] This remedy treats the plaintiff's use as an entitlement, and therefore as something that the plaintiff can insist upon exercising. Since the entitlement can be secured by the cessation of the nuisance, the remedy is to enjoin the defendant's conflicting use. In accordance with Kantian right, no considerations of community advantage or wealth maximization can justify the court's compelling the plaintiff to accept monetary damages in lieu of the exercise of the violated right.

Thus the doctrines I have outlined—what may be called the traditional law of nuisance—can be understood as the expression of corrective justice.[57] In this context, the principle of Kantian right that lies at the heart of corrective justice requires that the parties' uses be capable of coexisting with each other. To fulfill that principle, nuisance law treats as tortious the more particular of the competing uses. Its favoring of ordinary over extraordinary use, its concern for mate-

---

[55] Sturges v. Bridgman, 865: "[I]t would be…unjust, and, from a public point of view, inexpedient, that the use and value of the adjoining land should, for all time and under all circumstances, be restricted and diminished by reason of the continuance of acts incapable of physical interruption, and which the law gives no power to prevent."

[56] Shelfer v. City of London Electric Lighting Co., [1895] 1 Ch. 287 (C.A.). For my purposes, the exception to this rule (damages can be awarded where the injury is small, monetizable, and adequately compensable by money, and where an injunction would be oppressive) is not important. Nor is the general picture affected by the practice of postponing the injunction for a short period to allow the defendant to make an orderly transition to a different mode of operation.

[57] I am, of course, aware that many of these doctrines are controverted. For instance, there are judgments that restrict the right to build up: Prah v. Maretti, 321 N.W. 2d 182 (Wisc. S.C., 1982); T. H. Critelli v. Lincoln Trust and Savings Co., 86 Dom. Law Rep. (3d) 724 (Ont. H.C., 1978); Nor-Video Services v. Ontario Hydro, 84 Dom. Law Rep. (3d) 221 (Ont. H.C.); there are judgments that favor the prior use: Miller v. Jackson, [1977] 3 All Eng. Rep. 338 (C.A.); Spur Industries v. Del Webb Development Co., 494 P. 2d 700 (Ariz. S.C., 1972); and there are judgments that regard damages rather than the injunction as the primary remedy: Boomer v. Atlantic Cement, 257 N.E. 2d 870 (N.Y. C.A., 1970). It is sufficient for my purposes to point to a set of doctrines that are basic to the law of nuisance, that hang together as a coherent set, that are enunciated in what are generally regarded as leading cases, and that can be understood as expressing corrective justice. As noted in section 1.4.2, I do not claim that courts always get it right.

rial discomfort, its reference to the standard of the locality, its disregard of hypersensitive uses and trifling reciprocal interferences, its acceptance of building up, its disregard for temporal priority, its injunctive relief—all these articulate the normative implications of the Kantian idea of property in the interaction of one property owner with another.

7.4.4. Incomplete Privilege regarding the Preservation of Property: Vincent v. Lake Erie

Another possible example of strict liability is the incomplete privilege of using another's property to preserve one's own. The privilege consists in the law's recognition that the use of another's property is lawful, provided that the value of the property preserved exceeds the prospective damage to the property used. However, the privilege is incomplete because the use of another's property carries with it liability for any damage thereby caused.[58] This liability can be regarded as strict because the defendant is obligated to compensate for damage resulting from action that is not considered wrongful.

This doctrine arises from the famous but notoriously problematic case of Vincent v. Lake Erie Transportation Co.[59] In that case a violent storm arose while the defendant's boat was moored at the plaintiff's dock. To prevent the boat from drifting away and being sunk, the crew kept the lines fast, and replaced them as they parted or chafed. Meanwhile the storm constantly threw the boat against the dock, causing it damage. The court held that the defendant's conduct was not wrongful, but rejected the argument that the defendant should therefore not be liable for the damage to the dock. "[T]hose in charge of the vessel deliberately and by their direct efforts held her in such a position that the damage to the dock resulted, and, having thus preserved the ship at the expense of the dock, it seems to us that her owners are responsible to the dock owners to the extent of the injury inflicted."[60]

By holding the defendant liable for a lawful act, the court appears incoherently to divorce the legal response to the harm from the legal

---

[58]   Charles Bohlen, "Incomplete Privilege to Inflict Intentional Invasions of Property and Personality," 39 *Harvard Law Review*, 307 (1926).

[59]   Vincent v. Lake Erie Transportation Co., 124 N.W. 221 (Minn. S.C., 1910). For Epstein's treatment of this case to support his argument for strict liability, see above, section 7.2.1.

[60]   Id. at 222.

assessment of the harmful action. One would think that consistency requires the court either to base liability on the defendant's having committed a trespass to the dock or to absolve the defendant because the conduct is lawful. Instead, the court paradoxically annexes liability to lawful conduct.[61] If the case is correct,[62] the theoretical task set by its seemingly simple facts is extraordinarily complex: one must present mutually coherent justifications both for the lawfulness of using another's property and for the property owner's entitlement to compensation.

For this task, the standard tort analysis is of little help, because it places the privilege and the compensation on different justificatory foundations.[63] The basis ascribed to the privilege is that society maximizes its wealth by preserving the boat at the expense of the dock; the basis ascribed to the compensation is that justice between the parties requires the party who benefits from the act to bear its cost. From the standpoint of Kantian right, this pastiche of heterogeneous considerations, one of which is explicitly utilitarian, is inadequate on its face.

The resolution of the difficulty concerning the defendant's incomplete privilege lies elsewhere. Given the impossibility of construing the defendant's conduct as wrongful, we should not seek to explain the case on tort principles. Instead, we should look to principles that specifically allow for liability in the absence of wrongdoing. These principles are restitutionary.[64]

As shown in my survey of the categories of liability,[65] restitution does not necessarily presuppose wrongdoing by the defendant. Res-

---

[61] I am assuming for purposes of this discussion, as did the majority of the court, that the risk of damage to the dock was not allocated by contract. The privilege would apply even if, as in Ploof v. Putnam, 71 A. 188 (Vt. S.C., 1908), the parties were strangers who had no contractual dealings.

[62] One must keep in mind that *Vincent* is a two to one decision of the Minnesota Supreme Court and that it has been rejected by at least one other common law court; see Munn v. M/V Sir John Crosbie, [1967] 1 Exch. Ct. Rep. 94 (Can.).

[63] Bohlen, "Incomplete Privilege to Inflict Intentional Invasions of Property and Personality."

[64] For the treatment of *Vincent v. Lake Erie* as a problem in restitution, see American Law Institute, *Restatement of Restitution*, sect. 122; Robert A. Keeton, "Conditional Fault in the Law of Torts," 72 *Harvard Law Review*, 401, 410–418 (1959); Daniel Friedmann, "Restitution of Benefits Obtained through the Appropriation of Property or the Commission of a Wrong," 80 *Columbia Law Review*, 514, 540–546 (1970); John P. Finan and John Ritson, "Tortious Necessity: The Privileged Defense," 26 *Akron Law Review* 1 (1992).

[65] See above, section 5.6.3.

titution is the law's response when there is no juristic reason for allowing one person to retain a benefit received at the expense of another.
To be an expression of right under corrective justice, the transfer of
the benefit must be the execution of the benefactor's donative intent.
Otherwise, no matter how faultlessly the benefit was acquired, the
enriched party is not entitled to retain it.

The basis for ordering restitution is that the defendant's use of the
dock is a benefit measurable by reference to the damages that are its
attendant costs. The fact that the use of the dock was justified does not
mean that the defendant should retain the benefit of that use by avoiding its costs. Although lawfully used by the defendant, the dock was
nonetheless the property of the plaintiff. Restitution is required
because the privilege of using the dock was not the free gift of the
dock owner, but was mandated by law. Having benefited, the boat
owner must remove the detrimental effects of that use.[66]

The principal objection to the restitutionary account of the *Vincent*
case is that it does not fully capture the circumstances of liability.[67]
The dock owner's claim should succeed whether the boat was lost or
saved. As it happened, the boat in the *Vincent* case was saved. But if the
boat had been lost, the enrichment targeted by the restitutionary claim
would also have disappeared.

This objection misapprehends the enrichment. The enrichment consisted not in the continued existence of the boat, but in the use of the
dock. Throughout the storm the boat belonged to the boat owner and
was therefore not something that could be the locus of the boat owner's
unjust enrichment. To be sure, the survival of a boat that otherwise
would have sunk was a gain to its owner, but only a factual one. Although
the boat owner would have been poorer had the boat been lost, he realized no normative gain—no excess over what was normatively his by
right—by virtue of the continued existence of what already belonged
to him. In this transaction, only the dock belonged to the plaintiff.
Accordingly, the only basis for the plaintiff's complaint was the defendant's use of his dock, a use which, although lawful, was at the plaintiff's
expense because of the damage the dock thereby suffered.

---

[66] The boat owner's enrichment is similar to that of the hiker who survives a sudden blizzard
by breaking into another person's wilderness cabin and consuming the provisions stored there.
For this example of a justified infringement of rights, see Joel Feinberg, "Voluntary Euthanasia
and the Inalienable Right to Life," 7 *Philosophy and Public Affairs* 93, at 102 (1978). Both in *Vincent* and in the example of the hiker, the plaintiff's loss is the measure of the defendant's gain.

[67] George Palmer, *The Law of Restitution*, vol. 1, 140 (1978).

Of course, the defendant's use was motivated by the desire to save the boat, but the benefit was complete when the use was terminated, regardless of the boat's fate. In this respect the use of the dock is like the use of a service, where the restitutionary claim to the service's value does not depend on the outcome of the larger enterprise that made the service necessary. Just as if I use my resources to save you in a emergency, I can recover the value of the resources regardless of the success of my efforts,[68] so if you use my resources to save yourself or your property, I should be able to recover regardless of the success of your efforts. The enrichment is the same in both cases.

Considered, then, in terms of restitution rather than tort, the liability in the *Vincent* case is consistent with corrective justice. Can the same be said about the boat owner's privilege of using the dock?

At first glance, the answer seems to be "no." The standard justification of the privilege is expressed in utilitarian terms: allowing the dock to be damaged in order to preserve the boat maximizes aggregate wealth and therefore benefits society as a whole. Surely, one might think, this justification, which is inconsistent with corrective justice understood as an expression of Kantian right, is obvious.

Despite its obviousness, however, this justification of the lawfulness of the use of the dock is too broadly formulated. The law does not adopt as a principle the idea that wealth maximization legitimates the use of another's property. Suppose I wish to construct a high-rise building, and you refuse my offers to purchase the right to station a crane on your adjacent property. No matter how much society's aggregate wealth would be increased by my putting the crane on your property and proceeding with the construction, the law denies me the privilege of doing so. If I nonetheless station my crane on your property, the law stamps my conduct as tortious, and you are entitled to an injunction.[69] The crane example shows that it cannot be wealth maximization as such that justifies the defendant's privilege in the *Vincent* case.

---

[68]   Cotnam v. Wisdom, 104 S.W. 164 (Ark. S.C., 1907); Matheson v. Smiley, [1932] 2 Dom. Law Rep. 787 (Man. C.A.). See Friedmann, "Restitution of Benefits Obtained through the Appropriation of Property," 541.

[69]   In Graham v. K. D. Morris and Sons, [1974] Queensland Rep. 1 (S.C.), and in Lewvest v. Scotia Towers, 19 Real Prop. Rep. 192 (Nfld. S.C., 1981), the court granted an injunction to prevent the jib of the defendant's crane from swinging over the plaintiff's property. Contrast Woollerton and Wilson v. Richard Costain, [1970] 1 All Eng. Rep. 483 (Ch.), a decision about which the Court of Appeal reserved its opinion in Charrington v. Simons, [1971] 2 All Eng. Rep. 588, 592. Compare also Townsview Properties v. Sun Construction and Equipment, 42 Dom. Law Rep. (3d) 353 (Ont. H.C., 1973), awarding exemplary damages in an analogous situation.

To account for *Vincent*, the justification for using another's property has to respect the difference between that case and the crane example. In *Vincent* the defendant acts to preserve his property; in the crane example, I act to increase my wealth. Property and wealth stand on entirely different juridical footings. Whereas I have no entitlement to the prospective increase in my wealth, the defendant has a right to the boat. Of course, the boat has value and forms part of its owner's wealth. But private law is interested in that wealth not for its own sake but only to the extent that it is the value of something owned.

From the standpoint of Kantian right, one can make sense of the defendant's privilege in *Vincent* by focusing on the role of property in setting its precise contours. The privilege has two components: that a property owner must allow the use of his or her property to save the property of another, and that the value of the property saved must be greater than the prospective harm to the property used to save it. As I shall indicate, these components, when taken together, actualize the Kantian principle of right, which in this situation requires that the action of one property owner be compatible with the freedom of the other property owner. The privilege reflects the equal status of both parties as property owners because it restricts property to affirm property. To see this, we need to follow through on the implications of use and value as aspects of property.

Use is central to the first component of the privilege, that the owner must allow his or her property to be used to save the property of another, because the dock owner cannot prevent the boat from remaining moored during the storm by relying on his or her generally exclusive right to determine the use of the dock. As seen in the discussion of nuisance, Kantian right regards the owner's use of property as the realization of the owner's free and purposive agency. In determining the use of property, the owner asserts a right that others also have with respect to their property. Since the continued existence of a thing is the condition of all uses of it, the use of one's property implies the conceptually prior right to preserve one's property. However, one cannot assert this right for oneself without conceding it to others. As between property owners, therefore, the right to preserve property ranks ahead of the right to use it. Accordingly, no property owner can assert an exclusive right to determine the use of his or her property without conceding that others have a prior right to preserve their property. Inherent in ownership is the owner's right to preserve the thing owned, even to the extent of using what belongs to another.

Everyone's property is, as it were, encumbered by the servitude of being available for use to preserve someone else's property.[70] Thus in *Vincent* the dock owner's property right in the dock does not preclude the boat owner from using the dock to preserve his boat.[71]

The second component of the privilege, that the value of the boat exceed the prospective damage to the dock, is also intelligible from the standpoint of Kantian right. We need not think that comparing values signals a wealth-maximizing impulse, especially since the restriction of the privilege to the preservation of property is incompatible with such an impulse. Under corrective justice, value is the aspect of property through which commodities are regarded in abstraction from the particularity of their specific attributes or of the specific needs of a given owner. Value allows qualitatively different commodities to be treated as quantitatively comparable objects as they circulate through exchanges.[72] Accordingly, in corrective justice the normative significance of value is entirely dependent on that of property. Because the conception of property in Kantian right is not based on wealth maximization, neither is the conception of value.

The Kantian argument that the boat can lawfully be preserved at the expense of the dock only if the value of the boat exceeds the anticipated damage to the dock goes as follows. First, the boat owner's privilege of using the dock is based on the status of both parties as property owners. Therefore, the boat owner's use of the dock must be consistent with respect for the dock owner's ownership. Second, the ownership of something has significance for others only through the owner's control of the thing's use and through the thing's value. The former requires nonowners to abstain from interfering with the owner's decisions concerning use; the latter requires nonowners to purchase the commodity if they wish to own it. Third, in the *Vincent*

---

[70] These comments about the preservation of property are subject to the discussion about comparative values that is to come. As will become clear, the preservation is only of property that is of greater value than the anticipated damage.

[71] So understood, the privilege observes the distinction, central to Kantian right (see above, section 4.2.4), between nonfeasance and misfeasance. The exigence of the boat owner during the storm imposes no positive duty on the dock owner to assist; rather, the dock owner is under a negative duty to refrain from undoing or interfering with the boat owner's efforts. Thus the privilege reflects a tie between the agent's conduct and what the agent owns, and does not conscript the agency of anyone else.

[72] Hegel, *Philosophy of Right*, sect. 63. See Peter Benson, "Abstract Right and the Possibility of a Nondistributive Conception of Contract: Hegel and Contemporary Contract Theory," 10 *Cardozo Law Review* 1077, 1192–1193 (1989).

case, the party that does not own the dock, far from respecting the owner's control of the use, lawfully commandeers it. Therefore, respect of ownership must consist in respecting the thing's value rather than in the right to control the use. Fourth, value is the medium through which commodities—and thus the owners of these commodities—are related to each other by a quantitative comparison. Given that the dock is not being purchased, the only way for the boat owner to respect the value of the dock is to compare the value of the boat with the value of the anticipated damage to the dock and to act on the basis of this comparison. The upshot is that the use of the dock is lawful only if the value of the boat exceeds the anticipated damage to the dock. Since value is an aspect of property, it would not be an affirmation of property to save the less valuable at the expense of the more valuable.

Notice that despite the reference to value this argument makes no maximizing moves and makes no appeal to the social benefit of preserving property. The argument proceeds from the conception of property in Kantian right and from the idea that one can use another's property to save one's own. It then works out how a comparison of values is the condition under which the boat owner's privilege would be consistent with the conception of property in Kantian right.[73]

This account of the boat owner's privilege and the dock owner's entitlement to compensation resolves the difficulty with which this discussion began. The privilege and the liability in *Vincent*, having both been justified in terms of Kantian right, are no longer in tension. The entire case is informed by the parties' mutual recognition of each other as property owners. The boat owner's privilege of saving the boat at the expense of the dock represents the dock owner's recogni-

---

[73] For another nonutilitarian account of the privilege of using another's property, see Alan Brudner, "A Theory of Necessity," 7 *Oxford Journal of Legal Studies* 339, 365–368 (1987). Brudner confines the privilege to situations where the use of property is necessary for saving life, on the ground that moral agency—and life, which is indispensable to moral agency—are logically prior to property and must therefore be preferred to it in cases of conflict. Id. at 362. On his view Ploof v. Putnam, in which the dock owner set a boat adrift with its occupants in it, was correctly decided, but Vincent v. Lake Erie Transportation Co. was not. Id. at 366. I agree with Brudner's argument that an endangered person has the privilege of using another's property; under Kantian right (see section 5.4) bodily integrity is an innate right and thus prior to the acquired rights of property. But because from the standpoint of property itself preservation is prior to use, I consider *Vincent* to be correct in not confining the privilege to the saving of life. As he does elsewhere (see Chapter 5, note 32), Brudner presumably would reject the idea that corrective justice allows values to be compared.

tion of the status of the boat owner. The restriction of this privilege to situations where the boat is more valuable than the dock represents the boat owner's recognition of the status of the dock owner. And the liability for the damage is the remedial expression of the fact that, although legitimately used by the boat owner, the dock belongs to the dock owner.

7.5. Conclusion

Two conclusions emerge from this discussion of strict liability. First, the theoretical case for basing tort liability on the causation of harm without fault is inconsistent with the equality and correlativity of corrective justice and with the concept of agency that underlies Kantian right. Second, the four problematic doctrines do not exemplify liability based on causation alone. *Respondeat superior* and liability for abnormally dangerous activities can be understood as extending the operation of fault. And nuisance law and the incomplete privilege regarding the preservation of property embody corrective justice in the relationship of one property owner to another.

This and the previous chapter, when taken together, give an account of liability for unintended harms that is based on corrective justice and Kantian right. The two chapters thereby illustrate the relationship between the theory of private law and the operation of private law as a normative practice. The doctrines of negligence liability discussed in the last chapter and the four doctrines discussed in this one make manifest the efforts of the common law to express the dignity of self-determining agency in a coherent tort law.

Of course, private law is more than an ensemble of doctrines. It is also a set of public and authoritative judicial institutions that elaborate and enforce these doctrines in the context of specific controversies. But since institutional function corresponds to doctrinal structure, an understanding of doctrine contributes to the elucidation of the public and authoritative role of judicial institutions. That elucidation is one of the objects of the next chapter.

8

The Autonomy of Private Law

8.1. Introduction

In the preceding chapters I presented a formalist account of the private law relationship. As I noted, formalism concentrates on the linkage of a particular plaintiff to a particular defendant. To explicate this linkage formalism deploys three theoretical notions: First, the notion of form brings together the aspects of character, kind, and unity; when applied to the private law relationship, form reflects the justificatory necessity of coherence. Second, corrective justice, as the form of private law, represents the bipolar structure of doing and suffering. Third, Kantian right normatively grounds corrective justice in free and purposive agency. Understood in the light of these three elements, private law, as illustrated in my discussion of tort liability, treats the doing and suffering of harm as a single normative unit.

In this chapter I complete the circle of exposition by returning to the claim adumbrated at the beginning of this book, that private law is autonomous and nonpolitical. Turning from substance to process, from specific tort doctrines to the role of courts as expositors of juridical reason, I elucidate the public nature of corrective justice when actualized in an operating system of private law. By considering the relationship between the formalist idea of private law and the concrete particularity of the social life that private law governs, I attempt to show how private law can be autonomous without being detached from social reality, and how corrective justice can become public without being political.

Assumptions about the formalist conception of legal autonomy account for much of formalism's current disfavor. Scholars regard formalism as a necropolis of lifeless abstractions that repel meaningful contact with the movement and vitality of social interaction. Formalism is dismissed as "the dogma that legal forms can be understood apart from their social context."[1] The abstractness of formalism is equated with a withdrawal from social and historical situatedness. Formalism is therefore thought to be incapable of comprehending the concrete legal reality that it claims to illuminate.

This view of formalism's separation from the world is matched by a view of its operation on the world. The formalist is alleged to construe legal analysis as the geometrical working out of the logical conclusions of a limited number of axioms. Formalism's procedures are said to be deductive and to ignore the inevitable indeterminacy inherent in the application of legal rules. Such indeterminacy purportedly can be handled only by reference to the political.[2]

These criticisms originate in the conceptual nature of formalism. The formalist's concepts are thought to exist in a world divorced from human activity—they are, in Holmes's famous phrase, "a brooding omnipresence in the sky."[3] Accordingly, they are thought to vindicate the autonomy of law by resolving controversy without sensitivity to the nuances of context or recognition of the inherent indeterminacy of abstract norms.

Now it is true that the formalist account is avowedly and unabashedly conceptual. At the level of positive law, for instance, formalism focuses on the organizing concepts of coherent legal relationships. These concepts are the articulations of a single normative sequence from doing to suffering. In this way formalism funnels the particulars of the private law transaction through a set of conceptual categories.

Conceptualism also pervades the deeper recesses of formalist theory. The distinction between corrective justice and distributive justice is itself a conceptual one. The two forms of justice are the most abstract representations of different unifying structures for juridical relationships. Although manifested in circumstances that are socially and historically conditioned, the forms of justice (and the factors that differentiate them) are not themselves socially and historically conditioned. Their conceptual status guarantees for them a significance that embraces external interaction whenever and wherever it occurs and that, accordingly, transcends particular social and historical contexts.

---

[1] Robert Gordon, "Critical Legal Histories," 36 *Stanford Law Review* 57, 68 (1984).

[2] See, e.g., Duncan Kennedy, "Legal Formality," 2 *Journal of Legal Studies* 351 (1973); Mark Tushnet, "Following the Rules Laid Down: A Critique of Interpretivism and Neutral Principles," 96 *Harvard Law Review* 781 (1983).

[3] Southern Pacific Co. v. Jensen, 244 U.S. 205, 222 (1916).

As the categorically distinct abstractions underlying particular interactions, corrective and distributive justice are stable conceptual substrata that persist through the multifarious juridical relationships that realize them. In other words, the forms of justice are universals.

Kantian right too is replete with conceptualism. The ultimate presupposition of Kantian right is that purposive activity is a causality of concepts. Indispensable to agency so understood is the will's capacity to abstract from any particular purpose and to conform to the universality of its own inherently rational nature. From its point of unity in the abstracting will, Kantian right branches out into a set of juridical concepts. Hence the claim that law is a practical idea of reason that connects various doctrines and institutions to the abstracting free will of purposive beings.

In this chapter I contend that despite the acknowledged presence of conceptualism at every level of the formalist approach, the criticisms leveled at formalism are misguided because they fail to take seriously the immanence of corrective justice. Being immanent, corrective justice cannot be separate from the interactions it is immanent in. And the autonomy of private law consists not in the determinacy of its concepts, but in the self-regulative nature of private law's immanent rationality. To substantiate these contentions, I first consider the meaning of autonomy and the nature of the political domain from which private law prescinds. I then consider the relationship between corrective justice and social interaction, as well as the role of the judge in elucidating the public character of private law. Finally, to repudiate the myth that the formalist's conceptualism commits private law to a deductive moral geometry, I consider the ways in which corrective justice can be said to be both determinate and indeterminate.

8.2. The Significance of Autonomy

8.2.1. Immanence and Autonomy

As I have noted, formalism views private law as the locus of a rationality that works out, in the context of specific controversies, the normative correlativity of doing and suffering. The bipolarity of doing and suffering mirrors the relationship between the two litigants. Being correlative, doing and suffering constitute a single integrated sequence in which the justificatory considerations that bear on the doer necessarily bear on the sufferer as well. Accordingly, the rationality of private law consists in elaborating the categories expressive of corrective justice and Kantian right and in relating those categories to specific transactions.

The claim that private law is autonomous rests on the immanence of this rationality both in private law and in itself. The rationality is immanent in private law because, as a coherent justificatory phenomenon, private law presupposes both the structure of corrective justice and its grounding in Kantian right. The rationality is immanent in itself in a number of related senses. First, its moral force derives not from any ulterior good but from the inherently normative dimension of free and purposive action. Furthermore, the elaboration in private law of this inherent normativeness involves reference not to any external value but to the sheer correlativity of doing and suffering. Finally, because formalism construes the relationship as an intrinsic unity, the relationship as a whole is crucial to the intelligibility and normative significance of any of its parts.

This immanent rationality serves a regulative function for private law. Kantian right sets private law the task of governing the relationship of doer and sufferer in accordance with the principle of right. Similarly, corrective justice is the structure to which private law must conform if it is to be coherent, and it must be coherent if it is truly to be a justificatory enterprise. Thus corrective justice and Kantian right are dynamic principles that regulate the elaboration of private law from within.

The regulative function of corrective justice does not, of course, mandate the pursuit of any particular substantive end or ends. Being concerned merely with the correlativity of doing and suffering, corrective justice is indifferent to such ends. In corrective justice the doer can act for any end, so long as the action is consistent with the equality of the potential sufferer. Hence private law is a domain of prohibitions against misfeasance, rather than of positive commands promoting particular substantive ends against a background of nonfeasance.

If corrective justice does not mandate substantive ends, how is it regulative for private law? The answer is that corrective justice requires only that private law realize its own immanent rationality. Because of the correlativity of active and passive, the relationship of doer and sufferer has latent within it an inwardly articulated schema of justification whose components complement one another. In elaborating this justificatory ensemble into a legal reality, private law regulates and develops itself through the distinctive rationality that renders it the kind of normative ordering it is. For the formalist, the autonomy of private law refers to this process of self-regulation.

8.2.2. Law and Politics

Formalism postulates a morally differentiated world, marked by different kinds of justification. Aristotle's distinction between corrective justice and distributive justice is an expression of this moral differentiation. By reducing the morality of the doer-sufferer relationship to its most abstract representation and then by contrasting the structure of this relationship with that of distributions, Aristotle demonstrated that a categorically different mode of justification applies to private law than to other external relationships. The claim that private law is autonomous merely formulates the distinctive nature of private law justification in a particularly succinct way.

Distinguishing between law and politics is another way of expressing this differentiation. The distinction affirms that considerations germane to law differ in kind from those that apply to other domains of our collective lives. In contrast, the assimilation of law to politics denies the autonomy of private law.

Among lawyers, the question of whether law is distinct from politics manifests itself as a controversy about the courts' role in the development of legal doctrine. Adherents of the distinction see the judge as the guardian and expositor of whatever is nonpolitically legal, the nature of which emerges from a consideration of the limits appropriate to judicial, as opposed to legislative, lawmaking. Those who deny the distinction maintain that judges are policy makers serving an essentially legislative function.

Pointing to the courts' relative lack of institutional competence and democratic accountability, proponents of a distinct judicial role have used various formulations to demarcate legitimate court activity. One formulation anchors the courts' role in the preexisting body of rules, standards, policies, and principles from which courts move by a process of "reasoned elaboration."[4] Another requires the courts to distance themselves from the realm of "current political controversy," so that they are restricted to the area left unclaimed by the political agenda of the day.[5] While purporting to illuminate a crucial difference in principle between the juridical and the political, these formulations

---

[4] Henry M. Hart and Albert M. Sacks, *The Legal Process: Basic Problems in the Making and Application of Law*, 162–168 (tent. ed., 1958).

[5] Robert E. Keeton, *Venturing to Do Justice*, 92 (1969).

make this difference contingent on whatever happens to receive the attention of courts and legislatures, respectively. Whether a court can take account of a particular factor depends on whether that factor (or something from which it can be elaborated) has already ensconced itself in legal doctrine, or on whether it has, or can be expected to, become a matter of political controversy.

For the formalist these considerations are but shadows of the truth. The formalist seeks to connect this controversy about judicial role and the insight on which it is based—that "[t]o call a court 'political' is merely to deny it the character of a court of law"[6]—to the conceptual features of form that characterize and give coherence to juridical relationships. These features refer not to what may have come within the purview of judicial or legislative treatment in a given jurisdiction, but to the elements of structure that together constitute a coherent justificatory ensemble.

The formalist understanding of the juridical, as opposed to the political, centers on the immanence of form in the rationality of interaction. Corrective and distributive justice are not extrinsic impositions on private law transactions and on distributions, respectively. They are, rather, the justificatory structures that inhere in these two kinds of relationship. The forms of justice represent the modes of understanding that pertain to interaction from within; the expression of these forms in a way that remains true to their coherence and normativeness is the province of the juridical. The judge gives voice to the specifically juridical by elaborating and applying elements of positive law that express or specify aspects of these forms of justice. Thus the juridical can be defined as that which is contained within the internal rationality of interaction.

For the formalist, the political, in contrast to the juridical, refers to considerations extrinsic to juridical form. Political considerations owe their normative standing not to the coherence of the legal relationship in which they figure but to some ground outside that relationship. Whereas a juridical aspect depends on the form in which it participates, a political value purports to be independently desirable.[7]

---

[6] Michael Oakeshott, "The Vocabulary of a Modern European State (Concluded)," 23 *Political Studies* 409, 412 (1975).

[7] It is not necessary in this context to formulate a positive conception of the political. My intention is not to offer the rudiments of a political theory, but to give some indication of what the political might mean for purposes of drawing a contrast between law and politics. This contrast requires no more than a negative characterization of politics as what law is not.

8.2.3. The Nonpolitical Nature of Corrective Justice

To show the bearing on private law of so differentiating the juridical and the political, I propose to revisit Aristotle's contrast between corrective and distributive justice.

Distributive justice is the home of the political. In distributive justice the relation between persons is mediated by the criterion that assigns things to them in accordance with a proportional equality. The whole complex of persons, things, and criterion is an expression of a particular mediating purpose that is not immediate to the relationship of person to person but is brought to bear upon them from outside.

In the case of distributions, an external orientation is both possible and required. Distributive justice, it is true, is the internal integration of persons and things according to some criterion, so that the formal adequacy of a given distribution is a matter of integrating the elements constituting distributive justice's distinctive unity. But this internal aspect must be supplemented extrinsically. Although the elements of distributive justice are internally structured, the fixing of a particular distribution involves selection from among many possible different distributions. The juridical aspect of distributive justice goes to the inner coherence of a distribution, not to the choice of one distribution over another. The latter requires a political decision.

Assume, for instance, that one wanted to replace or supplement tort law by introducing a distributive scheme of compensation for personal injuries. A decision must be made as to the class of injuries for which compensation will be paid, the persons who will be burdened by the levies necessary to finance the scheme, the criteria by which recovery will be limited if the need for compensation exceeds the available financing, and so on.[8] Whether one settles in the end on a workers' compensation scheme, a crime-victim compensation program, an automobile insurance system, or a more general accident compensation plan, these are all different distributions, each with its own specific purpose and scope.

Because there are many possible distributions, the justification for any particular distribution is not immanent in distributive justice. For any such particular distribution one can require that its various elements fit with one another, but the notion of internal ordering is not sufficiently powerful to establish the boundaries or the criterion of the

---

[8] For a discussion of the relevant considerations, see Walter J. Blum and Harry Kalven, "Ceilings, Costs, and Compulsion in Auto Compensation Legislation," [1973] *Utah Law Review* 341.

scheme. To be sure, whatever distribution is chosen must live up to the coherence of distributive justice and accordingly it has juridical aspects, expressible through norms of constitutional and administrative law, that are subject to judicial review. Distributive justice, however, understood as the coherent ordering of persons, things, and criterion, cannot single out which of the available distributions is to be preferred. The selection of a particular distribution involves a decision about the desirability of a particular collective goal. The goal is extrinsic to form—and therefore political—because its justification is independent of the requirements of coherent ordering. For distributive justice, the political choice of an extrinsic goal must supplement the immanent rationality of a coherent distributive arrangement.

A particular distribution is the product of political institutions that have the capacity and authority to evaluate the full range of possible distributions, and that are accountable for their choices from among those possibilities. Hence considerations of institutional competence and electoral responsibility figure prominently in discussions of the limits of the legal process.[9] Since no particular distribution can be excluded *ab initio*, competence and accountability must be of a global character. The authorization of some distributions and the rejection of others involve decisions about the interests of all members of the community. Those responsible for these decisions should correspondingly be answerable to all. Judges, who have limited control over their own agendas, who see controversy through the prism of litigation about entitlements, who must funnel the effects of their judgments through litigants, and who are relatively insulated from accountability to the community, are not appropriately situated to select from among possible distributions.

The choice of distributive program is therefore political in its nature. A distribution must distribute something and it must distribute it to particular persons according to a criterion that embodies a particular purpose, to be chosen from the many available purposes. Distributive justice implies that a political authority must define and particularize the scope or criterion of any scheme of distribution. The purpose of a specific distribution is not elaborated from within distributive justice, but must be authoritatively incorporated into the schedule of collective aims. Until then, this distribution is merely one of the inventory of possible distributions.

The situation in corrective justice is categorically different. Correc-

---

[9] See, for example, Hart and Sacks, *The Legal Process*, 398, 662.

tive justice involves no decision as to the selection of a collective purpose. When construing a transaction in accordance with corrective
justice, the adjudicator does not choose one scheme of correction
over another but rather specifies the meaning of corrective justice
with respect to the transaction in question. The contrast with distributive justice is stark. The varieties of distribution are the various ways of
mediating relationships through different distributive purposes, but for
the relationship of doer and sufferer, a single conception of corrective
justice gets worked out in accordance with the transaction's particular
facts and history. Whereas the category of distributive justice encompasses different instantiating distributions from which the distributor
may choose, the category of corrective justice is a single conception
whose meaning is judicially elaborated in the different circumstances
of its application.

The rationality of corrective justice is entirely immanent. Since the
bilateral interaction between the parties is understood as immediate,
no extrinsic purpose intrudes. Of course private law may have political consequences and may result from a political decision to establish
the appropriate institutions of adjudication. However, *qua* realization
of corrective justice, private law has no political aspect. The parties to
a transaction are active and passive with respect to a single harm; the
significance of their interaction lies not in the specification by political authority of a collective external goal but in the normative correlativity of doing and suffering as each party pursues his or her own
goal. Corrective justice is therefore immune to the external purposes
that characterize distributions.

An external purpose is incompatible with corrective justice in at
least two ways. First, corrective justice holds the parties to the equality
inherent in their immediate interaction. An extrinsic purpose, however,
cannot be true to the unmediated relationship of doer and sufferer; it
must favor one of the interacting parties and thereby contradict the
transactional equality of corrective justice. For instance, the analysis of
tort law in terms of possible aims such as compensation or deterrence
is incompatible with the understanding of tort law as the operation of
corrective justice. The first of these aims refers to the plaintiff only, the
second to the defendant only. Yet the form of corrective justice postulates that each party has an equal standing and that neither is subordinate to the other or superfluous to their relationship.

The second way in which external purpose is incompatible with
corrective justice is that the purpose in question cannot necessarily be

limited to the interaction of the two parties to the transaction. The purpose must embrace all those who fall under it; the immediate link between plaintiff and defendant is irrelevant. Since a transaction does not realize a collective goal, there is no necessary reason that the scope of the transaction should be coextensive with the operation of any purpose. Again, take tort law as an example. If the purpose of tort law is considered to be the provision of financial support to those who suffer from personal injuries, the claim of a plaintiff can be no stronger than the claim of any person who is injured even nontortiously and who therefore falls within the ambit of the purpose. Similarly, if one conceives of the purpose of tort law as the deterrence of wrongful behavior, there is no warrant for restricting the deterring sanction to those instances of wrongful behavior that materialize in injury. The purpose as such is indifferent to the bipolar relationship of plaintiff and defendant.

These two incompatibilities between corrective justice and exogenous goals are connected as follows. Corrective justice represents the integrated unity of doer and sufferer. The extrinsic goal disassembles this unity by isolating an aspect that favors one of the litigants and then bending the entire relationship to the promotion of that goal. But once the transaction is decomposed into competing aspects, the preferred goal has a vitality of its own that cannot rationally be confined to the bounds of the transaction's now disintegrated unity. It must float free to cover all the instances that fall under its independent sway.[10]

---

[10] This conceptual dynamic is explained perfectly by Hegel in his critique of empiricism: "In an organic relation to the manifold qualities into which the unity is divided (if they are not simply to be enumerated), one certain determinate aspect must be emphasized in order to reach a unity over this multiplicity; and that determinate aspect must be regarded as the essence of the relation. But the totality of the organic is precisely what cannot be thereby attained, and the remainder of the relation, excluded from the determinate aspect that was selected, falls under the dominion of this aspect which is elevated to be the essence and purpose of the relation. Thus, for example, to explain the relation of marriage, procreation, the holding of goods in common, or something else is proposed [as the determinant] and, from such a determinate aspect, is made prescriptive as the essence of the relation; the whole organic relation is delimited and contaminated. Or, in the case of punishment, one specific aspect is singled out—the criminal's moral reform, or the damage done, or the effect of his punishment on others, or the criminal's own notion of the punishment before he committed the crime, or the necessity of making this notion a reality by carrying out the threat, etc. And then some such single aspect is made the purpose and essence of the whole. The natural consequence is that, since such a specific aspect has no necessary connection with the other specific aspects which can be found and distinguished, there arises an endless struggle to find the necessary bearing and predominance of one over

Thus, unlike distributive justice, corrective justice cannot be oriented toward an extrinsic objective. Corrective justice is the understanding of the relationship of doer and sufferer in terms of itself, through its immanent rationality. The selection of an extrinsic purpose has no place. As the elaboration of corrective justice, private law is purely juridical and completely nonpolitical.

8.3. The Detachment Issue

8.3.1. Immanence and Detachment

In the formalism I have been presenting, the autonomy of private law is justificatory in nature. The notion of autonomy embraces the mutually complementary features that constitute a coherent doer–sufferer relationship, the conformity of legal concepts and justifications to the normativeness presupposed in such a relationship, and the self-regulation of private law in accordance with its immanent form and normative grounding. As I have just noted, this notion of autonomy excludes extrinsic purposes.

Moreover, because private law is a distinctive normative phenomenon, it is also an autonomous body of learning. One comprehends private law by comprehending the mode of justification that animates it from within. This includes taking seriously the discourse through which a sophisticated system of private law aspires to express its rationality. Inasmuch as this rationality is immanent, it can be grasped from within and only from within. Just as one understands mathematics by working through a mathematical problem from the inside, so one understands private law by an effort of mind that penetrates to, and participates in, the structure of thought that private law embodies. Private law, accordingly, is not only self-regulating, but also self-illuminating.

This does not mean that other disciplines are irrelevant to private law. However, private law regards their insights from its own perspective and assimilates them to its own immanently rational purpose.[11] Conclusions of alien disciplines enter private law on its terms, not on theirs.

---

the others; and since inner necessity, non-existent in singularity, is missing, each aspect can perfectly well vindicate its independence of the other." Georg W. F. Hegel, *Natural Law*, 60 (T. M. Knox, trans., 1975).

[11] For example, in awarding damages for long-term injury, tort law must confront the significance of inflation—an exercise that requires recourse to the economist's ex-

Private law is autonomous without being detached from the world or from our cognition of it.[12] As the form of private law, corrective justice does not inhabit a world divorced from the juridical relationships it governs. Corrective justice is a regulative idea, not an ontological entity, much less one having an existence parallel to, but separate from, human interaction. The formalism of corrective justice therefore lies not in its existing somewhere apart from the social world, but in its representing the unifying structure of the doer-sufferer relationship. Because it renders the interaction of doer and sufferer intelligible from within, corrective justice takes the doing and suffering of harm—as well as the conditions under which such interaction occurs—for granted. Accordingly, corrective justice both draws on a social and empirical reality and impresses that reality with the stamp of its regulating form.

Although corrective justice and distributive justice are abstract and general, they admit—indeed depend upon—the particularity of interaction. In this the forms of justice differ from the forms of geometry. The relationship of corrective and distributive justice to the transactions and the distributions that they respectively govern is not that of a triangle in Euclidian geometry to a triangle drawn on the blackboard. Whereas the geometer's triangle is completely intelligible apart from the blackboard representation—indeed, the drawn triangle is always and necessarily a defective version of the idea that it supposedly renders—the forms of justice cannot be understood detached from the particularity of the external interactions that they govern and from the specific regimes of positive law that actualize them.

---

pertise. But this expertise is harnessed to the task of determining the present value of the plaintiff's entitlement under corrective justice. Similarly, personal injury cases require medical testimony about causation, but courts are not tied to medical standards of proof; see, e.g., Farell v. Snell, [1990] 2 Sup. Ct. Rep. 311 (Can.). Cf. the observation of Gunther Teubner that "social science constructs are not only transformed or distorted, but constituted anew, if they are incorporated into legal discourse. They are not imported into the law bearing the label 'made in science,' but are reconstructed within the closed operational network of legal communication." Gunther Teubner, "How the Law Thinks: Toward a Constructivist Epistemology of Law," 23 *Law and Society Review* 727, 749 (1989).

[12] That "the legal system is normatively closed and cognitively open" is a central insight of Niklas Luhmann's "autopoietic" approach. See, e.g., Niklas Luhmann, *A Sociological Theory of Law*, 283 (1985); Niklas Luhmann, "Operational Closure and Structural Coupling: The Differentiation of the Legal System," 13 *Cardozo Law Review* 1419, 1427 (1992). Luhmann's dictum can be taken as expressing the formalist position if one understands the normative (as Luhmann does not) in terms of the coherent justificatory structure immanent in juridical relationships.

The forms of justice do not operate in detachment from society or from history. Their significance as forms is understood through the relationships they inform. These relationships are necessarily social and historical ones. They are social in that they feature the interaction of one person with another and thereby do not construe the person as living isolated on a desert island. They are historical in that they are the products of events in history, since these relationships come into being and fade away in a world of temporality, flux, and change.[13]

8.3.2. Social Context in Kantian Right

One can make a similar objection to formalism—and a similar response—on the basis of its Kantian aspect. According to Kant, free will is the capacity to abstract from any particular object of desire. Action thus conceived presupposes an empty and detached self that can stand back from the context in which it finds itself and reflect upon how it might exercise its capacity to act. Since it is characterized by a capacity for choosing that is prior to whatever it might specifically choose, this self seems to be historically and socially deracinated. Contemporary thinkers have criticized this conception of the self for denying our experience as socially and historically situated beings con-

---

[13] A historicist critic of formalism might object that the formalist's pointing to the historical situatedness of juridical relations is beside the point because the real difficulty is with the historical intelligibility of those relations. The formalist postulates that though the forms govern historically situated relationships, the forms themselves *qua* abstractions are not historically situated. These forms are the historical residue that is exposed to the historicist objection.

It is noteworthy, however, that contemporary critics of formalism do not always press their attacks so far. Even while proclaiming their historicism they may recognize that the indeterminacies that reflect particular historical circumstances are embedded in an ahistorical framework of understanding. For example, Robert Gordon's justly celebrated account of historicism in legal scholarship begins with the statement that "law exists and must *to some extent* always be understood by reference to particular contexts of space and time." Robert Gordon, "Historicism in Legal Scholarship," 90 *Yale Law Journal* 1017 (1981) (emphasis added); see also id., note 1. Gordon appears to regard this statement about law's contextual existence as antithetical to the attempt—which he stigmatizes as "rationalizing the real"—to show that "the law-making and law-applying activities that go on in our society make sense and may be rationally related to some coherent conceptual ordering scheme." Id. at 1018. However, Gordon's qualification of his thesis by the words "to some extent" indicates that he does not believe that law can exhaustively be understood by reference to particular contexts of space and time. His formulation implies that a residue of intelligibility—in his words, "some coherent conceptual ordering scheme"—survives all the particularity of historical context.

stituted in some crucial sense by the communities in which we live and by the forms of life in which we participate. We know that we take our bearings, as one critic has put it, from "a common vocabulary of discourse and a background of implicit practices and understandings."[14] How can law be rooted in an acting self that transcends this vocabulary and these practices and understandings?

At issue in this objection is the nature of the Kantian will's capacity to stand back in reflection from any particular content.[15] However, the charge that free choice is independent of the choosing being's social and historical context misconstrues the Kantian integration of reason and purposive activity. As the principle immanent in free purposive activity, practical reason functions to realize a purpose; thus, in the circumstances of human agency, it operates within a social and historical context. The freedom of self-determination consists not in the absence of context, but only in an absence of determination by any particular context.

Moreover, in the Kantian understanding, practical reason necessarily has an external orientation; its focus cannot be exclusively internal to the actor. Only in ethics, where the actor acts out of duty, does practical reason assume a standpoint internal to the actor. However, as I noted in my account of Kantian right,[16] ethics itself presupposes the priority of external relationships under the concept of right. Practical reason cannot attend to action from an internal standpoint without already having attended to its external standpoint. The abstractly free will requires interaction with others.

The actor of Kantian legal theory is, accordingly, an inherently social being, far removed from the atomism that some have ascribed to liberal thought.[17] This sociability is not a matter of natural affection or of the wishing of another's good; it is based, rather, on the conceptual requirements of the free will. The will is social without being communal: it takes its bearings from the public world without losing in a larger collective will its individualized capacity for detachment.[18]

---

[14] Michael J. Sandel, *Liberalism and the Limits of Justice*, 172–173 (1982).

[15] See Bernard Williams, *Ethics and the Limits of Philosophy*, 68–69 (1985).

[16] See above, section 4.4.

[17] See Charles Taylor, "Political Philosophy," 2 *Philosophy and the Human Sciences*, 185, 187–210 (1985). Kant insists that even the state of nature can be a social condition. See Immanuel Kant, *The Metaphysics of Morals*, 121 [306] (Mary Gregor, trans., 1991); cf. John Rawls, *Political Liberalism*, 278–281 (1993) (discussing the profoundly social nature of human relationships in the Kantian view).

[18] What Kant calls the general will is not a collective will but practical reason operative in the external relations of individual free wills.

Although actors are abstractly equal embodiments of separate wills—egos who do not merge into a single willing organism—they live and move and have their being in a public forum.

8.3.3. The Publicness of Private Law

These remarks about Kantian right indicate that, far from being detached from society, private law under the formalist approach has a public character. Given the concern of corrective justice with the juridical intelligibility of interaction, this is no paradox. What needs to be emphasized, however, is that the public character of private law in no way signifies the presence of what I earlier characterized as political considerations.

Integral to the public character of private law is the role of positive law in linking corrective justice to the social world of doing and suffering. From the standpoint of corrective justice, the task of positive law is to actualize the justificatory structure latent in the relationship of doer and sufferer. A properly functioning positive law connects the particularity of a specific transaction to the generality of corrective justice through an ensemble of doctrines and procedures reflecting the structure of corrective justice. The components of this ensemble are themselves of varying generality—some are concepts, some are principles, some are standards, some are rules, some are mechanisms for very specific fact determination, and so on. In this way positive law gives concrete legal expression to the abstraction of corrective justice.

Moreover, positive law supplies institutions that authoritatively and impartially elaborate the law and relate it to specific instances of interaction. In treating the parties as equals, corrective justice precludes either of them from unilaterally determining the legal consequences of their relationship. Corrective justice thereby requires that disputes be authoritatively resolvable by a third party. Positive law establishes the impartial and disinterested institution—in our culture, the judiciary—that can decide the controversies in a way that is publicly recognized as valid and authoritative.[19]

The role of the judge, or of the jury deliberating under the judge's instructions, is to declare the public meaning of the parties' interaction. The judge operates as "justice ensouled,"[20] spelling out the rationality implicit in the dealings of a given doer and sufferer. In

[19] On the "impartial and disinterested third party," see Alexandre Kojève, Esquisse d'une phénoménologie du droit, 73–94 (1981).

[20] Aristotle, Nicomachean Ethics, 1132a22.

holding the transaction to corrective justice, the court declares the meaning of corrective justice in the context of the specific controversy at hand. Its judgment provides the publicly authoritative specification of how corrective justice manifests itself in a particular set of dealings.

This function is public but not political. In private law cases, the court elucidates the public meaning of the transaction at issue, but it does not orient the juridical relationship to any extrinsic purpose. Indeed, if it imported an extrinsic purpose, the court would no longer be elucidating corrective justice, because corrective justice is unreceptive to all such purposes.

One can, therefore, distinguish two public functions—one political, the other juridical—that formalism ascribes to the positivity of law. The first, restricted to distributive justice and therefore inappropriate to private law, is the selection of the goal to be embodied in a particular distribution and thereby to be authoritatively inscribed into the schedule of the community's collective purposes. This function calls for a political body that is recognized as the locus of collective decision making, that can evaluate the full range of possible distributions, and that is accountable to the community as a whole for the particular one it selects. Thus the setting up of a particular distribution is an act of a politically authoritative body that imbues its determinations with the validity of positive law. The reliance on an extrinsic purpose makes this function political.

The second function, exemplified by corrective justice,[21] is juridical: to interpret a particular transaction in accordance with its immanent form of justice. This function brings in no purpose extrinsic to the form. Rather, it requires the authoritative specification of the form's public meaning in a particular context. Being juridical, the function is entirely within a court's normative competence.

An English case on proximate cause nicely illustrates the distinction between these two functions. In Lamb v. London Borough of Camden,[22] a homeowner sued a municipality for the damage resulting from the negligent repair of a sewer pipe. Contractors employed by the defendant had breached a water main, and the resulting flood caused the plaintiff's house to subside. Because the house was then unsafe, the plaintiff used it only for storage as it awaited repair. While the house remained vacant squatters moved in. Subsequently, they were evicted, and the plaintiff boarded up the house. Nevertheless, squat-

---

[21] I do not mean to imply that this function is absent from distributive justice; see above, section 8.2.3. Its role there, however, is irrelevant to the idea of private law.

[22] Lamb v. London Borough of Camden, [1981] 2 All Eng. Rep. 408 (C.A.).

ters moved in again, and this time damaged the house's interior. The question for the court was whether the municipality was liable for the damage done by the second set of squatters.

This case is typical of situations where several causes, including the actions of third parties, intervene between the plaintiff's damage and the tortfeasor's original negligence.[23] Given the number and variety of possible causes, as well as the varying generality of the possible risk descriptions, courts never have—and doubtless never will—come up with a definitive verbal formula for resolving these disputes. Confronted with this indeterminacy, the members of the court took two different approaches.

Lord Denning declared that the case raised "a question of policy for judges to decide."[24] He thought the decisive consideration was that damage to property, including damage caused by criminal acts, is usually covered by the owner's insurance, and that the insurers whose business it is to cover the risk should not be allowed by subrogation to pass the cost on to the defendant. Through insurance "the risk of loss is spread throughout the community. It does not fall too heavily on one pair of shoulders alone."[25] Lord Denning accordingly ruled against liability.

Lord Justice Watkins came to the same result, but for a different reason. He made no reference to insurance or to loss-spreading; instead, he drew attention to "the very features" of the act or event for which liability was claimed. Among these were the nature of the event, the time and place of its occurrence, the identity and intentions of the perpetrator, and the responsibility for taking measures to avoid the occurrence.[26] Although these features could not be factored into a predetermining test, they inclined Lord Justice Watkins to the conclusion that the squatters' damage was too remote for the defendant's liability.[27]

Both Lord Denning and Lord Justice Watkins exercised their authority to issue public declarations of positive law. There is, however, this fundamental difference between them: Lord Denning's approach was political, whereas Lord Justice Watkins' was juridical. Lord Denning's judgment first required selecting the particular goal

---

[23] See William L. Prosser and Page Keeton, *Prosser and Keeton on the Law of Torts*, sect. 44, at 301–319 (5th ed., 1984).

[24] Lamb v. London Borough of Camden, at 414.

[25] Id.

[26] Id. at 421.

[27] Id.

of loss-spreading from among the various goals (including general deterrence, specific deterrence, and redistribution to the deepest pocket)[28] that his judgment might promote. It then necessitated electing to effect this goal through the homeowner's property insurance, not through the tortfeasor's liability insurance or through the municipality's self-insurance. Loss-spreading, however, like all external goals, is a matter for distributive justice and cannot be coherently achieved within the relationship of doer and sufferer. Nor is its positing the province of a judge, who is neither positioned to canvass the range of possible collective goals nor accountable to the community for the particular goal chosen.

Lord Justice Watkins, in contrast, did not attempt to achieve any goal external to the relationship between the plaintiff and the defendant. His judgment is an exposition of the nature of that relationship through attention to the link between the defendant's wrongdoing and the plaintiff's damage. For him proximate cause is not an occasion for "policy," but a juridical concept under which the court comprehends the nexus between the litigants by tracing the proximity of the wrongful act to the injurious effect. This concept does not exist independently of the interaction it regulates. Nor can the factors relevant to it be listed and weighted in a formula that, when applied to a particular situation, yields a uniquely determinate conclusion. Rather, the meaning he attributes to proximate cause in this case is simply what he regards as the most plausible construal of the relationship between the parties in light of the factors he considers relevant. Lord Justice Watkins' conclusion, reached through deliberation on the relationship between the defendant as doer and the plaintiff as sufferer, constitutes an authoritatively declared meaning of proximate cause for these facts.

In concentrating on the features of the injurious act rather than on a mediating goal, Lord Justice Watkins treats proximate cause as a concept that bears on the parties' relationship as doer and sufferer. Proximate cause so treated is one of the set of concepts through which a delictual interaction is understandable as corrective justice. In the *Lamb* case, Lord Justice Watkins does not use proximate cause as the occasion for a political operation. Rather, he specifies that concept's meaning in the context of the particular transaction he is judging.

To sum up: Corrective justice is not detached from society or from public understandings. Corrective justice is immanent in transactions and not independent of them. In drawing out the significance of cor-

---

[28] Guido Calabresi, *The Costs of Accidents*, 35–129 (1970).

rective justice for particular transactions, positive law functions juridically. Yet the court's role in publicly specifying what corrective justice means in particular cases differs categorically from the political role of selecting an exogenous end.

8.4. The Determinacy Issue

8.4.1. The Indeterminacy of Corrective Justice

This analysis of the *Lamb* case leads directly to the issue of indeterminacy. As Lord Justice Watkins' judgment in the *Lamb* case illustrates, corrective justice does not antecedently determine the uniquely correct result for particular cases. In *Lamb*, Lord Justice Watkins rightly treated proximate cause as a concept linking the doer to the sufferer of harm. His problem was whether the particular harm that the plaintiff suffered and the particular process through which she suffered it could fairly be described as falling within the risk created by the defendant's negligent repair of the sewer pipe. Viewing the problem in this way did not in itself determine its solution.

Such indeterminacy is not unusual in corrective justice. In the chapter on negligence, for instance, I noted that the issues of duty and proximate cause, construed from the standpoint of corrective justice, require a description of the risk that is neither too particular nor too general.[29] Similarly, lack of reasonable care consists in the creation of a certain degree of risk.[30] Clearly, these categories each refer to a qualitative spectrum that does not antecedently determine specific results.

For many contemporary scholars an account of law that admits such indeterminacy cannot construe the law as autonomous. For unless one can follow "the rules laid down"[31] to a determinate conclusion, how can those rules insulate law from politics? And to the extent that law is delegitimized by contamination with politics, indeterminacy cuts against the law's legitimacy.

Whatever its strength in undermining other approaches, the indeterminacy critique is ineffective against formalism. The formalist's assertion of the autonomy of private law depends not on the determinacy of the rules laid down but on the immanence of corrective justice in private law conceived as a justificatory—and thus as a normatively coherent—enterprise. The function of the posited private law

---

[29] See above, section 6.4.3.
[30] See above, section 6.2.
[31] Tushnet, "Following the Rules Laid Down."

is to express corrective justice through its doctrines and institutions, rather than to predetermine every case.

For formalism indeterminacy is merely the inevitable consequence of the relationship between general and particular. Legal formalism arrays the particulars of external interaction under a coherent set of juridical categories, and therefore ultimately under the forms of justice. Formalism thereby illuminates the particular through the general: the particulars are the inexhaustible ways in which persons can externally affect one another, whereas the forms are the general patterns that order these particulars in a juridically coherent way. The difference between the generality of the forms and the particularity of specific interactions is precisely what allows the former to be principles of ordering for the latter. It also prevents the law's treatment of all the possible particulars from being exhaustively specifiable by theory. Such exhaustiveness would mean that the particulars are theoretically as intelligible as the forms through which they are understood, and would render otiose the formalist's invocation of form. The predetermination of a uniquely correct result for every legal controversy, as the critics demand, would make formalism self-stultifying.

Adjudication of the particular in the light of the general is neither deductive nor determinate. A juridical concept does not carry with it instructions that allow it to be applied to any possible set of facts through the operation of deduction.[32] Nor do the facts themselves come pre-attached with labels that classify them according to juridical concepts and that simply have to be consulted to produce a determinate conclusion. Rather, adjudication involves the exercise of an articulated judgment that specifies what the judge considers to be the meaning of the concept in relation to a set of particular facts.[33]

Several aspects of the judge's legal context inform this exercise of judgment. One is the judge's familiarity with the analogous decisions

---

[32] Even if there were instructions, the problem of application to particulars would simply repeat itself for every instruction. As Kant remarks, "General logic contains, and can contain, no rules for judgment....If it is sought to give general instructions how we are to subsume under these rules, that is, to distinguish whether something does or does not come under them, that could only be by means of another rule. This in turn, for the very reason that it is a rule, again demands guidance from judgment." Immanuel Kant, *Critique of Pure Reason*, A133/B172 (Norman Kemp Smith, trans., 1929).

[33] An illuminating and succinct account of adjudication, on which this and the preceding section draw, is Michael Oakeshott, *On Human Conduct*, 133–141 (1975). As Oakeshott observes at 135, "meanings are never deduced or found, but are always attributed or given."

that form a repository of accumulated meanings for the concept in question and that serve as guides and exemplars for judicial decision.[34] Another is the professional training and experience through which jurists are inducted into a culture of reasoning and discussion concerning, among other things, the differences signaled by seemingly small variations in the contours of fact situations. A third is the requirements of judicial role (including knowledge of the legal categories, awareness of the need for systemic coherence, and commitment to professional integrity and independence), which preclude, or at least ought to preclude, the influence of improper and irrelevant considerations. A fourth, as Lord Justice Watkins' reference to "the very features" of the transaction illustrates, is the process of publicly formulating the factors considered significant, of "presenting and representing...those features of the case which *severally co-operate* in favour of the conclusion."[35]

---

[34] Kant, *Critique of Pure Reason*, A134/B173, draws the link between judgment and examples in the following terms: "[A] judge ... may have at command many excellent ... legal ... rules, even to the degree that he may become a profound teacher of them, and yet, nonetheless, may easily stumble in their application. For although admirable in understanding, he may be wanting in natural power of judgment. He may comprehend the universal *in abstracto*, and yet may not be able to distinguish whether a case *in concreto* comes under it. Or the error may be due to his not having received through examples and actual practice, adequate training for this particular act of judgment. Such sharpening of the judgment is the one great benefit of examples.... Examples are the go-kart of judgment." Kant goes on to observe that one of the dangers of examples is that, by weakening our capacity to understand universals, they "accustom us to use rules rather as formulas than as principles." Compare Lord Diplock in Home Office v. Dorset Yacht, [1970] App. Cas. 1004, 1060 (H.L.) (above, section 6.4, note 51).

[35] John Wisdom, "Gods," 75 *Proceedings of the Aristotelian Society*, 185, 193 (1944/45) (emphasis in original). Wisdom's description of casuistic legal argument is pertinent and evocative: "[T]he process of argument is not a *chain* of demonstrative reasoning.... The reasons are like the legs of a chair, not the links of a chain.... [I]t is a matter of the cumulative effect of several independent premises, not the repeated transformation of one or two. And because the premises are severally inconclusive the process of deciding the issue becomes a matter of weighing the cumulative effect of one group of severally inconclusive items against another group of severally inconclusive items.... This encourages the feeling that the issue is one of fact—that it is a matter of guessing from the premises at a further fact, at what is to come. But this is a muddle. *The dispute does not cease to be a priori because it is a matter of the cumulative effect of severally inconclusive premises.* The logic of the dispute is not that of a chain of deductive reasoning as in a mathematical calculation. But nor is it a matter of collecting from severally inconclusive items of information an expectation of something further, as when a doctor from a patient's symptoms guesses at what is wrong, or a detective from many clues guesses the criminal. It has its own sort of logic and its own sort of end—the solution of the question at issue is a decision, a ruling by

To bring general categories to bear on specific instances of interaction, formalism postulates precisely what law supplies: a set of institutional actors whose job it is to exercise a judgment that relates particulars to the relevant concept. Lord Justice Watkins' decision in the *Lamb* case is an example of the exercise of such judgment. Even more particular, because they are without precedential effect and thus limited to a specific transaction, are the judgments produced by juries applying the juridical concepts crystallized in the judges' instructions to them. If undertaken in good faith, these exercises of judgment are as nonpolitical as the concepts that inform them.

The thesis that indeterminacy transforms law into politics denies the possibility of legal judgment. The thesis rests on the assumption that exercises of judgment are necessarily political. This assumption is implausible. The nature of a judgment depends not on the very fact that it is a judgment, but on the issue being judged. If, as I have argued above, corrective justice is nonpolitical, judgments relating corrective justice to the transactions it governs are similarly nonpolitical. The fact that the meaning of a juridical concept needs to be specified through an act of judgment does not entail recourse to extraneous political considerations. However undetermined the judgment, it must still relate to the concept about which it is a judgment.[36]

The reason that the indeterminacy critique does not touch formalism is that the critique takes the positive law as its ultimate point of reference. According to this critique, the distinction between law and politics hinges on the leeways present in "the rules laid down." Politics obtrudes wherever those rules fail to prescribe a unique solution. And the entry of politics undermines the autonomy—and therefore the legitimacy—of law.

Formalism, in contrast, offers a conception of juridical relations that

---

the judge. But it is not an arbitrary decision though the rational connections are neither quite like those in vertical deductions nor like those in inductions that guess at what is to come; and though the decision manifests itself in the application of a name it is no more merely the application of a name than is the pinning on of a medal merely the pinning on of a piece of metal." Wisdom's description, in conjunction with the other aspects listed, reveals the infelicity of referring the exercise of judgment, as Lord Justice Watkins himself does in *Lamb* at 421, to an "instinctive feeling." By suggesting an immediate personal apprehension, the phrase fails to capture the significance of the legal context.

[36] Of course, the indeterminacy of judgment allows judges to escape detection if they use legal discourse as a cover for political decisions. But this problem of professional integrity does not deny—indeed, it presupposes—the possibility of exercising a truly legal judgment.

is prior to positive law and that positive law actualizes. Because the differentiation of the forms of justice is conceptually anterior to their expression in positive law, no criticism of the supposed limitations of positive law can suffice to undermine formalism. Moreover, the normative grounding of corrective justice in Kantian right means that legitimacy depends not on predetermined answers but on the subsumption of positive law under the concept of right. Although the external nature of Kantian right requires positive law to be as certain and predictable as the public significance of language allows, the law's inability to predetermine all cases is merely the consequence of the difference between the particularity of interaction and the generality of concepts and of their representations in language. Under Kantian right, what makes law legitimate is not its determinacy but its embodying of the rational freedom of purposive beings.

8.4.2. The Determinacy of Corrective Justice

There is, however, another sense in which corrective justice, although not excluding the exercise of judgment, is determinate after all. To determine something is to set the boundaries that mark it off from something else. A concept can be determinate even though it does not exhaustively predetermine the particulars under it, if it intelligibly performs the determining function of marking something off from something else.

In this sense, corrective justice determines its particulars through its contrast with distributive justice. Corrective justice demarcates the relationship of doer and sufferer as a unit of coherent justificatory significance. Because form goes to the character, kind, and unity of what it informs, corrective justice determines the character of a private law relationship by representing that relationship as having the justificatory structure that it has and that distinguishes it from distributions. Corrective justice thereby determines the mode of justification to which private law reasoning must conform. Private law being a justificatory enterprise, this determining function is fundamental.

Taken together, corrective justice and its companion form, distributive justice, determine juridical relationships in several ways. First, by setting out differing structures of justification that legal phenomena can express, they mark the boundaries within which coherent justifications subsist. Corrective justice and distributive justice are categorically distinct; as a result, any given juridical relationship must maintain itself within the confines of its appropriate framework. Second, these two forms of justice are schematizations of juridical coherence; their conceptual components demarcate the boundary between the juridical and the political. Third, the forms exhibit the different ways in which relations among persons can be understood as external; thus they demarcate modes of normativeness that are distinguishable from the moral excellences, such as love and virtue, that are internal to the agent. Accordingly, the forms of justice are determinative in that they make salient the boundaries of juridical intelligibility. In light of these forms, juridical relationships cannot be understood as a confusion either of the corrective and the distributive, or of the juridical and the political, or of the external and the internal. Since juridical relationships are formally determinable in these ways, legal phenomena are more than an indeterminate aggregate of particulars.

Determinacy, therefore, can refer both to the particularity of specific rulings and to the general abstractions under which they fall. In accordance with the meanings respectively appropriate to each, the particular and the general can be said to be mutually codetermining. A form of justice determines particular rulings by regulating them in accordance with its conceptual structure. Conversely, a particular ruling enunciated in positive law determines its form of justice by presenting the authoritative public manifestation of that form in the context of a specific interaction. The form marks out the conceptual specificity of the particular ruling, and the ruling marks out the contextual specificity of the form. Thus the form and the ruling are locked in an embrace of reciprocal determination.

Determinacy therefore relates in different ways to the generality of the forms and to the particularity of external interaction. Formalism comprehends both these ways in their interrelation. The forms of justice are both determinate and indeterminate. They are indeterminate in that they do not predetermine exhaustively the particular results they govern. They are determinate in that they establish the bounds of coherence for the particulars that fall under them. In determining the character, kind, and unity of juridical relationships, the forms of justice determine all that they need to, or can, determine as forms.

8.5. The Variability of Law

As orderings immanent in interaction, the forms of justice necessarily make contact with a social and historical world because they must be specified for particular cases. These specifications depend on the public meanings of such a world. Within the bounds of character, kind, and unity, the forms are constituted by the shared understandings of society, and the forms' particular public shapes are authoritatively declared by the functionaries of positive law. Thus although the forms as such, because they are conceptually distinguishable, have a historical universality, their manifestations in a legal system are relative to a set of public meanings that obtain at a given time and place. In its governance of juridical relationships, formalism is universality with a variable content.

This variability indicates that formalism does not move deductively from theory to the concrete arrangements of positive law in a given jurisdiction. One reason for the inapplicability of deductive reasoning is that formalism does not itself choose between distributive and corrective arrangements; it requires only that whatever mode of ordering a jurisdiction adopts conform to the rationality immanent in that mode of ordering. Deductive reasoning cannot leapfrog over the choice between these structures or over the selection of particular distributive arrangements.

Moreover, a deduction of the particularities of private law is unavailable even within corrective justice. Deduction is a logical operation, and logical operations cannot determine exercises of judgment within a context of public meanings. The critical dimension of formalism lies in determining not whether a given doctrine of private law can be deduced from corrective justice, but whether the doctrine is adequate to corrective justice. The test of adequacy is satisfied when the justification for a doctrine conforms to the structure of corrective justice. More than one doctrine concerning a given point may satisfy this test.[37]

Almost since the dawn of jurisprudence, formalists have recognized such variability. In his famous discussion of the relationship between what is just by nature and what is just by convention, Aristotle commented that "among us [as contrasted with what holds for gods] there are things which, though naturally just, are nevertheless change-

---

[37] Accordingly, the common law doctrine of *respondeat superior* and the German doctrine that the employer is liable only for personal fault—see Konrad Zweigert and Hein Kötz, *Introduction to Comparative Law*, 670–676 (Tony Weir, trans., 2nd rev. ed., 1992)—may both be adequate to the form of corrective justice. Or to take an example that may appear trivial to us but was much discussed in the system in which it arose: if the defendant tortiously kills the plaintiff's animal, is the defendant obligated to pay damages in the value of the animal or does the plaintiff retain the carcass as partial payment? See *Babylonian Talmud, Baba Kamma*, 10b–11a (I. Epstein, ed., 1935). Both alternatives recognize the role of tort damages in corrective justice.

able."[38] This sentence can now be interpreted as including the following understanding: The intelligibility of juridical relationships is not merely a conventional opinion, because corrective justice and distributive justice are the timeless justificatory structures through which the coherence of such relationships can be conceived. The way in which the forms of justice are realized in legal systems is, however, subject to the variations inherent in their public interpretation and application. Thus the forms of justice coexist with indeterminacies whose resolution can vary from time to time and from culture to culture.

Formalism, as I have presented it, is neither positivist nor historicist. Legal positivism and historicism construe the law's positivity and its history respectively as the exhaustive modes of understanding law. Formalism is not positivist, because corrective justice and distributive justice are conceptual categories that inform the content of law without themselves being posited by legal authority. It is not historicist because the forms of justice are not valid for a particular social and temporal context. But although formalism transcends positivity and history, it is not detached from them. Because formalism inquires into the immanent rationality of juridical relations, the object of its attention is the historical domain of social interaction and the public announcements by positive law of the terms of that interaction. In comprehending the social and historical arrangements established by positive law as the possible expressions of a coherent order, formalism does not ignore the history, positivity, and social reality of law. Rather, formalism claims to render them juridically intelligible.

8.6. Conclusion

Over the last generation legal scholarship has both lengthened its reach and shortened its ambition. The lengthening of reach is evident in the appeal beyond law to other disciplines and modes of thinking: economics, literature, history, and so on. The shortening of ambition is evident in the assumption that law is not systematically intelligible in its own terms. The lengthening of reach and the shortening of ambition are parts of the same phenomenon: the comparative richness of interdisciplinary work reflects the supposed poverty of the law's own resources.

---

[38] Aristotle, *Nicomachean Ethics*, 1134b29.

Nowhere is this more evident than in scholarship about private law. For the last several decades economic analysis has dominated the theory of private law. As for the adversaries of economic analysis, their opposition to its systematizing pretensions led them to more skeptical or more fragmented interpretations of private law. Few attempted to arrest what one acute observer called the "declining expectations" of private law theory.[39]

In contrast, formalism attempts to retrieve the classical understanding of law as "an immanent moral rationality."[40] This conception of law has a long history, beginning with Aristotle's sketch of the justificatory structures for legal relationships, and continuing through the accounts of normativeness found in the great natural right philosophies of Kant and Hegel. Seen as the actualization of corrective justice, private law is neither an enterprise in social engineering nor an occasion for moral skepticism, but an elaborate exploration of what one person can demand from another as of right. By attending to the distinctive morality that marks coherent legal relationships, formalism asserts the autonomy of private law both as a field of learning and as a justificatory enterprise. Formalism thus claims to be the theory implicit in private law as it elaborates itself from within.

Half a century ago, in an unjustly neglected article, Michael Oakeshott observed the chaos of what was then passing for jurisprudential explanation.[41] After tracing the competing claims of historical, economic, and other jurisprudences, he pointed out that a truly philosophical jurisprudence could not simply accept the conclusions of special disciplines. It must start instead with what we already know about law and work back through the presuppositions of this knowledge to a clearer and fuller knowledge. This, he wrote, was the procedure followed by all great philosophers, including the giants of natural law and natural right. Jurisprudence, Oakeshott concluded, must regain a sense of this tradition of inquiry. Unfortunately, the passage of time has not appreciably diminished the pertinence of his observations.

The importance of recalling the classical conception of private law goes beyond the mere critique of current academic fashion. Despite

---

[39] George P. Fletcher, "Fairness and Utility in Tort Theory," 85 *Harvard Law Review* 537 (1972).

[40] Roberto Unger, "The Critical Legal Studies Movement," 96 *Harvard Law Review* 561, 571 (1983).

[41] Michael Oakeshott, "The Concept of a Philosophical Jurisprudence," [1938] *Politica* 203 (part I), 345 (part II).

the rise of the administrative state, private law remains a pervasive medium of social interaction. It also provides the most extensive and most durable manifestation of public reason in our social life. We must therefore ask: Can we understand private law as an expression of self-determining freedom? Can the elaboration of private law be a coherent justificatory enterprise? Can private law be anything other than a set of political operations? In short, can private law exemplify the autonomy that we associate with the rule of law? These, ultimately, have been the questions animating this exploration of the idea of private law.

Index

Administrative law, 211
Agency: normativeness intrinsic to, 84, 92–94; free and purposive activity, 89–92; rights as juridical manifestations of freedom inherent in, 122, 128–129, 176–177, 191; relationship to particularity, 127–129, 131; and risk creation, 151–152, 166; incoherent conception of implicit in strict liability and subjective standard of care, 179–183. *See also* Free will; Practical reason
Andrews, Justice William, 159–164
Aquinas, Saint Thomas, 6, 80
Aristotle, 6, 19, 55, 56–83, 84, 85, 97, 98, 114, 117, 126, 140, 208, 228, 230. *See also* Corrective justice; Distributive justice; Ethics; Justice

Bailment, 107
Benson, Peter, 51–53
Bolton v. Stone, 149, 150

Cardozo, Justice Benjamin, 134, 159, 160, 164, 165
Causation of injury: central to private law, 2, 10, 11–12, 28; independent of loss-spreading, 37–38, 39; in economic analysis, 47–48; in negligence liability, 153–167, 169, 170; in strict liability, 171, 173, 178, 184, 203
Character: private law's salient features as indicia of, 9–11; as aspect of form, 22, 26–28; of juridical relationships, 28; embraced by corrective justice, 75–76
Classifications, 68–70

Coherence: private law strives toward, 12, 13, 19, 30, 42, 146; and internal intelligibility of private law, 12–14, 42–45; and misconceptions about formalism, 30–32; applies to relationship's justificatory considerations, 32–33; different from consistency, 33; requires intrinsic not accidental unity, 33–36; absent from functionalist justifications for tort liability, 36–38, 39–42, 45–46; as justificatory necessity, 38–42; and positive law, 42–43; keeps private law separate from politics, 45–46; and the forms of justice, 72–75, 226–227; and idea of reason, 85–87, 87–88, 100. *See also* Unity
Compensation. *See* Tort law
Constitutional law, 211
Contract: and morality of promising, 50–53, 124n; irrelevance of private intention, 104; as embodiment of agent's external freedom, 128–129; and corrective justice, 136–140; expectation damages, 136, 139–140; offer and acceptance, 137; consideration, 137–138; unconscionability, 138–139
Corrective justice: as the form of the private law relationship, 19, 56, 75–76, 114; grounded in Kantian right, 19, 58, 81–83, 84, 97–98, 114, 126, 176–177, 179, 204; distinguished from distributive justice, 57, 61–63, 70, 75, 77–80, 210–214; formalism of, 57, 66–68; lacuna in Aristotle's account of, 57–58, 76–80; implicit in transactions, 61–62, 209; features

Corrective justice (*continued*)
quantitative equality, 62–63, 119n;
bipolarity of, 63–66; and the logic of
correlativity, 78; role in Kantian
progression to public law, 85, 104;
concerned with the correlativity of
normative, not factual, gain and loss,
115–120, 194; conditions of
correlativity within, 120–123, 142;
right and duty as the applicable
correlatives, 122–126; relationship
between the normative and the
factual in, 126–129; and tort law,
134–136, 145–203; and contract law,
136–140; and the law of restitution,
140–142; regulates private law from
within, 206–208; as juridical not
political, 211–214, 219; immanent
rationality of, 212; public character
of, 218–222; determinacy and
indeterminacy in, 222–227; allows for
the variability of legal ordering,
227–229. *See also* Justice
Courts. *See* Judge
Criminal law, 104

Denning, Lord, 220, 221
Deterrence, 108. *See also* Tort law
Distributive justice: distinguished from
corrective justice, 57, 61–62, 70–73,
77–80, 210–214; implicit in
distributions, 61–62; features equality
of ratios, 62; tort goals of loss-
spreading and compensation as
instances of, 74–75, 121; has both
political and juridical aspects,
210–212, 219. *See also* Justice

Economic analysis: instance of
functionalism, 3–4; inadequacy of,
46–48, 147; deals with welfare, not
right, 130, 132–133; dominance of,
190, 230
Epstein, Richard, 171, 172–177
Equality: in corrective justice, 19,
57–58, 62–63, 63–66, 76–83, 84, 114,
126, 176, 179, 204; in Aristotle's
account of justice in holdings, 60–61;

in Aristotle's account of distributive
justice, 62
Ethics: Aristotle's account of, 58;
distinguished from law in Kantian
philosophy, 94, 99; conceptual
priority of law to, 110–113, 217
Excuses, 53–55, 109

Fletcher, George, 53–55, 112–113, 230
Form: and intelligibility, 25–26;
character, kind, and unity as aspects
of, 26–28; applied to juridical
relationships, 28–30; corrective justice
as, 75–76; and determinacy,
226–227
Formalism: centrality of form to, 18,
25–26; as internal understanding of
law, 22–24, 146–147; current
academic attitude to, 22, 204–206;
distinction between law and politics
in, 22, 23, 25, 45–46, 208–214,
218–222; Unger's critique of, 23;
treats law as immanent moral
rationality, 23–24, 206–208, 230; as
integrative notion, 24; method of,
24–25; role of coherence in,
29–32; distinguished from
essentialism, 30–31; distinguished
from a semantic project, 31–32;
conception of coherence in, 32–36;
importance of coherence for, 38–45;
contrasted with other contemporary
theories, 46–55; of Aristotle's account
of justice, 57, 66–68; of Kantian right,
86, 91–92, 97, 111; of procedure in
identifying norms of correlativity,
120; and the concepts of negligence
liability, 146–147, 170; conceptualism
of, 205–206, 218–222; not
undermined by indeterminacy,
222–227; recognizes the
variability of legal ordering,
227–229; not deductive, 228
Fortuity of injury, 20, 145, 155–156
Free will: and purposive activity, 81–90;
and causality of concepts, 89, 90, 91,
93, 94, 98, 99, 106, 112, 206;
distinguished from animal will, 90,

96; free choice and practical reason as aspects of, 90–92; as ultimate precondition of legality, 92; and normativeness, 92–94; and concept of right, 95–100; as first stage in progression to public law, 100–109; relation to particularity of, 127–132; absence of prospect of injury not manifestation of, 157; operates within a particular social and historical context, 216–218. *See also* Agency; Practical reason

Fried, Charles, 50–53, 55, 112–113, 124n

Functionalism, 3–8, 11–12, 16

Grotius, Hugo, 6

Hand, Justice Learned, 148, 149, 150, 189

Hegel, Georg W. F., 6, 230

Historicism, 216n, 229

Holmes, Oliver Wendell, 3, 172, 177, 180–181, 205

Idea of reason. *See* Kantian right

Indeterminacy, 166–167, 222–226

Instrumentalism and noninstrumentalism, 48–55, 85, 110, 112–113, 132, 170, 175

Interdisciplinary approaches to law, 6–7, 17–18, 214, 229–230

Internal account of private law: contrasted to functionalism, 8, 11–12, 16, 170; understands legal concepts in their own terms, 8, 146–147, 170; characteristics of, 11–14; and private law's self-understanding nature, 14–16; critical dimension of, 16, 228; three theses constituting, 18–19; relationship of law and theory in, 19–21, 146, 170; formalism as, 22–25

Judge: functionalist and internal understandings of adjudication contrasted, 12; as agent of rectification in corrective justice, 65, 117; role under Kantian right, 84, 105–107, 132, 144; controversy about

role of, 208–209; role under distributive justice, 210–211; role under corrective justice, 218–222; exercise of judgment, 223–226, 228

Juridical: meaning of, 24; distinguished from the political, 208–209, 218–222

Juries, 225

Justice, Aristotle's account of: justice as directed toward another, 58; justice as coextensive with virtue, 58–59; justice in holdings, 59–61; corrective and distributive justice as forms of justice, 61–63; Kelsen's critique of, 66–68, 75; neither form valued over the other, 67, 228; nature of classification in, 68; conceptualism of, 69–70, 205–206; juridical significance of, 72–75; relevance of social and historical context, 214–216; variability of manifestations of justice, 227–229. *See also* Corrective justice; Distributive justice

Justificatory nature of law, 12, 32, 39, 42, 106

Kant, Immanuel, 6, 51, 58, 81–83, 84–113, 230

Kantian right: as ground of corrective justice, 19, 58, 81–83, 84, 97–98, 114, 126, 176–177, 179, 204; as idea of reason, 84–100, 122, 206; prior to the good, 87, 109–113; normativeness of, 92–94; distinguished from ethics, 94, 96, 99; relation to free will, 94–100; defined, 95; universal principle of, 98, 99, 101, 102, 104, 109, 112, 129, 131, 132, 152, 176, 182, 191, 200, 207; movement from free will to public law, 100–109; operates within a particular social and historical context, 104, 216–218; role of judge under, 105–107, 132; rights as juridical manifestations of free will, 122, 128–129, 176–177, 179; correlativity of rights and duties, 122–123, 133–144, 162, 163, 172, 178–179, 205; articulated unity of right and duty in,

Kantian right (*continued*)
123–126; role of particularity in,
126–129, 131; right to bodily
integrity, 128, 157; rights to external
objects of the will, 128–129; makes
freedom, not welfare, primary,
130–133; conceptualism of, 206;
regulates private law from within,
206–208; legitimacy not dependent
on determinacy, 226
Kelsen, Hans, 66–68, 75
Kind: as aspect of form, 22, 26–28; of
juridical relationships, 28–29; as
embraced by corrective justice, 75

Lamb v. London Borough of Camden,
219–222, 225
Langdell, Christopher Columbus, 3
Law and politics: functionalist
assumptions about, 7–8; formalism's
distinction between, 22, 23, 25,
45–46, 208–214; role of coherence in
distinction between, 45–46; claim
inseparability of, as denying the
possibility of legal
judgment, 225

Negligence liability: challenge to
corrective justice, 20, 145; concepts
constitute a single normative
sequence, 145–147, 168–170; standard
of reasonable care, 147, 178; American
approach to reasonable care, 147–148;
English and Commonwealth
approach to reasonable care, 147–152;
misfeasance, 153–154; factual cause,
154–158; probabilistic causation,
156–158; duty of care and proximate
cause, 158–166; negligence resulting
in unforeseeable injury, 158–164;
indeterminacy of duty of care and
proximate cause, 166–167, 219–222;
defenses, 169n; subjective factors in
standard of care, 183n
Nonfeasance and misfeasance: centrality
of distinction between, 10; distinction
grounded in Kantian right, 97; in
negligence liability, 153–154

Oakeshott, Michael, 230

Palsgraf v. Long Island Railroad,
159–164, 165
Parties, relationship of: directness of, as
central feature of private law, 1, 10–11,
28, 43–44; failure of contemporary
theory to account for, 11, 47, 49,
50–55; basic unit of formalist analysis,
24–25; role of coherence in, 32–36,
42; corrective justice account of,
56–57, 63–66, 73, 74, 75–76; governed
by the concept of right, 98; reflects
correlativity of right and duty, 123,
125–126; constructed through
ensemble of negligence concepts,
145–170; significance of idea of risk
for, 168
Personal injury, possible legal regimes
for, 45–46, 67, 70, 210
Positive law: distinguished from the
juridical, 24; and intrinsic and
accidental unity, 35; possible
incoherence of juridical relationships
in, 42; links corrective justice to the
social world, 218; political and
juridical aspects of, 218–222; juridical
relations conceptually prior to,
225–226. *See also* Public law
Positivism, 229
Practical, Kant's conception of the,
88, 91
Practical reason: as determining ground
of purposive activity, 90–91; as aspect
of free will, 91; relationship to free
choice, 91, 93, 94, 99, 110–111; abstract
and formal standpoint of, 91–92; as
ground of normativeness, 93–94; and
principle of right, 98–100; and the
progression to public law, 101–102;
implies possibility of interaction, 103;
judge as institutionalized
embodiment of, 106; and the priority
of the right, 110–113; correlative right
and duty as expressions of, 123, 124;
relation to particularity, 127–129;
operates within a particular social
and historical context, 216–218

Property: social meaning of acts of appropriation, 104; and good faith purchase, 106; and restitution, 118, 140, 141, 142; embodiment of agent's external freedom, 128–129, 176–177, 191, 200; based on right, not welfare, 131–132; in Epstein's argument for strict liability, 173, 175–176; use and value as aspects of, 184, 191–196, 201–203; owners related through nuisance law, 190–196; owners related through privilege to preserve property, 196–203; distinguished from wealth, 200

Public law: and functionalism, 7, 48, 85; under Kantian right, 84–85, 100–102, 105–109; juridical function of publicness, 218–222

Purposive activity. *See* Agency; Free will

Rationality: in formalism, 23; and autonomy of private law, 206–208, 214; immanence of, 207

Reid, Lord, 149–152, 164

Remedies: injunctions, 56n, 144n, 195; shaped by bipolarity of corrective justice, 65; publicly authorized coercion, 107; nominal damages, 116; punitive damages, 135n; expectation damages, 136, 139–140; maintain the correlativity of right and duty, 143–144

Restitution (law of): correlativity in, 114–115, 118, 140–142; mistaken improvement of another's property, 116; relevance of distinguishing from reparation of loss, 133–134; reflects corrective justice, 140–142; as basis of liability for damage done while exercising privilege to preserve property, 197–199

Risk: as relational concept, 147, 160, 168; American and Commonwealth approaches to creation of, 147–152; theory that exposure to risk counts as injury, 156–158; general and particular descriptions of, 164–167; of abnormally dangerous activities, 188–189

Sales law, 106

Seavey, Warren, 159

Strict liability: definition, 171; Epstein's case for, 172–177; has defects that parallel those of subjective standard, 177; unequal treatment of parties, 177–179; right and duty not correlative, 178–179; implies incoherent conception of agency, 179–183; inconsistent with principle of right, 182–183

Subjective standard: has defects that parallel those of strict liability, 177; unequal treatment of parties, 177–179, 193; right and duty not correlative, 178–179; implies incoherent conception of agency, 179–183; inconsistent with principle of right, 182–183

Sumner, Lord, 158

Tort law: deterrence and compensation as justifications for, 3, 4, 38, 39–42, 43, 45–46, 64n, 121–122, 124, 212, 213; loss-spreading as goal of, 36–38, 39–40, 74–75, 143, 220–221; products liability, 36, 184n; argument for abolition of, 41–42; Fletcher's theory, 53–55; normative correlativity in, 114, 115, 117–118, 119, 134–136; nominal damages, 116; reflects corrective justice, 134–136, 145–203; liability for economic loss, 134n; doctrine of transferred intent, 135n; punitive damages, 135n; *respondeat superior*, 185–187, 228n; liability for abnormally dangerous activities, 187–190; nuisance law, 190–196; tort analysis inapplicable to incomplete privilege regarding preservation of property, 197. *See also* Negligence liability; Strict liability

Traynor, Justice Roger, 36, 37

Ulpian, 86, 100, 101, 103

Unger, Roberto, 23–24, 45

United States v. Carroll Towing Co., 148

Unity: aspect of form, 22, 27–28; of juridical relationships, 29, 30–31; paramount aspect of formal intelligibility, 29; intrinsic and accidental conceptions of, 33–36, 37, 44, 75, 159, 170; embraced by corrective justice, 75; in Kantian idea of reason, 85, 87–88. *See also* Coherence

Value, 138–139, 201–202
Vaughan v. Menlove, 178, 180, 182
Vincent v. Lake Erie Transportation Co., 173, 196–203

Watkins, Lord Justice, 220, 221, 222, 224, 225
Welfare, 4, 130–133